SLEEPERS, MOLES AND MARTYRS

Sleepers, Moles and Martyrs
Edited by Regina Bendix & John Bendix
Copyright © 2003 Ethnologia Europaea, Copenhagen
Printed in Sweden by Grahns Tryckeri AB, Lund 2004
ISBN 87-7289-987-5

Reprint of Ethnologia Europaea. Journal of European Ethnology 33:2 (2003)

Cover illustration: "Snowwhite and the Madness of Truth" (Stockholm Historical Museum, 2004).
Photo: Dror Feiler & Gunilla Sköld Feiler.

The publication of this volume was made possible with the generous support of the
Stiftung der Georg-August-Universität Göttingen, Germany.

Museum Tusculanum Press
University of Copenhagen
Njalsgade 94
DK-2300 Copenhagen S
www.mtp.dk

Sleepers, Moles and Martyrs

Secret Identifications, Societal Integration and the Differing Meanings of Freedom

Edited by

Regina Bendix

&

John Bendix

MUSEUM TUSCULANUM PRESS ❋ UNIVERSITY OF COPENHAGEN
2004

Contents

John Bendix & Regina Bendix: Introduction 5

PART I. DISCOURSES: GENERATING AND COMMENTING ON SLEEPERS

Sabina Magliocco: The Opposite of Right Society: Witches, Terrorists and
    the Discourse of Evil 13
Véronique Campion-Vincent: The Enemy Within: From Evil Others to
    Evil Elites 23
Regina Bendix: Sleepers' Secrets, Actors' Revelations 33

PART II. SENSE-MAKING IN SHADOWY CONTEXTS

Oskar Verkaaik: The Nation and its Shadow: Imagining Subversion in
    Post-'911' Pakistan and Holland 45
Friedrich Kratochwil: Moles, Martyrs and Sleepers: The End of the Hobbesian
    Project 57
Dorothy Noyes: Alias "Yusuf Galán": Neighbors, Sleepers, and the
    Violence of Recognition in Urban Spain 69

PART III. MARTYRS IN VISUAL AND LINGUISTIC CONTEXTS

Ulrich Marzolph: The Martyr's Way to Paradise: Shiite Mural Art in the
    Urban Context 87
Galit Hasan-Rokem: Martyr vs. Martyr: The Sacred Language of Violence 99

PART IV. MURMURS AND SILENCES

Jonas Frykman: Making Sense of Memory: Monuments and Landscape
    in Croatian Istria 107
Barbro Klein: Silences, Cultural Historical Museums, and Jewish Life
    in Sweden 121

Introduction

John Bendix & Regina Bendix

The symposium "Sleepers, Moles, and Martyrs: Secret Identifications, Societal Integration, and the Differing Meanings of Freedom" was held on October 6–8, 2002 in the conference facility Waldschlösschen in Reinhausen near Göttingen, Germany. Occasioned by the social, political and mass media discourses after the bombings of New York's World Trade Center on September 9, 2001, an interdisciplinary group of scholars came together to explore the connotations and implications of the term "sleeper".

The German and American press often used the term "sleeper" in the immediate aftermath of the Sept. 11th 2001 attacks on New York and Washington. It was shorthand for describing how major acts of destruction could be planned by foreigners living in Western Europe or North America, in a sense under the very noses of the authorities. It was an easy way for the media to characterize what now seemed a façade: those who appeared well integrated in host societies and cultural environments not their own in fact had remained secretly devoted to ideals not just alien to the environment they lived in, but when awakened or called to their "true nature," devoted to destroying their hosts. In the vocabulary of Kenneth Burke's theory of rhetoric, "sleeper" became a way to name the problem.

Since then, a more complex picture has emerged, for along with the irrefutable reality of the destruction and the clear symbolic import of the targets, it also became necessary to identify not just how the acts were carried out, but where to locate the direct perpetrators in social, cultural and political terms. While the term "sleeper" seemed particularly suited to Mohammad Atta, as the personification of the unassuming long-term resident from another country who awakens to action and violence, the term "sleeper" itself comes, among other connotations, out of an older secret service context in which agents are deliberately planted within other societies to spy and be "moles." Even the animal allusions that have been attached to such spy work – the nosiness and furtiveness attached to "ferreting" out information; the subterranean work of burrowing in like a mole in its dark, night-like environment – are noteworthy, for they readily become attached to this more recent imagery of the terrorist "sleeper." Real and imagined secrecy, or keeping rather than revealing secrets, has been the focus of past work in a variety of disciplines, but the Sept. 11th events lent a sense of urgency, in geopolitical terms, to understanding it better against this backdrop.

At the same time, the self-destruction Atta and his compatriots engaged in, coming in an era marked by suicide bombing as a political (and religious) act in the Middle East, suggested the presence of a strain of martyrdom that deserved greater scrutiny. In Western public discourse and perception, self-destruction as a radical form of political speech has become rare and is more seen as belonging to a distant if not "backwards" past. Self-immolation has been an episodic feature of political protest in various nations since 1945, but examples have tended to be horrifying cries by individuals wanting to be heard by governments or by the population at large. The intent has been not to destroy others in the process, but if anything to halt – through a dramatic, ultimate gesture – further destruction, almost as though the sacrifice of the one would help save the many. Recent political suicides seem also to stem from a mixture of a recognition of personal failure, desperation, and an attempt to wrest one's public biography, through this ultimate performance, from the discourse of scandal (Noyes 2002).

There have also been many cases of innocent bystanders being killed as a byproduct of groups left, right, religious, and regionalist making statements through violence rather than words. Here the desire may be to destroy specific individuals seen as embodying whatever is despised, or to bring down (or at least force the hand of) a government by sowing terror in public spaces. Yet while there are exceptions, such acts often do not come at the expense of a bomb-layer or assassin's life, and there are even cases of deliberate attempts to keep bystanders safe by issuing warnings ahead of time. Some of the groups who use such methods also are aware that wanton destructive acts with many casualties may well reinforce public support for the state rather than for the group's cause, and cast their violence in symbolic and material terms instead.

Religiously inspired and politically motivated martyrdom performed on a global stage that costs a perpetrator his or her life and deliberately destroys bystanders who are judged guilty by association seems to be a new story, performed for an audience that is larger than ever. Terrorism often targets specific governments, but the acts of September 11th were also directed explicitly against value systems or lifestyles. Yet as some contributors point out, we may simply be the victims of bad memory, as there are antecedents in various traditions for martyrdom even of this kind. New is that the mass media today ensure global coverage and thus globalized knowledge of such acts.

Television coverage has been a feature of hostage crises in recent years, and perpetrators have not infrequently manipulated this access. That CNN and other television networks aired the destruction on Sept. 11th live not only turned the morning news into visual trauma, but definitively put an end to an idea that has circulated since the 1960s, namely that 'the revolution will not be televised'. Immediacy and instantaneous transmission have multiplied the cultural interpretations and personal angles from which to approach the terrorist acts many times over.[1] It is then not surprising that the Bush administration quite successfully enlisted the media's support in fighting the war on terrorism by in essence restricting what they could report about it. Being a witness to destruction, live on the television screen, also meant witnessing the visual narrative the terrorists wanted to relate and thereby potentially also seeing more than one side of a global conflict.[2] An administration arming to go to war has little interest in its citizens wondering why there is such anger and hatred against American values and American citizens. The image of the burning and collapsing twin towers, replayed again and again since then, also repeats the story of these suicide flyers, demonstrating that "the act of turning physical defeat into narrative victory" is a rhetorically most powerful operation (Edwards 2002:181). As Oskar Verkaaik said during our discussions, "death is very convincing." Al-Qaeda very effectively utilizes existing media imagery to fuel not only terrorist imaginations but also to participate in shaping global narratives about power, belief and justice. Terrorists might be drawing inspiration from extant (Western) print or film fiction, but the regular use of documentary and interview footage, along with recordings from unknown locations, clearly feeds into a desire to create the public perception of a "shadowy" style of power being used by Al-Qaeda's chief ideologues or "dreamaturges", if one wants to put it the language of sleep.[3]

The biographies of the 911 perpetrators have proven rather more complex than initially thought, deserving more sophisticated treatment than the many conspiracy theories have been able to offer.[4] Discovering that "sleepers" exist who reveal their hidden selves in final performances of enormous violence has troubling implications for liberally-minded (and Judeo-Christian) societies that for decades have wrestled with questions of integration (esp. of Muslims) and multiculturalism. While the military, the police, and the secret services in various countries have tried to address "shadowy" networks and presumed "links" between past, present, and future perpetrators – in the process themselves building networks and practices of secrecy[5] – the symposium "Sleepers,

Moles, and Martyrs" that formed the basis of the papers assembled here was oriented more toward making a contribution to the discussion of what the implications now might be for host societies, polities, and cultures in Europe and North America.

Disciplinary Encounter

The symposium brought together ethnologists, folklorists, anthropologists, political scientists, literature scholars and sociologists from six countries. It is then not surprising that though the conference was in English, a variety of disciplinary tongues were spoken, and a fair amount of translation between fields and perspectives took place. To ethnologists who tend to emphasize the importance of the particular, the idea of the "sleeper" is already embedded in the fieldwork they engage in. Fieldwork requires the researcher to engage in documentation and participant observation, and such behavior creates numerous ethical dilemmas and to those being visited, interviewed, and watched, the motivations for gathering information may be quite obscured or even suspect.[6] Political scientists, who tend to emphasize the importance of the general, must resign themselves to the fact that their scholarly work may be of immediate interest to agencies of the state that have vested interests in being secretive about what they are doing with this knowledge.

In the context of the interaction at this conference, a number of the reservations that disciplines hold towards others were fruitfully brought into the open. Some of the social scientists would have liked to see ethnographers add meaning and interpretation to what they gathered from informants, even as they enjoyed the new perspectives on narrative and symbolic evidence ethnologists and folklorists provided. Some folklorists and anthropologists, in turn, would have liked to see their social science colleagues descend a bit from their fascination with typologies and generalization and address what their theoretical constructs actually looked like in the field. By the same token, however, it was important for the ethnologists present to recognize that some social scientists would still like to be able to rely on them for assessments of cultural wholes, even though it is today more impossible than ever to provide a clearly defined concept of culture and the notion of cultural wholes has, within the discipline, long been criticized if not abandoned. The social scientists in turn came to recognize that though ethnologists can provide detailed, context-rich, cultural information, it would often come in forms hard to abstract or fit into predictive formats. To that extent, one of the fruits of interdisciplinary encounters of this kind is the discovery of latent – if not sleeping – images that other disciplines hold about one's own.

Overarching Themes of this Volume

It seemed both undesirable (and near-impossible) to find one overarching explanation for the sleeper phenomenon, but it was possible to point to several recurring major themes and sub-themes: the role of modernization (and its attendant divergent modernities) in relation to identity formation; the need to relativize perspectives and language; and, most frustrating, the difficulty of trying to investigate what by its very nature is not intended to be revealed.

The "traditional" narrative of modernity generally foregrounds its relevant components – industrialization, democratization, dislocation. Yet our discussions confirmed what scholars of modernization have been saying: modernity comes in multiple and competing forms. Thus "fundamentalism" as embraced by the perpetrators of 911 cannot be labeled a threat emanating from the "residual". It is rather a competing, extreme modernity. In the medicalizing language that also surfaces around the sleeper complex, competing modernities generate not viruses but rather something akin to autoimmune disease. From this perspective, sleepers and the ideologues who provide them with their script do not want to participate in the collective modernizing project and practice a seemingly non-modern intolerance. But in developing their strategies, they nonetheless employ thoroughly modern techniques and technologies, culminating in what is again a highly modern desire for maximum visibility.

At the level of the individual, modernization

presents the self with differing options or identification choices. The culture of one's family or background differs in aspect from the culture that needs to be adapted to upon migration. The culture of background may itself be transforming in an incomprehensible manner or in a manner individuals deeply object to. There is an option to adopt the socio-economic status one is born into as opposed to the economic and professional status one aspires to, or there may be a choice to identify later in life with moral or religious precepts different than those one was socialized into.

The self may experience these options as empowering, valued facets of modern life. But the self may also experience such choices as painful, incongruent demands to be rejected, even violently so, and this latter aspect is difficult to understand in the context of Western societies that positively value the changes modernization brings. The typical expectation in the West has been that leaving what is labeled as "traditional" for the promise of the "modern" is inherently a good thing, carrying as it does implicit judgments about progress versus stagnation. The devaluation of what is thereby declared "not modern" does not go unnoticed among those so labeled.

At the societal level, the question is how the different kinds of modernities, in their order, values and predictabilities, can be grasped and brought into perspective. What 911 has shifted into plain view is the Panglossian conceit and sense of comfort with how things in the Western world are. In light of individuals who use the tolerant, comfortable, modern surroundings to act in very intolerant, destructive, and seemingly un-modern ways it is unavoidable that we reconsider the economic and political "order of things" from the highly local to the global.

Faced with real destruction, not abstractions or simulacra suitable for postmodernist or deconstructionist analysis, a more realist[ic] ethnographic and analytic practice is in order. The ethnological or anthropological project has been to make the mentalities of places conceptualized as Other understandable. While this effort must continue, there is a need to increase efforts to understand the niches "we", or small groups of "us", fashion. In immigrant contexts with established and emerging mixed neighborhoods and urban spaces, there is a palpable uncertainty over what the "we" might look like both culturally and socially, what the rules will now be, and what borders of tolerance are shared. Notions such as "loyalty" or "shared memory" which might inform social collectives from neighborhoods to entire polities carry multiple referents. The Hamburg neighbors, teachers, fellow-students and acquaintances of Mohammed Atta were caught, in hindsight, in a dilemma: were they witnessing increasing religious devotion or should they instead have been alarmed (or even notified the authorities)? Such overt uncertainties must be emphasized but so must research into the realms of the shadows, the darker and less talked about aspects of our societies and polities.

The papers are grouped in four loose categories. The first section brings together three analyses of the discourses about sleepers: historical antecedents (Magliocco), communicative and narrative mechanisms (Campion-Vincet), and semantic operations (Bendix). The next section, using the notion of "shadow" and its multiple meanings, makes efforts to come to terms with known but hidden or unspoken aspects of the state and its history (Verkaaik), what examining the foundations of our theories of the secular state can tell us (Kratochwil), and the unfolding of self vis-à-vis the state in the tension between neighborly secrets and public display (Noyes). The third section combines officially endorsed yet subtly changing depictions of martyrdom (Marzolph) with a paper documenting the violence done to the term "martyr" itself (Hasan-Rokem). The two case studies in the final section probe into cultural secrets and public silences surrounding war memorials (Frykman) and knowledge production (Klein).

Prof. Dr. John Bendix, Institute for Political Science, Universität Bamberg, Feldkirchenstr. 21, D-96045 Bamberg. E-mail: johnbendix@hotmail.com

Prof. Dr. Regina Bendix, Institute for Cultural Anthropology/European Ethnology, Georg-August-Universität Göttingen, Friedländer Weg 2, D-37085 Göttingen, e-mail: rbendix@gwdg.de.

Notes

Acknowledgments

The following institutions are thanked for their financial support: the Humboldt Stiftung for TransCoop Funds awarded to Fritz Kratochwil and Ned Lebow and used to support the conference on which this volume is based; the *Stiftung der Universität Göttingen* for its generous support both for the conference and for the printing of this volume. The symposium also took place under the auspices of the *Société Internationale d'Ethnologie et de Folklore* (SIEF). Numerous individuals assisted in shaping the contours of the meeting, though many were unable to attend, but are to be thanked for their interesting ideas and partial paper drafts: Peter Niedermüller, Andre Gingrich, Gita Dharampal-Frick and Julia Kristeva all assisted in the early stages, and Doris Bachmann-Medick, Dario Biocca, Martin Heisler and Mick Taussig all intended to participate until life's circumstances interferred. Present at the conference but not represented in this volume are Marianne Gullestad (see Gullestad 2003), Thomas Hauschild, Ted Hopf, and Ned Lebow. James Davis, Tatjana Eggeling, Wolfgang Knöbl and Gerhard Lauer as well as John Bendix participated as lively discussants during the meeting. A few of the papers from Reinhausen (Bendix, Marzolph and Noyes) and an additional one included in this volume by Sabina Magliocco were also presented at the panel "Sleepers, Secrets, Sacrifices" at the American Folklore Society Meetings in Rochester, NY, October 2002. All participants at the Reinhausen symposium are thanked for their willingness to engage in the modalities of this venture. Dorothee Hemme assisted in the practical planning phase, and Stephan Gill was our assistant during the actual meeting and also transcribed all the discussions. Karin Ilten helped enormously with the bureaucratic paper work. Jeffrey Beckman was our editorial assistant.

1. For a poignant account of a reaction unfolding alongside media coverage, mixing the personal, cultural and political, cf. Bowman (2001). A first assessment of 911's impact on journalism can be found in Zelizer and Stuart (2002).
2. Visual narration touches us aesthetically, intellectually, affectively and effectively – most poignantly evident in the controversy surrounding composer Karlheinz Stockhausen's response to 911: "Rushing in where angels fear to tread, Karlheinz Stockhausen voiced what some may have felt, but none dared say. For him, the crashing planes and collapsing towers felt like art: ',What happened there is: now you must re-adjust your brain. The greatest work of art imaginable for the whole cosmos. Minds achieving in a single act what we in music can only dream of, people rehearsing like mad for ten years, preparing fanatically for a concert, and then dying. You have people who are that focused on a performance and then 5,000 people who are dispatched to the afterlife, in a single moment. I couldn't match it. Against that, we – as composers – are nothing.' Surely the guy is crazy? In Stockhausen's defence, he did go on to admit it was a crime, because part of the 'audience' was 'not consenting'. This demur didn't soften Gyorgy Ligeti's retort: 'Stockhausen should be locked up in a psychiatric hospital" (Watson 2001).
3. The idea of "sleepers and dreamers" was developed in Thomas Hauschild's conference contribution. He built connections between examples of Al-Qaeda video-footage and alternate models of leadership and loyalty.
4. For the second anniversary of 911, the German news magazine *Der Spiegel's* title story surveyed an astounding number of publications devoted to explaining the events with the use of (mutually contradictory) conspiracy theories (Cziesche et al. 2003:58–76, cf. also Campion-Vincent in this volume).
5. Some of this was discussed orally by conference participants with first-hand knowledge, information which even when presented in generalized terms was deemed unpublishable – for security reasons! Edward Shils's *The Torment of Secrecy* (1956) about the U.S. administration and bureaucracy makes the point that even legitimate governments that otherwise promote transparency find it necessary to have shadowy realms. One has difficulty, it seems, even openly discussing the secrecy surrounding secrecy.
6. The Albanian novelist Ismail Kadar's fictionalized rendition of Milman Parry and Albert Lord's fieldwork, undertaken in search of epic song in the Balkans in the first half of the 20th century, develops the "ethnographer perceived as spy" marvellously (1999).

References

Bowman, Glenn 2001: Thinking the Unthinkable. In: *Anthropology Today* 17, No.6: 17–18.

Cziesche, Dominik *et al.* 2003: Panoptikum des Absurden. In: *Der Spiegel* 38, Sept. 9, 58–76.

Edwards, David B. 2001: Bin Laden's Last Stand. In: Ghosh, Gautam, ed.: *Civilization, Vulnerability and Translation: Reflections in the Aftermath of September 11th*. In: *Anthropological Quarterly* (Special Issue) 75: 179–81.

Gullestad, Marianne 2003: Mohammed Atta and I: Identification, discrimination and the formation of sleepers. In: *European Journal of Cultural Studies*:6(4):529–548.

Herrmann, Richard and Richard Ned Lebow, eds. 2004. *Learning form the Cold War*. New York: Palgrave, 2004.

Kadar, Ismail. 1997: *The File on H*. Transl. by David Bellos. London: The Harvill Press.

Shils, Edward A. 1956: *The Torment of Secrecy*: The

Background and Consequences of American Security Policies. Glencoe.

Noyes, Dorothy 2000: Authoring the Social Drama: Suicide, Self, and Narration in a French Political Scandal. In: *Narrative*, 8(2000): 210–231.

Watson, Ben 2001: Music, Violence, Truth. In: http://www.militantesthetix.co.uk/violence.html *(consulted October 2003)*.

Zelizer, Barbie & Stuart Allen, eds. 2002: *Journalism after September 11*. London.

Part I

Discourses:

Generating and Commenting on Sleepers

The Opposite of Right Society
Witches, Terrorists and the Discourse of Evil

Sabina Magliocco

> Magliocco, Sabina 2003: The Opposite of Right Society: Witches, Terrorists and the Discourse of Evil. – Ethnologia Europaea 33:2: 13–22.
>
> This paper explores cultural antecedents for the idea of the "sleeper," the terrorist who appears to adapt to a host culture while secretly harboring plans to destroy it, in the discourse of European and American witch hunts. The idea of an evil infiltrator, who lives hidden within a society, clandestinely conspiring to overthrow it, has deep historical roots. The language used by American political leaders to describe Al-Qaeda echoes that of medieval inquisitors and New England witch hunter Cotton Mather, ferreting out diabolical conspiracies threatening to destroy the foundations of society. In this paper, I explore the similarities between the discourse of witch hunts and that of terrorism, arguing that language which creates an enemy simultaneously alien and internal to the host society accomplishes two rhetorical goals: it projects evil onto a racial, cultural, gendered or social Other, allowing the host culture to see itself as "pure" and "good;" and it dehumanizes the Other, making it easier to deprive him/her of basic human rights.
>
> *Prof. Sabina Magliocco, Department of Anthropology, California State University – Northridge, 18111 Nordhoff St., Northridge, CA 91330, USA.*
> *E-mail: sm32646@csun.edu*

Almost immediately after the attacks of September 11, 2001 on the World Trade Center and the Pentagon, news stories began to circulate about the terrorists who had perpetrated this heinous crime. According to reports, Mohammed Atta and his henchmen did not fit the profile of the typical terrorist drawn up by the FBI and the CIA: that of a poor, young male driven to fanatical acts by the desperation of his life circumstances. The terrorists who blew up the towers were of a different stripe: middle-aged, middle class, educated and by all appearances "average" immigrants to the United States who did not appear to be radical fanatics. They dressed in Western garb, smoked cigarettes, drank alcohol and in other ways blended in with their neighbors in the anonymous suburban apartment complexes where they resided. They were, it is said, "sleepers:" infiltrators "long in place but not yet activated" (Saffire 2001).

New York Times columnist William Saffire, writing his weekly piece "On Language" barely two months after the attacks, observed that the word, which has many meanings, was first used in this sense in the context of the Cold War: "a member of the Communist Party whose whole life was dedicated to the one big moment," according to mystery novelist Holly Roth in a 1955 book by that title (Saffire 2001).

In 1976, *The Times of London* observed, "There almost certainly exists within our political establishment, what is known as a 'sleeper' – a high-level political figure who is in fact a Soviet agent, infiltrated into the system many years ago." As the cold war ended, the word surfaced again with a slightly different meaning: in 1990, Prof. Paul Wilkinson, a British terrorism expert, told the Press Association that Iraq was unrivaled in the technique, with sleeper squads, known as "submarines," already in position (Saffire 2001).

The word surfaced again in 2000, when Benjamin Weiser reported in the New York Times that a former U.S. Army sergeant told the FBI about "networks of terrorists known as 'sleepers' who lie low for years but do not need to be told what to do." The sergeant, according to Weiser, knew that "that there are hundreds of 'sleepers' or 'submarines' in place who don't fit neatly into the terrorist profile" (Saffire 2001).

Two years later, the word "sleeper" became part of the national vocabulary.

"The pattern of bin Laden's terrorism," wrote Evan Thomas and Mark Hosenball in *Newsweek* two weeks after September 11, "is to insert operatives into a country where they are 'sleepers,' burrowed deep into the local culture, leading normal lives while awaiting orders" (quoted in Saffire 2001).

Yet the idea of a "sleeper," the terrorist who appears to adapt to a host culture while secretly harboring plans to destroy it, an evil infiltrator who lives hidden within a society, clandestinely conspiring to overthrow it, is not new in American culture. It has many historical antecedents; in fact, I will argue that it is part of a pattern of American political discourse that draws heavily from folklore to create an enemy simultaneously alien and internal to the host society, upon whom political problems can then be blamed. In American history, this discourse has often been used to project evil onto a racial, cultured, gendered or social Other, allowing the dominant culture to preserve an image of itself as "pure" and "good." It has been used to dehumanize it the Other, making it easier to deprive him/her of basic human rights. And by using the language of moral absolutes, of "good" vs. "evil," it has obscured the role of the state in creating the conditions in which political opposition and resistance leading to terrorism can flourish.

I wish to state at the outset that it is not my intent to justify terrorist actions, especially those of the hijackers on September 11. These crimes against innocent civilians remain unconscionable under any circumstances. Nor do I mean to cast doubt upon the very real fact that there are terrorist groups in many parts of the world, including the United States, engaged in plotting future crimes. Instead, I want to call attention to the ways in which the language of terrorism used by the current administration, and picked up by the news media, represents a long-standing pattern in American politics. This language transforms human beings with human motivations into political and folkloric symbols, ultimately blinding us to more subtle understandings that could help us sway or undo them.

One of the earliest antecedents for the idea of the sleeper terrorist lies in the European folklore of witchcraft. *The Canon Episcopi*, a 9th century ecclesiastical document, describes witches literally as sleepers: women whose bodies remained in bed at night while they journeyed in spirit to the meetings of secret societies headed by a fantastical supernatural woman known by a variety of names: Diana, Herodias, Dame Abonde, Signora Oriente, la Signora del Giuoco. There, they would feast, dance, sing and receive advice from the queen of the assembly (Bonomo 1959:15–20; Ginzburg 1989:65–98). While early accounts of these nocturnal journeys emphasized their spiritual nature, around 1100, the Catholic Church's interpretation of these legends shifted, and the nighttime revels were understood as having taken place in the flesh (Muraro Vaiani 1976:142). That is, what was once commonly understood as cultural fantasy with heretical content was now understood as real. Thus was born the legend of the witches' sabbat, which came to dominate Europe and, later, the Americas for several centuries. While the original purpose of these folkloric night time assemblies was not to do evil, inquisitors inevitably interpreted these reports as wicked, or at the very least heretical, in intent, since the leaders of the assemblies could be understood as challenging the primacy of God and Christ. Even though the women who confessed to having participated in the "games of Diana" did not believe they were doing evil, they were nevertheless executed as witches (Bonomo 1959; Caro Baroja 1965; Ginzburg 1989; Muraro Vaiani 1976).

Belief in witchcraft was brought to the new world by the English Puritans, who believed humans existed in a state of constant struggle against the forces of Satan and his demonic army. These were not mere figures of speech or metaphors for them, but represented a genuine dualistic cosmology. Puritan witch hunter Cotton Mather described witches as part of a "vast Power, or Army of Evil Spirits, under the Government of a Prince who employs them in a continual Opposition to the designs of GOD" (Mather, quoted in Dorson, 1973:32). Mather used the language of the state, with a political leader, an army and a strategy of opposition, to describe the role of witches. Witches were thought to have a covenant, or contract, with the devil, their political leader, that could compel them to do things they would never otherwise consider (Dorson 1973:33). According to Richard Dorson, "In the eyes of the Puritans, witches in covenant with the devil and his army of demons threatened the fabric of their holy communion with their black magic aimed at ... subverting the true church" (Dorson 1973:35). It was but a small step from the idea of witches subverting the church to that of witches as subverting the state: colonial diarist John Evelyn wrote that witches wished to subvert the government, and in the very next line discussed a conspiracy discovered among African slaves on Barbados to overthrow and kill their masters (Dorson 1973:41). It is clear that for Evelyn, the planned slave rebellion was on par with the overthrow of the colonial government by witches. Witches and slaves both existed as minorities living alongside the dominant culture, appearing to conform to its rules while secretly plotting its destruction. They were, in a sense, sleepers: dangerous infiltrators who were at once both insiders and evil aliens, whose presence was simultaneously both hidden and manifest. Their presence was rendered apparent by their difference: gender, in the case of most witches,[1] and race, in the case of African slaves.

The language of difference, especially that of darkness, both racial and spiritual, was already long in use in the witchcraft persecutions. Europeans had a history of equating light with goodness and dark with evil, and of presuming that an individual's physical aspect revealed their moral character. In the American colonial context, these assumptions extended to racial attributes. In court documents from American witch trials, for example, the devil was often referred to as a "black man" or a "dark stranger" (Dorson 1973:49). One of the first to be accused and prosecuted in the infamous Salem witch trials was Tituba, a slave variously described as Afro-Caribbean or American Indian (see Norton, 2002b) whose own religious practices, intended to rid the girls of their ailment, were misunderstood or misrepresented as witchcraft by the prosecutors.

The discourse of witchcraft as difference is not unique to Western cultures; anthropologists have found similar constructions in many societies. Witchcraft discourses generally portray witches as embodying the opposite of right society: the antithesis of what is considered to be proper, decent social behavior (Mair 1969:36–37). "The image of the ways witches behave, which is associated with the reasons why they should seek to destroy others, is an image of evil, of the antithesis of good," explains anthropologist Lucy Mair in a comparative, cross-cultural study of witchcraft beliefs (1969:38). Witches are often imagined as transgressing a number of social norms: they may have insatiate lusts for power, food, goods, and sexuality. They break fundamental rules in the social contract, killing relatives and attacking their neighbors. Disregarding life itself, they think nothing of murder, and are often also accused of cannibalism, incest and turning into animals, all actions which violate fundamental rules of human conduct that societies everywhere imagine separate humans from non-humans (Mair 1969:36–39). While such exaggerated portrayals belong to what Mair calls the "nightmare witch," a creature of fantasy, real-life, everyday witches—"the person who may actually be living among you, suspected or unsuspected" (Mair 1969:37) — also embody oppositional qualities: in this case, they are the opposite of the type of person one would wish to have as a neighbor. And those who repeatedly violate social norms for one reason or another, or who are considered socially or economically marginal to the community, are particularly vulnerable to being accused of witchcraft, since according to this system of reasoning, those who break one type of social rule may easily violate others (Mair 1969:37).

Witches in colonial New England were no exception to this cross-cultural pattern. Existing legend complexes depicted them as evildoers whose ordinary activities included copulation with the devil and his minions, sexual perversions, and the murder of children for cannibalistic purposes. According to the work of historian Mary Beth Norton, the language of difference accompanied the language of witchcraft in the Salem witch trials. The Salem witch trials emerged at the same time as settlers were engaged in renewed, violent warfare against local Indians. The principal accusers belonged to families which had suffered great losses in the Indian wars. In their testimony, they claimed to have seen the devil in the shape of an Indian, and blamed the defeat of colonial soldiers by the Indians on sorcery (Norton 2002a). In this construction, the accused were not only guilty of conspiring with the devil, but of aiding and abetting the enemy. As Boyer and Nissenbaum's study of the Salem witch trials illustrates, accusations tended to follow existing political divisions, with the accused belonging to one and accusers to a rival faction (Boyer and Nissenbaum 1997). The language of witchcraft proved the ideal discourse to bring down political opponents.

The language used by American political leaders to describe Al-Qaeda terrorists echoes that of medieval inquisitors and New England witch hunters ferreting out diabolical conspiracies threatening to destroy the foundations of society. Attorney General John Ashcroft described the terrorist conspiracy as "A calculated, malignant, devastating evil [that] has arisen in our world. Civilization cannot afford to ignore the wrongs that have been done" (*The New York Times,* 2/24/02:4/1). According to this construction, the United States as well as many other parts of the world are filled with sleepers, dangerous terrorists who masquerade as ordinary citizens, but await word from their leader to explode into rageful, evil action. These sleepers are part of a vast, secret, worldwide network with tentacles in every nation, whose aim is nothing less than the overthrow of Western civilization itself. Like Satan's army of darkness, this network is headed by Osama Bin Laden, the mastermind of a great subversive plan. Without the direction and financing of Bin Laden, the current administration imagines, terrorists would never even conceive of their evil plans. Parallels between Bin Laden and the devil quickly emerged in popular culture as well. Less than a week after the attacks of September 11, an email began to circulate featuring a photograph of a huge cloud of smoke rising from the ruined towers. Texts accompanying the photograph interpreted the shape of the smoke cloud as the face of Satan, the head of Bin Laden, or both.

In the autumn of 2002, Saddam Hussein's name was added to the roster of terrorist financiers and sympathizers as the United States prepared to go to war against Iraq, even though the evidence of this link was later deemed to be manufactured. Whether Bin Laden or Hussein, the alleged mastermind takes on the role of the devil in the witchcraft conspiracies, creating covenants with his followers that force them to take on suicide missions and carry out other actions they would otherwise never think of themselves. Bin Laden and Hussein are portrayed as the masterminds of the operation, much as Satan was imagined by colonial witch hunters as the prince of a great army of minions ready to carry out his evil plans. Indeed, the capacity of both leaders to elude U.S. forces thus far has occasionally been depicted as almost preternatural.

During the Iraq war, media reports often focused on rather trivial details of Hussein's personal life and that of his family members in an effort to portray their moral debauchery and hypocrisy. When U.S. soldiers uncovered the abandoned house of Hussein's son in the spring of 2003, images of his extensive collection of pornographic videotapes were broadcast by CNN, ABC, CBS and NBC. Reports also focused on his stash of alcoholic beverages, which he held in apparent violation of Islamic law.

As was the case of the language of witchcraft, the language of terrorism converges with the discourse of difference, focusing on those deemed to be not fully members of the larger community. As the U.S. administration began its investigation of the September 11 attacks, suspicion focused increasingly on Others within American society: Muslims (non-Christians) as well as Middle Easterners, Central Asians, African Americans and Latinos (non-whites). Within one year of the 9/11 attacks, over 5000 Arab and Muslim Americans and immigrants had been rounded up and interrogated, and 1200 of these were detained. Detainees are being held without recourse to lawyers and without charges being filed while their alleged links to terrorist sleeper cells are investigated. Those who are U.S. citizens have been designated as "enemy combatants," stripping them of due process and allowing them to be detained in military prisons and tried in military tribunals, without access to legal counsel or knowledge of the specific crimes of which they are accused. "We have documented many instances of immigrants from the Middle East and South Asia ... face[ing] cruel and degrading treatment at the hands of U.S. authorities," said William F. Schultz, the executive director of Amnesty International, in an interview with *New York Times Magazine* writer Matthew Brzezinski. "Those are the sort of practices we usually see in the most repressive regimes in the world" (M. Brzezinski 2002:52).

The state's focus on individuals of Middle Eastern provenance and Muslim faith as potential terrorists led to an alarming reaction of suspicion and hatred towards these Others among the general population. In Los Angeles county alone, 118 hate crimes were committed against Middle Easterners, South Asians and people of Arab descent between September 11, 2001 and September 11, 2002. According to LAPD (Los Angeles Police Department) figures, this represents a 200% increase in the number of hate crimes against these minority groups since the previous year.[2] Some of the murdered individuals were mistakenly identified as Middle Eastern or Muslim by their attackers, including a Coptic shopkeeper, several Sikh men and a number of Latinos.

The American Civil Liberties Union (ACLU), a watchdog political organization, began tracking the stories of individuals affected by anti-Muslim persecution following the state sponsored crackdown on potential terrorists. In an October 2002 issue of its newsletter, the ACLU documented the personal narratives of several victims of hate crimes. Among them was Ali Akbar, the Pakistani owner of a halal restaurant in Orange County (southern California).

"On the night of September 26, 2001, I saw my hard work and my family's source of income burn to the ground. The week before the fire, people were driving up to my restaurant honking and screaming. They saw the name of the restaurant, I think. They were very angry. Maybe they set the fire, I don't know. The Buena County Fire Department told me that the arsonist broke the glass door, poured fuel into the restaurant, then set it on fire. As a result of the fire, I had zero income for six months" (*Open Forum* 76/4 [2002], p. 5).

In the intensified political climate of California, all non-citizens became the focus of renewed suspicion. An NPR/ Kaiser Foundation poll in the autumn of 2002 showed that the majority of Americans believe that naturalized U.S. citizens should not have as many rights if arrested as those born in the United States and holding only U.S. citizenship.

Attorney General Ashcroft's intensification of the FBI's authority to spy on U.S. residents, and his institution, in August 2002, of the TIPS (Terrorist Information and Prevention System) program in which neighbors and workers with access to homes and apartments were encouraged to report suspicious activities to the authorities, only heightened an already-existing trend. Already in October 2001, only weeks after the attacks, Suzanne Goodman of Islip, NY wrote to the *New York Times*' editorial page, suggesting that all landlords and motel operators were in a particularly good position to discover illegal activities among their tenants and guests:

"The sleeper terrorists aren't staying in American caves or in the backs of their cars. They're living anonymously among us, and it's the people who unwittingly provide shelter who are in the best position to detect the evildoers" (*NYTimes* Editorial Page 10/31/2001).

Shortly after the TIPS program's institution, Eunice Stone of Cartersville, GA reported to the authorities a conversation she overheard in a Shoney's restaurant between three men of Middle Eastern descent. Apparently, she mistook their black humor and discussion about transporting cars to Illinois, where they were to begin a medical residency program, as evidence that they were planning terrorist acts. She also expressed amazement that the men, two of whom are American citizens, spoke with "perfect American accents." Perhaps she believed that this was part of the sleepers' trick of blending in, since it was otherwise inconceivable to her that "foreign-looking" people might lack a distinctive accent. The men were arrested, detained, extensively questioned and eventually released for lack of evidence. Unfortunately, they also lost their positions as medical residents in a Florida hospital.

Popular sentiment against Muslims and Middle Easterners was fomented by the publication of Steven Emerson's book *American Jihad: the Terrorists Living Among Us* (2001). Emerson, a former CNN correspondent with an M.A. in urban studies, attended the meetings of many Islamic organizations across the United States, where he heard fiery tirades filled with rhetoric against Western "idol worshippers" and "enemies of Allah." He also discovered that because of its constitutionally guaranteed protections, the United States provided Islamic militants with an ideal location from which to organize political movements, raise funds, and disseminate propaganda. Rushed into print following September 11, the book became an instant best seller. Yet while Emerson was being hailed as a modern-day Cassandra by many on the right, critics argued that his warnings verged on paranoia, and that many of the individuals and organizations mentioned in his book have been cleared of any wrong-doing by judicial inquiries (Block 2002:42).

Besides their obvious racial and ethnic difference, potential terrorists are also portrayed as incomprehensibly irrational, or childishly emotional. They are "cowards" who "hate our freedoms" and despise Western culture because of their religious beliefs, or they are "jealous" of American material success. But studies show that far from hating Western-style democracy, Muslim public opinion the world over strongly favors representative government, individual liberties and education (Atran 2003). Muslim religious beliefs themselves are distorted in an effort to further dehumanize terrorists: soon after the 9/11 attacks, the hijackers' suicidal acts were explained in many media accounts with the rationalization that Islam promises martyrs a heaven filled with sexually alluring virgins.

These misinterpretations are symptoms of more than just cultural and religious prejudice. They successfully divorce the concept of terrorism from any U.S. political actions that may have inspired it. As Zbigniew Brzezinski argued in a *New York Times* editorial a year after the attacks, "It is as if terrorism is suspended in outer space as an abstract phenomenon, with ruthless terrorists acting under some Satanic inspiration unrelated to any specific motivation" (Z. Brzezinski 2002). In fact, he continues, "almost all terrorist activity originates from some political cause and is sustained by it as well" (Brzezinski 2002). The problem is not that terrorists don't like American values; it is American *actions* they dislike. For many years now, historical documents have demonstrated a relationship between U.S. foreign policy and increased terrorist threats against the United States (Atran 2003). According to a United Nations report, Al-Qaeda recruitment increased in thirty to forty nations around the globe as soon as the United States began its military build-up against Iraq in the fall of 2002. Recruiters did not have to scour the bushes to find volunteers; they were "beating down the doors to join" (Atran 2003).

It should be evident by now that a number of parallels exist between the language used by witch hunters to make witches appear to be "the opposite of right society," and that of the American administration and media in portraying sleeper terrorists after the 9/11 attacks. The existence of these similarities is not accidental. Both discourses are part of a pattern of what Alan Dundes has termed "projection" and "projective inversion" in folklore (Dundes 1980: 1991:354). Projection, a term Dundes borrows from psychoanalytic theory, is a psychological defense mechanism consisting of the repression of emotions and experiences deemed unacceptable by the individual or society, and the projection of these characteristics onto an object (a person or a group of people). Projection is further characterized by a lack of empathy with what is projected and a feeling of distancing or estrangement from the object onto which the reviled characteristics have been projected (Kernberg 1987:94). In other words, through projection, the individual or society disowns feelings, characteristics and emotions considered inappropriate or intolerable, and sees them as existing outside of the self in the person of an Other. The Other, stripped of humanity through the mechanism of projection, becomes a container for these negative qualities, and can be hated with impunity, while the projecting individual or society maintains an image of itself as entirely good. Moreover, the belief can then develop that by eliminating the Other, the negative characteristics can somehow be eliminated or purged altogether.

According to Dundes, projective inversion, a variant of the defense mechanism of projection, is in operation when A accuses B of doing something A would in fact like to do, or perhaps is already doing, but needs to keep hidden (Dundes 1991:355). It is the psychological mechanism at work behind the legend of the blood libel, used for centuries as a justification for the persecution of Jews in Europe. Jews were falsely accused of murdering Gentile children to use their blood in the making of Passover matzos. We see a similar motif of ritual cannibalism at work in the legends about witches, Catholics during the 1800s (Hofstadter 1966), and contemporary Satanists (Victor 1991), narratives which are clearly cultural fantasies without any factual elements whatsoever. While these legends all contain elements of projection, Dundes argues that the blood libel legend is a case of projective inversion, since it was the Christians who engaged in communion, a symbolic consumption of the body and blood of Christ, as the central ritual act of the mass. He maintains that their own ambivalence about the act of communion, with its symbolic cannibalism, was projected outside their group onto an Other that could be hated and reviled — in this case, the Jews. Historian Carlo Ginzburg argues that medieval depictions of cannibalism in witches' sabbats were drawn from the blood libel legend of anti-Jewish persecutions, which predated the witch craze by several centuries (Ginzburg 1989:36–61).

Projection is evident in American politics whenever minorities or imagined infiltrators are blamed for existing political and social ills. Historian Richard Hofstadter, writing not long after another episode of this nature, the hearings of the House Committee on Un-American Activities in the 1950s, called this pattern "the paranoid style in American politics" (Hofstadter 1966). He identified the basic elements of the style as:

- the idea of a vast, sinister conspiracy as the primary moving force behind historical events;
- the apocalyptic nature of the conspiracy – its intent to bring down entire ways of life;
- the portrayal of this conflict in absolute moral terms, good vs. evil;
- the personalization of the enemy, and his depiction as a model of malice;
- the dehumanization of the enemy through a focus on alleged acts of extreme cruelty and sadism;
- the perception that decisive events are caused by the enemy's personal will, rather than by a confluence of historical factors;
- the special attention and authority granted to renegades and apostates (Hofstadter 1966:29–39).

Hofstadter traced this style throughout American history, beginning with the colonial witch hunts, which we have already discussed. During the 1700s, as the colonial government gave way to the early Republic, fears of Masonic and Illuminati conspiracies to bring down the emergent nation became rife. During the 1800's, Catholics were suspect because of their alleged involvement in papist anti-government plots as the United States warred first with France, then with Spain for control of their former colonies on American soil. In the Cold War years following the Second World War, anti-Communist hysteria culminated in the McCarthyism of the 1950s, which journalists eventually dubbed a "witch hunt." One could add to this sad litany the murders of Sacco and Vanzetti, along with other innocent Italian immigrants imagined to be socialist agitators, at the turn of the 20th century; the internment of Japanese and Italian Americans during the second World War; and the Satanic panics of the 1980s, which led to the imprisonment of many innocent victims of accusations of ritual sexual abuse (Hofstadter 1966; Ray 2002; Fox 1990; Victor 1993). We can observe many of the same characteristics in the current discourse on terrorists as sleepers — characteristics rooted in the mechanism of projection.

But can the same psychological mechanism really be at work in our portrayal of sleeper terrorists today? Terrorists are clearly not "nightmare witches" in Mair's sense of the word: a fantasy embodying the opposite of right society. Their existence is well documented, and the results of their actions are blatantly evident. Yet it is not the reality of terrorists that I am calling into question by comparing the language of terrorism to that of witchcraft persecutions. Rather, I wish to demonstrate how, when faced with a serious threat, old, familiar discourses can easily take hold in society, with two unintended results: innocent people are invariably caught in the net meant for criminals, and the complex political relationships between self and other, state and terrorist, are reduced to essentializations. Black-and-white distinctions between good and evil, so characteristic of projection, protect the state from seeing its own part in creating the very circumstances that lead to the emergence of terrorism. Just as in the case of psychological defense mechanisms, they allow the state to exist in an imagined universe in which it is purely good, and all the evil is projected outside the boundaries of society onto foreign terrorists. By obliterating that evil through a protracted "war on terrorism," a state of purity can ultimately be achieved.

In order for projective inversion to be at work, according to Dundes' definition, the state, which accuses terrorists of plotting the demise of the American government and its entire way of life, would have to be engaged in exactly those same actions – or at least harbor a desire to do so. An examination of recent United States policy in the Middle East illustrates that in multiple settings, the United States is aiding or directly involved in planning military attacks against non-white Muslim populations or states. Since September 2001, the United States had made war on Afghanistan and Iraq. In each case, it fought against governments it had helped establish, supply and arm in order to combat Soviet expansionism, in the case of Afghanistan, and Iran's Fundamentalist Islamic regime, in the case of Iraq. The United States has historically been inimical to any regime which might restrict American access to valuable oil reserves in the Middle East and Central Asia. When it has supported Islamist states, they have often been governments which deny their citizens the very freedoms it claims to champion and cherish, and which it accuses the terrorists of coveting, as in the case of Saudi Arabia. Moreover, recent American foreign policy in Israel and Palestine has upheld the repressive policies of the Sharon government. It would be relatively easy for an outsider to interpret these facts as a desire on the part of the United States to destroy Islamist states and deprive their citizens of liberty and prosperity. This brief overview alone suggests that it is possible to interpret the discourse of sleeper terrorists as a case of projective inversion.

The discourse of the evil sleeper terrorist hiding among us, waiting to strike may reflect actual intelligence gathered by the FBI and CIA; but it is part of a continuing discourse in American history that blames social and political ills on evil infiltrators. Yet this apocalyptic narrative of moral struggle distracts public attention from the very real political causes underlying this situation. Moreover, discourses that contrast symbolic opposites – "good" vs. "evil" – without a more subtle delineation of cause and effect create an ideal medium for the growth of counter-cultural narratives of resistance. Targeted minority groups inevitably feel marginalized by these simplistic schemes, especially when they only heighten negative sentiments about them in the dominant culture.[3] In some cases, targeted groups may choose to identify with the negative pole of the symbolic system, reclaiming the narrative as one of heroism, martyrdom and sacrifice. It is not surprising, given this tendency, that in the two years since the attacks on the World Trade Center and the Pentagon, terrorist attacks against the United States and its perceived allies have increased, rather than decreased. The August 19, 2003 bombing of the United Nations headquarters in Baghdad illustrates that, as terrorism scholar Jessica Stern writes, "... America has taken a country that was not a terrorist threat and turned it into one" (Stern 2003). Columnist Maureen Dowd put it even more bluntly:

"The Bush team has now created the very monster that it conjured up to alarm Americans into backing a war on Iraq. Rushing to pummel Iraq after 9/11, Bush officials ginned up links between Saddam and Al Qaeda. They made it sound as if Islamic fighters on a jihad against America were slouching towards Baghdad to join forces with murderous Iraqis. There was scant evidence of it then, but it's coming true now. Since America began its occupation, Iraq has become the mecca for every angry, hate-crazed Arab extremist who wants to liberate the Middle East from the 'despoiling' grasp of the infidels (Dowd 8/20/2003)."

These reactions illustrate the perils of state discourses based on projection or projective inversion. While it seems likely that such discourses may arise spontaneously at times when states and social groups feel threatened by social change or outside pressures, their espousal by the state is a disturbing development. As the history of the witch trials illustrates, and as folklorist Bill Ellis points out in his study of the role of folklore in the spread of legends of Satanic activities in the 20th century United States (Ellis 2000), when popular discourses are instrumentalized by the state for political purposes, the results can be deadly and counter-productive. As poet W.H. Auden wrote:

"I and the public know
What all schoolchildren learn:
Those to whom evil is done
Do evil in return."

Notes

1. The majority of witches tried and executed in the American colonies were female, although some were male – notably the farmer Giles Corey, who was pressed to death as a punishment for allegedly causing sleep paralysis in his victims. Likewise, the majority of European victims were female, except in certain areas of Europe – Iceland, Finland and Estonia – where they were male.
2. During 2002–2003, hate crimes against perceived Middle Easterners or Muslims once again returned to their pre-September 11 levels, according to LAPD statistics.
3. According to a Los Angeles Times poll, only 14% of Americans have a favorable view of Islam (Watanabe, 2002).

References

Atran, Scott 2003: "Who Wants to Be a Martyr?" *The New York Times*, May 5.
Auden, W. H. 1976: "September 1, 1939." In: Edward Mendelson (ed.): *W.H. Auden: Selected Poems*. New York.
Bamford, James 2002: "Washington Bends the Rules." *The New York Times*, August 27.
Block, Zachary 2002: "One Man's War on Terror." *Brown Alumni Monthly*, November/December, pp. 39–45.
Bonomo, Giuseppe 1959: *Caccia alle streghe*. Palermo.
Boyer, Bruce and Steven Nissenbaum 1997: *Salem Possessed. The Social Origins of Witchcraft*. New York.
Briggs, Robin 1996: *Witches and Neighbors: the Social and Cultural Context of European Witchcraft*. New York.
Brzezinski, Matthew 2002: "Hady Hassan Omar's Detention." *The New York Times Magazine*, October 27, pp. 50–55.
Brzezinski, Zbigniew 2002: "Confronting Anti-American Grievances." *The New York Times*, September 1.
Caro Baroja, Julio 1965: *The World of the Witches*. Chicago.
Dorson, Richard M. 1973: *America in Legend*. New York.
Dowd, Maureen 2003: "Magnet for Evil." *The New York Times*, August 20.
Dundes, Alan 1980: "Projection in Folklore." In: Alan Dundes: *Interpreting Folklore*. Bloomington.
Dundes, Alan 1991. "The Ritual Murder or Blood Libel Legend: A Study of Anti-Semitic Victimization through Projective Inversion." In: Alan Dundes (ed.): *The Blood Libel Legend: a Casebook*, pp. 336–376. Madison.
Ellis, Bill 2000: *Raising the Devil: Satanism, New Religions and the Media*. Lexington.
Emerson, Steven 2001: *American Jihad: the Terrorists Living Among Us*. New York.
Fox, Stephen 1990: *The Unknown Internment. An Oral History of the Relocation of Italian Americans during World War II*. Boston.
Ginzburg, Carlo 1989: *Storia Notturna: una decifrazione del sabba*. Torino.
Goodman, Suzanne 2001: Letter to the Editor, *The New York Times*, October 31.
Halbfinger, David M. 2002: "Terror Scare in Florida: False Alarm, but Televised." *The New York Times*, September 14.
Hofstadter, Richard 1966: "The Paranoid Style in American Politics." In: *The Paranoid Style in American Politics and Other Essays*, pp. 3–40. New York.
Hufford, David 1982: *The Terror that Comes in the Night: an Experience Centered Study of Supernatual Assault Traditions*. Philadelphia.
Kernberg, Otto F. 1987: "Projection and Projective Identification: Developmental and Clinical Aspects."

In: Joseph Sandler (ed.): *Projection, Identification, Projective Identification*, pp. 93–116. Madison.

Krugman, Paul 2002: "Connect the Dots." *The New York Times*, April 2.

Mair, Lucy 1969: *Witchcraft*. New York.

Muraro Vaiani, Luisa 1976: *La signora del gioco: episodi della caccia alle streghe*. Milano.

Norton, Mary Beth 2002a: *In the Devil's Snare: the Salem Witchcraft Crisis of 1692*. New York.

Norton, Mary Beth 2002b: "They Called It Witchcraft." *The New York Times*, October 31.

Open Forum 76/4 2002.

Ray, Bipasha 2002: "Sacco-Vanzetti anniversary raises fresh questions about executions, treatment of immigrants." *The Boston Globe*, August 22.

Saffire, William 2001: "The Way We Live Now: On Language." *The New York Times*, November 11.

Scheer, Robert 2002: "We've Had Enough Witch Hunts." *The Los Angeles Times,* June 4.

Sontag, Susan 2002: "Real Battles and Empty Metaphors." *The New York Times*, September 10.

Stern, Jessica 2003: "How America Created a Terrorist Haven." *The New York Times*, August 20.

Victor, Jeffrey S. 1993: *Satanic Panic: the Creation of a Contemporary Legend*. Chicago.

Watanabe, Teresa 2002: "Frustrated U.S. Muslims Feel Marginalized Again." *The Los Angeles Times*, September 27.

Worth, Robert F. 2002: "A Nation Defines Itself by Its Evil Enemies." *The New York Times* February 24.

The Enemy Within
From Evil Others to Evil Elites

Véronique Campion-Vincent

Campion-Vincent, Véronique 2003: The Enemy Within: From Evil Others to Evil Elites. – Ethnologia Europaea 33:2: 23–31.

The idea and expression of "the enemy within" is briefly explored in its multiple uses. Arising parallel with the emergence of individualism, this notion was first tied to the religious ideals of purifying the self, later secularized and revived with the development of the idea of the unconscious. It is especially close to the notion of conspiracy. In folklore, the description of Others, through tales, is mostly ethnocentric and negative. A tentative classification of tales, with respect to visibility and origin, is suggested, and the detours and ambiguities that characterize folklore discussed. The contemporary orientation of conspiracy theories – present in the three realms of folklore, popular fiction, and social protest movements – to denounce "evil elites" is briefly commented on: these theories were widespread in explaining the September 11th, 2001 terrorist attacks in the U.S. However, the story of "the compassionate terrorist," one that reflects the detours and ambiguities of folklore, is the most representative of the spontaneous lore linked to terrorist attacks.

Véronique Campion-Vincent, MSH, Maison des Sciences de l'Homme, 54 boulevard Raspail, F-75006 Paris. E-mail: campion@msh-paris.fr

The Notion of "the Enemy Within"

This expression is very widely used. An August 2002 Google search for "the enemy within" returned links to 31,700 pages – and more than 1,300,000 if the quotes were omitted[1] – many of which were connected to activists and extremists of all kinds, from Lyndon La Rouche to anti-Islam fanatics. The expression is widely used in the self-help literature, advising readers to fight the internal enemy with special diets or spiritual exercises. It is a catch phrase for science fiction and strategy computer games. L. Ron Hubbard wrote a novel entitled *The Enemy Within* (1986)[2] that is still promoted by the Church of Scientology, and references to this book account for many of the above-mentioned websites. Computer security experts often use the expression in their promotional literature, and medical specialists, in promoting their conferences, often use "the enemy within" as a metaphor for cancer.

While this list accounts for the most commonplace usages, this expression demarcates a discourse and domain in academic political science as well. This is reflected not only in book-length studies and in the special issues of journals such as *Cultures et Conflits* (2001), but also in dedicated databases and coordinated research programs[3] that study the various uses of this expression. Historically, the state apparatus in non-democratic regimes, including the Nazi, Communist, and various dictatorships, has labeled elements dangerous to the regime as "the enemy within" and used it as a call to arms and tool for political mobilization. Examples range from the designation of entire categories as "enemies of the people" (e.g., the "Kulaks" in Russia during the late 1920s), to having dictators demonize growing opposition groups as "unnatural" or "enemies of the nation," particularly when such leaders are losing power. The expression has also been widely used by politicians and leaders of factions in democratic contexts, from Senator Joseph McCarthy denouncing suspected Communists and the "Red Menace" during the 1950s in the U.S. to the British Prime Minister Margaret Thatcher attacking trade unions, especially those that represented coalminers in the 1980s.

Conceptions of the Individual

The notion of "the enemy within" is also linked to the emergence of individualism in European thought since the 16th century. That tradition of self-examination, as taught in both Catholic and Protestant denominations, was aimed at purifying the sinner haunted by the menacing presence of evil in the human soul. In that era the temptations of sex, as well as odors and the sense of smell, were demonized whereas the sense of vision – linked to light – was advocated, as the eye was considered the gateway to the soul (Muchembled 2000: 119–147).

After the rediscovery of the unconscious, first through the promotion of hypnosis (in the era of Charcot and the Salpêtrière School in the late 19th century) and later with the founding of psychoanalysis, the psychoanalytical notions of the id and of repression renewed and secularized the concept of the interior Other. The emergence during the 1980s in the U.S. of the controversial hypothesis that there was a psychiatric condition called "multiple personality disorder" (Mulhern 1991), as well as the attention at the time paid to Satanism, increased this tendency to perceive "the enemy within."

"Sleepers" Unknowingly Harboring Violence

Historians who have studied the behavior within the Nazi elite, especially the SS, have used the notion of "sleepers." John Steiner (1980), who conducted research on the psychological profiles of SS members who voluntarily entered the force, first applied the notion to the violent tendencies some individuals harbored, tendencies which remained latent until they could flourish under conditions that cultivated and encouraged such behavioral tendencies, such as the exceptional circumstance of being an active member of a professional corps that encouraged the use of violence. In the wider scope of the study of genocide and group violence, Ervin Staub (1989) further elaborated Steiner's hypothesis, stressing that sleepers who harbored violent tendencies were very common in the general population.

Conspiracies

The idea of the expression "the enemy within" refers to the wider notion of a conspiracy and it denounces a group that threatens the very existence of the society that it has infiltrated. Americans have a long history of conspiracy fears, having been agitated at one time or another by the imagined dangers posed by Catholics, Jews, Freemasons, Communists and fellow travelers, capitalists, trade unions agitators and workers, witches, slaves, blacks, carpetbaggers, the Ku Klux Klan, white slavers, and racketeers. The list can readily be expanded, and this tendency has been very ably captured in the classic essay "The Paranoid Style in American Politics" (Hofstadter 1966). Yet Fenster (1999) has attacked Hofstadter's approach as having labeled dominant groups as normal while erroneously designating all those outside it and all political protesters as pathological (20); the forms of symbolic expression in protest are not analyzed, nor is "the political and cultural role of conspiracy theory in popular conceptions of power" recognized (62). Conspiracy theories are wrong, but they have legitimacy, as they address structural inequities and respond to the weakening of civil society and the corresponding concentration of power in oligarchies (67).

The development of alternative media has permitted a kind of conspiracy community to emerge, one that apes the academic community of scholars at its "assassination conferences," and these are occasions at which individual researchers intermingle briefly and discuss theories of conspiracies (182). Rather than identifying "with the lives of those who interpret and enter into the narratives of apocalypse and conspiracy," their approach often mixes fascination with irony. "Recognizing and conceptualizing the excitement and laughter of 'finding' and 'following' conspiracy is a crucial step in understanding the contemporary cultural fascination with conspiracy theory," Fenster notes (1999:201), and the Bible for such conspiracy 'theorists' is the trilogy *Illuminatus!*

(Wilson & Shea 1975), which itself has been expanded into fictional sequels and "prequels", essays and aphorisms, role-playing and board games (Fenster 1999: 202–203). Such transformations parody the fear of conspiracy and subvert conspiracy theory through humor. In addition, today's conspiracies are often asserted to have come from organized crime, which is depicted "as a confederation of Mafia families" whose power extends beyond the sphere of organized crime into the control of government and legitimate businesses[4] (Best 1999: 82).

What is more surprising for Europeans in this context, given the American belief in conspiracies, are their denunciation. Satanism, for example, is depicted as a blood-cult with numerous followers, whose hidden and unsuspected members sacrifice several thousand babies on a regular basis in their efforts to conquer and retain power (Richardson, Best, Bromley 1991). Similarly, the idea exists that evil extraterrestrials (in conspiracy with government insiders to whom they grant extraordinary powers through advanced military technology) are engaged in a takeover of society, though it is mostly pursued as "entertaining" fiction, as in the successful *Men In Black* movies, and in a darker vein, the increasingly fantastic *X-Files* television series. In popular fiction, one should also note, the image of the benevolent extraterrestrial warning us against the madness of our civilization – along the lines of Steven Spielberg's *E.T.* – competes with this negative, evil alien aspect.

Since popular fiction in Europe is thoroughly dominated by American entertainment, such themes also exist, but they evoke little social emotion. In the U.K., France and Belgium, however, there is a strong public belief in a conspiracy that unites a huge network of pedophiles (who are considered a powerful segment of society and capable of coordinated action) with elites. This conspiracy is largely imaginary, but belief in its existence is correlated with the existence of a general resentment against incompetent (or indifferent) official responses to sex crimes perpetrated against children.

The Many, and Mostly Evil, Aspects of "Others"

There are various "others," mostly evil, in the universe of folklore and particularly in contemporary legend, and it is to these that I next turn. We are no longer in the realm of the strident denunciation of the social activist who denounces conspiracies, but rather in the biased realm of folklore. In today's multicultural societies, the tales told about immigrants and minorities are mostly ethnocentric and negative, and in the performance of such tales one sees the delineation and definition of the limits of ethnic boundaries. It seems that the positive portrait of "us" emerges discreetly, and as an indirect result of the positive halo the negative image of tales about "them" casts.

Visibility and Origins

We can distinguish among outsiders based on their visibility and origin: are they visible or do they, purposely, make themselves invisible? Do they come from without or from within the society where they are located in which the relevant tale is told?

visibility:	visible:	invisible origin:
from without	ethnic minorities (color language or religion)	jews
from within	deviants (offensive lifestyles, drug addicts, punks, drunks)	deviants (acting normal, secret cults, pedophiles)

Ethnic minorities have become more visible as they refuse to forget or refuse to sacrifice their heritage in the name, or on the altar, of acculturation. Once common goals weaken, and the ideal of what is 'good' in terms of manners, speech, and clothing becomes less agreed upon. Deviants are also visible, because though they originate in our society, they do not behave or belong with the normal "us," as their lifestyle is offensive. They were yesterday's heretics, witches, lepers, and sodomites; today they belong to dangerous cults, are HIV carriers, or lesbians or gays who parade proudly each year through cities. In a development that parallels the growing visibility of ethnic minorities, these deviants have also become more visible.

As for invisible outsiders, we think we can spot these dangerous ethnic minorities that seem assimilated but remain hidden outsiders, with their agenda of aggression and their determination to take control over their host society. The denunciation of such dangerous outsiders belongs more to the universe of social activists and the realm of popular fiction than it does to the universe of folklore, where humor often provides a counterweight to denunciation. The basic subtext of anti-Semitism was that the Jew was all the more dangerous precisely because he seemed to be one of "us." Those deviants who seem normal, but have hidden aspects, are especially feared, as was the case when "secret" cults started to be denounced in the 1970s. The criminal pedophile, leading a seemingly normal life that is only discovered to be deviant after he's done his worst, is the best example of this today.

These depictions of visible and invisible outsiders are especially interesting not at the level of social protest movements, since those who denounce outsiders appeal mostly to the extremist fringes of society, but at the level of popular fiction and of folklore, both of which have a wider audience. These three realms are complementary. It is striking, for example, that the worst offenders to today's sensitivities, such as pedophiles, are branded by activists and terrifyingly portrayed in popular fiction but by and large ignored in folklore and contemporary legend.

The Detours and Ambiguities of Folklore
In Denmark, Tangherlini (1995) has shown that many contemporary legends featuring immigrants or minorities have close parallels with earlier legends that featured supernatural creatures. Stories of young Danish girls narrowly escaping kidnapping in Arab shops in Paris, their fate to be forced into prostitution, are echoed in traditional legends of supernatural forest creatures stealing young girls (41–43). The food scare that swept Western Europe in 1977, when a Palestinian organization in Holland claimed to have injected mercury into Israeli oranges,[5] has parallels in the legend told by a man poisoned as a young boy when he ate a tempting fruit he found on the road, a fruit that was placed there by an unknown evil hand (49–50). Horror stories are told about the theft, by immigrants, of household pets to be used for food. The owner chases the immigrant and rescues the pet just as it is about to be sacrificed in the immigrants' kitchen, or alternately, the police arrive at the thieves' house too late: "dinner was just finished. The entire family of Turks sat around the table and only the gnawed bones were left" (51). These echo stories about the *ellefolk* (elves) of yesterday who stole bread from shepherds and cats from village houses (52). Deviants (rather than immigrants) are targeted in the story of the severed fingers: a nurse traveling back home at night narrowly escapes attackers (often described as a motorcycle gang), by slamming her car door and driving away at full speed, only to find severed fingers in the car's door when she returns to her garage. This story parallels traditional tales of "failed attacks," especially when the traveling horseman cuts the hand of one of the robbers (52–57). The Danish legends of both yesterday and today center on instances of interacting with the Other who is far closer than we think, pretending to be one of "us" and operating in the inner circles of our society.

In the realm of contemporary legend, which draws its persuasive strength from the detour of the narrative – the quaint, funny, or scary incident said to have "truly happened" – seems to "naturally" lead to a conclusion denouncing a hidden evil Other. Thus, the story of the snake in the store, still told in the 1980s though noted already in the late 1960s describes the death of a (generally female) customer after she's been bitten by a creature hiding in an exotic item (a blanket, a rug, even a garment) for sale at a discount store.

It denounces the foreigner, here metaphorically designated through his products, in a manner similar to the 1970s story of the rat bone. Here the bone in question is discovered when a dentist removes it from a client's throat after a good lunch in an ethnic restaurant[6] – not merely a denunciation of poor restaurant health standards but pointing to voluntary pollution on the part of the miserly foreigner.

A parallel can be drawn with the globally known 1980s story of the rat dog (the American variant is called the Mexican pet). An innocent and kindhearted, but a little oblivious, female tourist brings an animal back from an exotic holiday, thinking it's a cute dog that can make a nice pet. It turns out to be a – very sick – rat after it kills a local pet. It is tempting to see a metaphoric equivalence here between the rat dog and the immigrant who not only deceives those who naively welcomed him about his aggressiveness (hidden on arrival but revealed later), but also about his state of health (seemingly healthy but in fact sick). They make him a menace to those among whom he now lives.

These examples of animal contamination that contain different messages reflect the distinctive use of masking and detours that are characteristic of folklore. Folklore is a generally ambiguous device as well, as can be seen in the seemingly "nice" and "funny" anecdote of "the helpful Mafia neighbor." In this story, soft-spoken and well-dressed newcomer neighbors advise a couple whose home has just been burglarized not to report it to the police until they "make a few phone calls and see what can be done." Indeed, the next morning the victimized couple finds all their stolen possessions neatly piled on their front porch. This example is not devoid of anxieties, for the extraordinary powers the Mafia neighbors possess could well be employed for evil purposes (Brunvand 2001: 191).

Still, this ambiguity also permits folklore to sometimes redress the balance and ridicule the expression of ethnic prejudice, as in the anecdotes of The Elevator Incident, Sharing by Error, and The Eaten Ticket whose messages seem to be to preach tolerance.

- "The Elevator Incident tells the story of three provincial women lost in the city who are extremely frightened by the presence of a big black man and his dog with them in their elevator. They misunderstand the command 'Sit!', which was addressed to the dog, and sit down on the floor of the elevator, expecting to be robbed. The black man, who usually is a renowned figure in sports or pop music, laughs; subsequently, he pays their hotel bill or sends them flowers. His good humor and generosity shows the foolishness of the women's fright and that the menace was imaginary. The specificity of the situation is typically American, and probably explains why the story has not really become international. Non-American versions in New Zealand (Brunvand 1989: 71), Germany (Brednich 1991: No. 59: 81–2, media source) or South Africa (Goldstuck 1990: 178–181, Hind 1990), locate the incident in a large American city, the heroine an elderly and proper New Zealander or South African visiting U.S. relatives; the heroine of the German version is an American" (Campion-Vincent 1995: 22).

- In Sharing by Error, set in a train station snack shop or a department store cafeteria, a proper middle-aged woman shares a table with an immigrant, or deviant, and mistakenly helps herself to his packet of biscuits or his meal. The immigrant or deviant lets himself be wronged, and the punchline of the story is the discovery of her error by the confused woman. The story is a variation on the older Theft by Error theme, in which a protagonist imagines having been robbed and robs in revenge, only to discover later that his suspicions were unjustified and that he has now perpetrated a robbery and cannot redeem it since "the aggrieved party is unknown and out of reach." This story has been widely diffused since its appearance in the 1970s, and has inspired at least five short films, one of which (the 1989 American film *The Lunch Date* by Adam Davidson) "received the Grand Prix du Court Métrage in Cannes (Palme d'Or) in 1990, and a Short Film Oscar in 1991" (Campion-Vincent 1995: 22).

- The story of The Eaten Ticket appeared in Denmark in the 1980s, and soon spread to neighboring countries. Located in a city bus or tram, it features a prejudiced lady who misbehaves by expressing – loudly or through disgusted gestures and expressions – the displeasure she feels at being seated near a conspicuous punk. The punk does not react, but when the ticket controller arrives and the lady holds up her ticket he suddenly grabs, chews, and swallows her ticket. The controller does not accept the lady's accusation ("He ate it!"), and as no one in the bus supports her, she has to pay a heavy fine. When a publicity film promoting seasonal bus passes used the incident in Oslo in 1987 (the punk showed his season card to the controller), the anecdote received public exposure when the film was aired at the 1988 Cannes's Festival of TV and Film Commercials. Oral versions than started to circulate in Switzerland and France, but in these the punk had been replaced by an immigrant, the fact of whose blackness and threats were significant[7]. Two other short films with this theme were made in 1993: the Belgian *La dame dans le tram* and the German *Schwarzfahrer* (by Pepe Danquart; it received an Oscar in 1994).

These three stories "appear to comment on the typical conditions of modernity, and to exploit a set of problems very present in modern society – 'non-places', public behavior, and a world full of strangers. In these circumstances, the message of the three anecdotes is not unambiguous – it oscillates between tolerance and the justification of prejudice" (Campion-Vincent 1995: 28).

Our Evil Elites

Compared with their past counterparts, today's conspiracy theories have loosened their links to religion: then, it was the devil who was the ultimate conspirator. Now conspiracy theories can be considered instead as a sort of folk social science or folk history, a "subculture of intellectual dissent" (Eliason 1996). They aim to provide meaningful and accurate explanations of the world's condition, which is seen as increasingly complex as the media become more and more omnipresent via TV and instant transmission.

Conspiracy theories have become a thriving industry, from which whole sectors of literature and the media draw their substance. They have recently evolved towards denouncing the powerful in society, rather than branding outsiders such as foreign powers or cultures. This is clear when we consider, for example, the recent evolution of themes such as the Kennedy saga, Marilyn Monroe's sad fate[8], Jack the Ripper's identity[9], or the suggested conspiracy that links the government to evil extraterrestrials. This evolution accompanies the spread of such themes in the general public, which (beyond the small groups of the active conspiracy 'theorists') is increasingly receptive to suggestions that things are not what they seem, or that our own leaders are deceiving us even though we elected them.

The expression of denunciation of evil elites and their conspiracies are numerous in folklore. To stay with our previous examples of contamination, the designated villains today are less likely to be foreigners than to be greedy corporations who are a part of our society but behave like enemies and spread poisons in their unchecked pursuit of profit. Persistent rumors alleging that a fast food chain, or a clothing manufacturer, or a food company is affiliated or owned by a racist group (and that its founder or CEO has made racist or bigoted statements on TV) exemplify these folk denunciations of "corporate malfeasance." Allegations of government conspiracies to create or spread the HIV virus (so as to wipe out undesirables), or of plans to limit religious activity, or sell the country to the UN, etc. are also widespread and circulate in the most diverse strata of American society.

The theme of conspiracy by an evil elite is especially widespread in popular fiction, and for over a hundred years we have had depictions of mad scientists, today often placed in the group of evil elites as doctors in the thriving sub-genre of the "medical thriller." The conspiracy of the powerful (together with evil extraterrestrials) is the subtext that links the various episodes of *The X-Files* television series together. In the public protests that denounce globalization, national or cultural frontiers among protesters but also the objects of protest themselves seem to have disappeared. A brotherhood of dissenters protests the acts of the elites – dominated by the West but with cohorts in all nations – and those elites are consistently depicted as "enemies of the people" who are linked together in malevolent conspiracies that aim to throw the powerless into the clutches of "the market."

After 911

Have there been changes in these conceptions of enemies following the terrorist attacks of September 11th, 2001? Reality is of course far removed from conspiracy theories, and without doubt, the attacks were perpetratred by a group of enemies who are complete outsiders. They hold values different from those of the materialistic Western World dominated by the U.S. However, the concept of "our" evil elites is so strongly embedded in contemporary culture that it has played a large part in trying to interpret what could have been behind these ominous attacks. This is reflected in apparently minor facts such as the popularity of Noam Chomsky's book on 911 (2001)[10], though it was by and large ignored by the media.

The disproportionate attention paid in the media to the many extremists who asserted the attacks were actually a U.S. conspiracy also seems relevant. The surprising success in France, but also among English speakers, of books stating that no plane crashed into the Pentagon and that the U.S. organized the attacks (Meyssan 2002a, 2002b), is based on tapping into a whole array of conspiracy theories (that one can find on the Internet, and mostly of American origin) that name the U.S. government as the real perpetrator (Dasquié & Guisnel 2002).

Rather than explaining the attacks, such conspiracy theories partly deny their existence, and instead of raising methodical doubt adopt a generalized doubt close to a form of instant revisionism. Facts are not simply re-evaluated or contested, but denied practically at the same time as they happen and are told. Rather than focusing on the conspiracies of obscure outsiders, they mostly accuse the media, who are considered the heralds of the authorities. In this interpretative system, the media obstruct the truth, transmitting official versions of it whose undisclosed aim is actually to hide the conspiracy: as accomplices of the authorities, they are participating in the conspiracy (Taïeb 2003: 12–14).

The Compassionate Terrorist

The threads of folklore are more consoling than those of the conspiracy theories that today seem the real promoters of "the enemy within" approach. Many are familiar with the story of the compassionate terrorist, which, in the version I received (in mid-October, 2001), goes as follows:[11] "In London, a young girl sees a wallet falling from the pocket of the male character, a man of Middle Eastern appearance, strolling in front of her. She picks it up, runs after the man and gives it to him. He thanks her and says: 'Stay out of London tomorrow (the 18th of October) for there will be an attack'. The girl thanks him, but finds this strange and goes to the police to report the advice. The police show her pictures of terrorists and in one of them, she recognizes her benevolent adviser."

The story points to a conspiracy: everything is planned, and it is to be carried out by Middle Eastern foreigners. But the story is also in the realm of folklore, given how ambiguous its message is. It is racist to the extent that an Arab or an Afghan knows what others like him are doing (they are all accomplices, all in on the conspiracy) and anti-racist at the same time, because the sensitivity of the enemy means he can act as a friend – and yet we don't think of that because our prejudices hamper our judgment (Taïeb 2003: 7). We have difficulty in perceiving the Other, or perceiving the nature of the Other's identity. In French versions, the story often is located in the subway, a place where we meet unknown characters who are difficult to identify, especially in troubled times like these. What are we to make of this man who is a deeply suspect enemy in the know about forthcoming attacks, yet also a "friendly enemy capable of feeling gratitude and sensitivity" (Taïeb 2003:8).

The trouble of identity is maximal: the man is an enemy, but a friendly enemy, who does not correspond to the image of an enemy since he shows gratitude and sensibility. The story could be closed on this conflicting image but the closure would not be satisfactory; the Other has to be identified clearly. And it is the police, a body of law and order that is going to decide, by showing pictures of known terrorists from which she identifies him. The man is clearly identified, and as an enemy.

The story seeks to comprehend the motives of terrorists, imputing empathy of a sort characteristic of the lifeworld of the narrator him- or herself. Personal relations are, to this fictional terrorist, more important than politics and thus he responds to a gesture of solidarity with a life-saving warning (Fine and Khawaja 2003). The legend belongs to the larger thematic complex of "the friendly enemy" which psychologically serves to exorcise the narrators' fear of the aggressor. Marie Bonaparte collected anecdotes about the victorious yet compassionate enemy who provided crucial warnings saving the narrators during the Second World War (1947). In the present story, the exchange with the terrorist begins over a lost wallet, invoking the motif *immunity from disaster as reward*[12] in which a supernatural being amply rewards a small favor received from a human (Campion-Vincent & Renard 2002:246–247). The legend has reappered in France at the end of 2002, with warnings mostly concerning shopping malls in large cities like Marseille, Lyon, Grenoble and Strasbourg. It may express the belief or at least wish that the enemy from within or without, who is so difficult to spot, can be tamed.

Notes

1. In September 2003, the same search returned links to 66,700 pages, and more than 2,180,000 without the quotes.
2. It was the third tome of his multivolume *Missing Earth*.
3. In particular, the research project conducted by the Slavics Department of the University of Zurich that examines Socialist propaganda, and that is supported by the Swiss National Foundation.
4. Let's recall that in 1960, Robert Francis Kennedy published The Enemy Within reporting the McClellan committees' activities against corrupt labor unions.
5. It was echoed in Italy by another announcement concerning cyanide injected into Israeli grapefruit.
6. The restaurant was said to be Greek when the story was told in Sweden, North African or Yugoslav when told in Germany, and Chinese when told in France or the UK.
7. In a Lausanne newspaper, a reader's letter narrating the incident was entitled: "The Lady and the Cannibal". In oral versions circulating in Grenoble, the black told the lady: "Next time, it's you I'll eat."
8. She is supposed to have been murdered by Bobby Kennedy (Anthony Summers: *Goddess: The Secret Lives of Marilyn Monroe*, 1986).
9. He is said to have seen a high placed member of the Royal Family, protected by an elite conspiracy.
10. Chomsky's publishers in New York describe 9–11 as "the most influential counter-narrative of dissent" and specify it sold "over 300,000 copies" and was "#1 paperback in Canada throughout 2002", while his French publisher calls it "a bestseller that sold millions of copies all over the world, the bedside book of all the anti-war" [le livre de chevet de tous les anti-guerre].
11. In the U.S. variant, the girl is warned not by a chance acquaintance but by her Arab or Afghan boyfriend; that version barely circulated in Europe.
12. Motif Q150 (Thompson 1969).

References

Best, Joel 1999: *Random Violence. How we Talk about New Crimes and New Victims*. Berkeley/Los Angeles/London.
Bonaparte, Marie. 1946: *Myths of War*. London.
Brednich, Rolf Wilhelm 1991: *Die Maus im Jumbo-Jet. Neue sagenhafte Geschichten von heute*. München.
Brunvand, Jan Harold 1989: *Curses! Broiled Again. The Hottest Urban Legends Going*. New York.
Brunvand, Jan Harold 2001: *Encyclopedia of Urban Legends*. Santa Barbara.
Campion-Vincent, Véronique 1995: Preaching Tolerance? *Folklore*: 21–30.
Campion-Vincent, Véronique & Jean-Bruno Renard. 2002 : *De source sure. Nouvelles rumeurs d'aujourd'hui*. Paris.
Chomsky, Noam 2001: *9–11*. New York [11/9. Paris].
Cultures et Conflits 2001: Special Issue – Construire l'ennemi intérieur.
Dasquié, Guillaume & Guisnel, Jean 2002: *L'effroyable mensonge. Thèse et foutaises sur les attentats du 11 septembre*. Paris.
Eliason, Eric 1996: Conspiracy Theories. In: J.H. Brunvand (ed.): *American Folklore. An Encyclopedia*. New York/London: 157–158.
Fenster, Mark 1999: *Conspiracy Theories. Secrecy and Power in American Culture*. Minneapolis/London.
Fine, Gary Alan & Irfan Khawaja. 2003. Celebrating Arabs and Kindly Terrorists: Rumor and the Politics of Plausibilitiy. Unpublished paper presented at the Conference on "Rumor". Bellagio, Italy.
Goldstuck, Arthur 1990: *The Rabbit in the Thorn Tree. Modern Myth and Urban Legends in South Africa*. Johannesburg: 178–181.
Hind, Cynthia 1990: South Africans in Elevators. *Foaftale News* 20 (December): 10–11.

Hofstadter, Richard 1966: *The Paranoid Style in American Politics and Other Essays*. New York.

Meyssan, Thierry 2002a: *September 11, 2001. The Big Lie*. Paris.

Meyssan, Thierry 2002b: *The Pentagate*. Paris.

Muchembled, Robert 2000: *Une histoire du diable. XII–XX siècle*. Paris.

Mulhern, Sherrill 1991: Satanism and Psychotherapy: A Rumor in Search of an Inquisition. In: J.T. Richardson, J. Best & D.G. Bromley (eds.): *The Satanism Scare*. New York: 145–172.

Richardson, James T., Joel Best & David G. Bromley (eds.) 1991: *The Satanism Scare*. New York.

Staub, Ervin 1989: *The Roots of Evil: The Origins of Genocide and Other Group Violence*. Cambridge.

Steiner, John 1980: The SS Yesterday and Today: A Sociopsychological View. In: J.E. Dimsdale (ed.) *Survivors, Victims and Perpetrators: Essays on the Nazi Holocaust*. Washington: 431–444.

Taïeb, Emmanuel 2003 : De quelques rumeurs après le 11 septembre. *Quaderni* 50/51: 5–22.

Tangherlini, Timothy R. 1995: From Trolls to Turks: Continuity and Change in Danish Legend Tradition. *Scandinavian Studies* 67: 32–62.

Wilson, Robert A. & Shea, Robert 1975: *Illuminatus!* New York.

Sleepers' Secrets, Actors' Revelations

Regina Bendix

> Bendix, Regina 2003: Sleepers' Secrets, Actor's Revelations. – Ethnologia Europaea 33:2: 33–42.
>
> The paper addresses three sets of questions: What is the semantic reach of the term "sleeper" and what ambiguities derive from the divergent contexts and genres within which the term has been used? What is the link between sleepers and secrecy, and how do terrorist sleepers interfere with the culturally accepted workings of secrecy in social and political life? What narratives are set lose when sleepers reveal themselves in unexpected action? The paper is guided by Georg Simmel's recognition of secrecy's role in social life and seeks to demonstrate the problematic encounter of multiple codes of secrecy in culturally heterogeneous societies.
>
> *Prof. Dr. Regina Bendix, Institute for Cultural Anthropology / European Ethnology. Georg-August-Universität Göttingen, Friedländer Weg 2, D-37085 Göttingen. E-mail: rbendix@gwdg.de*

Introduction

There were many things to remark on after September 11, 2001, but in the confusion and horror after the World Trade Center catastrophe, I was particularly struck by the appearance of the term "sleeper". It was used to describe Al-Qaeda terrorists who had prepared, in the seemingly adjusted life style of students, for acts of tremendous destruction against the Western societies that hosted them.[1] The word appeared, briefly, in English, but was particularly evident in German mass media discourse, its use meant to invoke a link to secret agency and the broader evil lurking amongst us. Employing the term called attention to the ambiguity of "sleep" itself, as well as to the broad semantic connotation associated with the word "sleeper", and my intent here is to explore this semantic reach along with the potential and agency the term circumscribes within culturally heterogeneous societies.

At the heart of the notion of sleepers lies the knowledge, hope, and fear of secrecy. Georg Simmel described secrecy already in 1908 as a powerful invention and tool. Secrecy is not only central to religious and political power, it is also a cultural practice in everyday life by which groups and subgroups form, relationships achieve their specific contours, and through which we regulate communication (Simmel 1991:338–445).[2] Yet ethnography would only begin to pay heed to the theatricality of everyday interactions – which of necessity involved a hidden, secret, backstage domain – in the wake of a social interactionist theory in which to place them (Goffman 1959). So cultural analysts have only relatively recently turned to studying the modes of secret-keeping in action and discourse.

It is true that early anthropological work on native North Americans documented the existence and power of secret societies and noted the role of secrecy in various religious formations. Anthropologist Michael Taussig has offered a reading of Simmel's "secrecy magnifies reality" as well, in an effort to illuminate an array of cultural practices from private secrets (such as lying) to the public secrets encoded in ritual (1999: 49–97).[3] Though ritual scholarship has seldom emphasized the point[4], the liminality of ritual naturally allows for displays of what is normally held secret or hidden (and even forbidden), be this in behaviors or in the parading of a whole array of scary, wild or feared figures kept firmly locked away and "asleep" during the ordinary course of the year. Stratified and multicultural societies contain more complex modes of secret-keeping, with different subgroups developing mechanisms of hidden communication and identification. James Scott's *Domination and the Arts of Resistance* (1990) is a widely cited work that examines discursive patterns that establish secret resources. Folklorists and social historians have documented vernacular evidence of the power of secrecy in African-American subcultures (Levine 1977, Abrahams 1992), for example. Finally, a substantial scholarship exists on secret societies, their cultural practices and their social role(s) in history.[5]

Secrets come in many forms and at many levels, from the smallest, interpersonal interaction to the largest social and political arenas. Inventorying or classifying secrecy forms and levels is not the point here; instead, the interest is to develop the semantic, social and political ties between sleepers and the cultural practices of secrecy. However, secrecy is a domain of cultural practice that has not seen sufficient ethnographic attention, perhaps because the cultures of secrecy are used by the strong and because the research itself may endanger the ethnographer. We have large, if understandable, lacunae in the ethnographic record: where is the ethnography of secret service cultures when we need it most? The cultural practices of such a culture is the model – and in some cases has even been the teacher – of the very terrorist agents we now fear. So I would argue that attention to the ambiguity and partial social legitimacy of secrecy can inform our understanding of the sleeper complex. An examination of the semantic reach of the term sleeper itself is a first step in this direction.

Sleep, Sleepers and Their Cultural Meanings

Sleepers come in many forms and reside in many contexts.[6] There are those who "sleep like a baby" in the midst of the noise or chaos that surrounds them. One observes with wonder how the pupil who has performed poorly for years "suddenly wakes up" and shows interest or talent. Financiers blame themselves for having "slept" through golden opportunities. There are a variety of creatures (such as owls or bats) whose propensity to spend the day asleep and to stir at night has kept them (at least at a time before zoos allowed us to see their harmless doings close-up) in the category of suspect or feared creatures, and the invisibility or stealth of other animal predators (such as foxes or wolves) have led humans to surround such creatures with a host of legends and beliefs associated with danger and evil. There are more curious associations as well: the edible or fat dormouse (*glis glis*) is known as the *Siebenschläfer* (lit. the 'seven-sleeper') in German, with a folk etymology of the term stating either that this creature sleeps seven months a year or that the name derives from the legend of seven persecuted Christian brothers who were walled in and only awoke 200 years later[7].

There are gloomier associations as well. Viruses are described as "sleepers" that awaken to attack biological systems at unpredictable times, the immunological discourse thereby permitting a comparison to be drawn between terrorist sleepers attacking the state and sleeping viruses attacking the body.[8] In the world of toys, we find the yoyo called the "Grim Sleeper"[9] which received its name due to the capacity of "all modern yoyos" to 'sleep', that is, to turn freely when the string is fully extended.[10] This allows for all kinds of spectacular tricks that are not possible with the "classic" yoyo. Special techniques can considerably prolong the usual yoyo sleep time of 1–2 seconds, but "a sleeping yoyo that cannot be woken up would be pointless. [Waking] occurs with a quick tug of the string or a slap on the hand."[11] Calling a material object in stasis that has a capacity to revert to sudden motion a sleeper is not that unusual, though some examples deserve the adjective "grim" rather more than does the yoyo: time bombs or landmines awoken from their sleep by being disturbed long after the time for their mission has passed. Their waking up is indeed pointless, as the hidden goal for which they were prepared – to serve as deterrents to action – is no longer viable.

Legendry knows of sleepers who are not feared but in whom great hopes rest such as King Barbarossa, said to be asleep in the Kyffhäuser mountain in Thuringia, Germany. In the war and starvation-torn time in which the legend formed, the memory of his rule shone brightly, holding out the promise of sleep and awakening rather than death.[12] So many legends about powerful, righteous leaders asleep in a mountain or cliff exist in so many places, that a reference tool of the early 20th century even invented the term "translated-into-mountain" (*bergentrückt*) to describe the state these figures were in.[13] This religious meaning of "translation" – to convey to heaven or to a nontemporal condition without death – can be found in one of the legends surrounding Charlemagne, as he is to awake in time to fight the Anti-Christ. In the framework of Shiite Islam, of course, we also encounter the twelfth Imam, assumed to be removed but ready to reawaken (Halm 1994:41–50). All of these are figures who rest in secrecy and their awakening would bring justice, or a new golden age, or the world's end, or the entry to paradise. The assumption of such coming can serve as encouragement, but it can also be a means to keep a population in check.[14] The nearly magical disappearance of Osama bin Laden post-September 11 and of Saddam Hussein during the US attack on Irak in spring 2003 hold within them the potential of sleeper-legendry to come.

Once historical and comparative windows are opened, we can recognize that the term sleeper, with its related semantic field and associations, has been used for a great many phenomena other than Islamic fundamentalist terrorists. Not only fear of destruction but also hope for liberation is within the sleeper's semantic reach. All such associations refer back to the natural process we call sleep, and to understand the potency of the term as applied to secret agents, spies, moles, or terrorists, one needs to reflect on the phenomenon of sleep itself, and its elements of perceived secrecy or duplicity.[15]

Many expressions and traditional songs celebrate sweet and peaceful sleep, and thus honor the physiological need for rest and recovery that sleep grants. Yet some sleepers, breathing quietly and inaudibly, raise uncertainty and fear. It is not for nothing that "eternal sleep" is a metaphor for death, or that numerous traditional expressions point to the seeming proximity of sleeping and dying.[16] Sleep possesses us, much as death does, and our normal, communicative countenance is quiet.

Yet there is also a duality to sleep, since the sleeper is also communicating with an inner world closed to an onlooker. The sleeper's countenance reassures us that the conscious self is resting peacefully, yet the sleeping body and mind are simultaneously engaged in invisible activity. Dreams take the sleeper to an alternate world, closed to those with whom conscious life is shared. "Sleepwalking" or somnambulism is a striking phenomenon in this regard, fuelling the metaphoric use of "sleeper" as an externally controlled being or as possessing hidden identities. Psychological experiences in a sleep-dream state produce motor activity and can lead the sleeper to rise and move as if awake.[17] Outside of a context of medical explanation, such activity naturally raises suspicions and fear of the individual, or of the "unknown power" that seems to be controlling her. The German expression *mit schlafwandlerischer Sicherheit* (with the sureness of sleep-walking) furthers this mistaken impression. While medical advice urges family members to protect sleepwalkers precisely because their waking perception of danger is "asleep", the popular image of sleepwalkers – who often proceed in straightforward, seemingly determined fashion – emphasizes their uncanny directedness and certainty, and further recommends the term "sleeper" as a designation for an individual controlled by an invisible power.[18] A further, obvious component of sleep's semantic range is its normal context of night and darkness. Sight, one of our primary senses, is severely restricted, opening the door to real or imagined secrecy, for unlike the expression "the light of day," that alludes to openness, to say something occurs "under cover of darkness" hints at all kinds of illicit or subversive activity.

Democratic Rights and Secrecy's Role in (Multi-)Culture

Democracy grants each individual a measure of privacy, and while privacy itself is not declared "secret", this allows for a shielding from public gaze. Our religious preferences, food habits, personal finances, family and sexual relationships are our own business, though they are subjected to greater or lesser degrees of social control. As long as what we do does not publicly harm others or threaten the safety of the social collective, it is acceptable, and as curious as we as humans are – the more sensationalist daily papers prove there is a very large market for satisfying what seems an incessant curiosity – we remain reluctant to peer in on our neighbors. We cherish the knowledge that others share in a reciprocal reluctance and in a common social and cultural context for privacy: it might be termed a democratic elaboration of secrecy's fundamental power.[19] Jan and Aleida Assmann have argued that "The invention of the secret is the founding act of culture. In the world of animals there is hiding and dissimulation, but no secret. ... The secret is a prerequisite and characteristic mark of all civilized forms of human co-existence which we summarize under the term culture." (1997: 7).

Society, Georg Simmel claimed nearly a century ago, cannot do without secrecy, for some very basic aspects of personal freedom reside in privacy and thus secrecy. Simmel's observations focus largely on the microlevel of interpersonal behavior, where he discusses the fine-grained spectrum between full self-disclosure and lying. Concealing and deceiving assists members of a social group to create structures and hierarchies. The same mechanisms are employed when individuals evaluate particular relationships vis-à-vis others. Different levels of self-disclosure in the realm of friendship and love can be modified so as to achieve distance or intimacy (1999[1908]: 386–401).

To Simmel, these practices at the interpersonal level are fundamental ways to differentiate public from private spheres, and thus essential methods to structure society. Secrets are essentially hidden knowledge that gain their potency through differential access. The innermost sanctity of a religion may be the privilege of a select few who have earned the right through training, ritual, and devotion, to partake of its revelations, but also to control the access granted to others. For less devoted or skilled adherents, those secrets will remain hidden, and thus hierarchies arise, much as they did in secret societies such as the Illuminati or the Freemasons. The irony is that in the revolutionary era of the late 18th century, such secret societies had liberation and revelation as their goals (Schindler 1983; Berger and Grün, 2002).

Elias Canetti, in *Crowds and Power*, depicted the secret as the "innermost kernel of power."[20] He argued that "the doubts which one harbors against freer forms of governance ...are connected with their dearth of secrets. Debates in parliament take place among hundreds of people; their actual purpose is to reside in the public sphere" (1992[1960], 339, my translation). Yet even if democratically elected parliaments were to make political processes transparent, governmental systems almost inevitably function by using secrets: the examples of alliance formation or negotiating exclusion illustrate that governmental decisions are often based on only partly deploying or even completely withholding knowledge (Nedelmann 1985).

Culturally heterogeneous societies face the problem that their members partake of multiple notions of secrecy which have differing valence depending on the context within which a person acts or observes. In addition to cultural norms of secrecy there are also divergent norms in negotiating public and private spheres. This presents problems both on a group or social and political level as well as at the individual level of identification.

On the social level, the European discourse on integration expresses a concern that new immigrants learn to dissimulate their own norms so as to not to burden the existing norms of the host society, with the very term "assimilation" speaking to this desire.[21] Under the surface similarity, individuals would be granted the right to privately exercise their difference. Yet no matter how assimilated, a groups' otherness may still be feared, for under the smooth surface might slumber a raging danger. Each subgroup within a heterogeneous society is familiar with the workings of secrecy and the capacity of any social actor to be engaged in it. Thus, whether a group assimilates or whether it carries its ethnic differences visibly, the fears of secret practices and conspiratorial plots, hidden or asleep under a calm surface, can germinate in the host, majority society.[22] Alan Macfarlane would likely connect this mechanism with what he perceives as a latent presence of the fear of evil among all members of a society (1985:58). And, again adapted to a culturally heterogeneous setting, what is considered "evil" may differ from one socio-cultural segment to the next.

Beyond the social level of the public, neighborly sphere there is, once again, the political level. All states have the propensity to protect themselves with the very mechanisms that are so feared at the neighborly level: secret services are part of any state apparatus. Their agents – who may be "sleepers" (programmed and waking up only once alerted), "moles" (actively digging for information under a surface of normalcy), or simple analysts (plowing through often public information and in the process extracting potential secrets...) – ideally never emerge as actors. Their working identity is to remain secret so as not to jeopardize the protective functions of the state, and the underlying purpose is to allow members of the polity to remain safe, even ignorant, of the threats to their normal lives.[23] In terms of the practices of secrecy, though, those active for the state and those active for a terrorist group employ much the same techniques of assimilation and dissimulation. Both aim to assert their legitimacy, the former by shoring up and asserting its power, the latter through provoking terror (Nedelmann 1999: 383).

It is only, and terribly, in these actions that reveal the ultimate goal of the terrorists that the difference emerges. The sleeper turned suicide bomber, or as Raphael Israeli (1997) puts it, the 'Islamikaze', reveals an identity and a cause. Israel takes issue with calling recent instances of Islamic "human bombs" suicide bombers, as he sees them as more akin to Japanese kamikaze fighters: devoted agents of a larger cause. From my point of view, however, individual Islamic terrorists likely diverge in their motivations, which stem in turn from the different ways individuals cope with beleaguered identification. Yet this coping response shows itself only in the narratives that unfold after sleepers have become revelatory actors.

Sleepers Awoken, Narratives Revealed

"We had no idea that...", or "I would never have suspected he would be capable of such acts" – these are the types of responses heard from neighbors, landladies, fellow students and professors of the 9/11 terrorists who once resided in the Hamburg area. Much the same was heard in the spring of 2002 when a student in Erfurt, Germany, shot and killed several teachers, fellow students, and himself. Family members and friends of young Palestinian suicide bombers have uttered similar sentiments. In the absence of precise knowledge and precisely because social life rests on the mutual respect of (albeit culturally differential degrees of) private realms, there is a customary assumption of peacefulness and normalcy. The burden of suspicion otherwise mounts intolerably, particularly in heterogeneous societies (and history provides countless examples for the violence that then ensues). Thus, the values of a shared humanity underlying cultural difference at the very least provide an ideal informing life within the same social space. Infractions of such values correspondingly lead to a sense of disappointment, self-doubt and fear echoed in such statements. The unwritten but presumed to be shared social or even familial contract is broken.

Only hindsight leads to a closer examination of possible signs of calamities to come, and to the tormenting recognition that a telling sentence or a new interest should have been recognized as "a sign" rather than fleeting thoughts or passing obsessions. The determination to commit a violent act had been hidden, slumbering within, or instilled by a "shadowy unknown" (such as a charismatic leader or a terrorist network) and the question that poses itself is what circumstances, internal and external, triggered the waking up.

Much effort is placed in socializing children to recognize if not learn to inhabit normative types. Dress, occupational choice, sexual preference, and the all-permeating standards of communication belong to the toolkit of fashioning and projecting a coherent self. Depending on personality, the different roles and identifications we have to enact or at least project in everyday life are integrated in better or worse ways. For some personalities, representing an unambiguous and socially accepted type is of paramount importance, but for others the possibility to be more than one type may be just as important. The levels of social control in a given setting provide individuals with greater or lesser freedom for varying their public or visible personhood. It is hard to venture guesses on the benefits or drawbacks of a relatively homogeneous environment – for even in an ethnically homogeneous environment there is the possibility of socially unacceptable difference in the realm of sexuality, political ideology, and religion. Class further restricts social experience.

Some societies may have surpassed the zenith of identity politics; after the struggle for ascertaining recognition for one particular (ethnic, racial, sexual) identity, there is both play with and commodification of identities (Bendix 2000). Still, such culturally heterogeneous polities likely contain more cases where individuals struggle, in more or less dramatic ways, to integrate the expectations of host culture and class with those of the culture and class of origin. While there will be immigrants and second or third generation hyphenated ethnics who recognize but cope with this dilemma, for others, the tension is sufficient cause to seek a "narrow path", a singular identification.[24]

Here, the presentation of self in everyday life, to invoke Irving Goffman (1959), rests on a complicated, ever shifting script. Individuals cope in different ways, and those who show accomplishments in their new settings may be celebrated as examples of successful integration. Yet the psychological costs they pay, the regrets they suffer[25], and the distance they increasingly feel from those less well "integrated" are not digested equally readily. Somatic and psychological consequences are well known and may take some seemingly extreme forms, such as the case of a 19th century country girl sent as a servant to a new region: she ended up drowning a child and was diagnosed with severe homesickness (Jaspers 1909). Life led with culturally heterogeneous demands and differential class-based expectations can force aspects of identification into a state of "sleep" – either an instance of true psychological suppression or as a social experience of needing to dissimulate and hide. Within this "sleep," nightmares of violent proportions may be dreamt in solitude or, as in terrorist groups, under the guidance of master ideologues.

Historically and cross-culturally, we can observe how societies have provided frameworks within which norms are lifted and hidden facets of personhood can manifest themselves. Carnival and other ritual moments within year and life cycles are moments of liminality rather than normality, where world, role, and gender reversals (or expansions) are allowed. They thus provide opportunities to briefly awaken aspects of the self that slumber during the course of the year. Immigrant societies, whether identified as such or not, struggle to bring culturally different norms into some kind of framework. Berlin's effort to harness this under the heading "Carnival of Cultures" is an interesting and typical example, as this event asks cultural groups to offer festive representations of their cultures within a fairly orderly framework, on the assumption that this provides a unique opportunity for expression.[26] Yet the place and function of this event hardly corresponds to the capacities of the carnivalesque observed in ritual scholarship. Rather, it is a consumer culture festivity, where cultures are "expressed" in order that others may witness them. True, the liberating potential inherent to carnival can be present in events of this sort – food and drink are flowing, and costuming abounds – but it is not clear that such events permit hidden facets of personhood or culture to be revealed. In fact, the very fact of putting on an outward, public face to one's culture may well hide away those aspects that are regarded as particularly important, whether within that culture itself or to the individuals who are culture-bearers.

This of course does not explain what makes a particular person develop hidden desires and aggressions. But to reduce an individual migrant's experiences to a singular identity suitable to be displayed in the context of numerous other migrant groups who are also putting a singular identity on display – particularly when that individual by the very fact of migration has added any number of additional facets to their identity – shows problem of utilizing a "holocultural" framework. It points as well to the centuries-old yet escalating processes of commodifying fragments of culture.[27] These kinds of commodity-based attempts to achieve harmony among diverse cultures are almost a perfect example of the effect global capital flows can have on "cultural" integrity. Rather than harmony, they may instead fuel aggressive assertions of fundamental identity.

Conversely, and this needs to be stressed in the context of any "sleeper" discussion, there are individuals who awaken to lead and to liberate, be this in a political or a religious framework. Indeed, this is the perception that terrorist "martyrs" might well wish to engender amongst those for whose sake they see themselves engaged. The individual who is privy to hearing the demanding voice of God and acts upon it, who speaks in tongues, or whose "conscience" (the positive counter-term to hidden evil) wakes him into action, moving him to speak out against oppressive, totalitarian rule, can – depending on the historical moment and the sociocultural circumstance – be received as special, chosen, saintly, and a promise to humanity, or as dangerous, heretical, or (since the development of psychiatry) as ill. Joan of Arc's biography is a case in point: "hearing voices" at age 14 awoke her from her role as peasant daughter and transformed her into a spiritual and military leader in the war against France, dressed as a man and with the permission of Charles VII. Regarded as heroine, martyr, and saint by some (she was pronounced a saint only in 1920), she was nevertheless burnt at the stake as sorceress and heretic in 1431. Her biography sharply puts the point that one may be both saint and sinner, and that one can be "asleep" to one's talents as leader and visionary. Once awakened and aroused to action, one may then become too much of a danger.[28] Her late 20th century rebirth in the Japanese animé *Kamikaze Kaitou Jeanne* gives the awakened sleeper another unexpected twist.[29]

The awakened terrorist sleeper chooses to tell a story, for in acts of destruction, sleepers turned actors practice revelation. The complexity of multiple allegiance and troubled identification seems to be resolved into a single narrative and a single cause. When Susan Sonntag, in an outspoken first reaction to 911, chastised those who called the culprits "cowards", she stressed this agency and urge toward revelation: "If the word 'cowardly' is to be used, it might be more aptly applied to those who kill from beyond the range of retaliation, high in the sky, than to those willing to die themselves in order to kill others. In the matter of courage (a morally neutral virtue): whatever may be said of the perpetrators of Tuesday's slaughter, they were not cowards" (2001:32). There surely are worlds of difference between suicide bombers, Islamikaze or lone individuals deciding to create a bloodbath at their school, but the need to shape and enact a single story out of the profusion of potential offerings, demands, and expectations is surely revealed in their last acts.

Conclusion

Many sleepers deny their agency. But suicide bombers choose to lift their secret, and narrate through their acts that which has tormented them. Their deaths not only reveal their cause, but also free a path for their potential celebration as martyrs among like-minded individuals or groups. The glorious life in paradise and the promise of being remembered as a hero and a martyr appear to be motivating factors, judging by interviews with those who failed and were captured in Palestinian refugee camps. Given the context within which young suicide bombers are growing up, such promises may indeed hold greater appeal than life.

Exploring the frame of reference of the term "sleeper", its overt and latent meanings in discourse, its associations in legend, and its use in politics or in the secret services should assist us in understanding the potency of the term on the one hand, and its capacity to stir both hope and helplessness on the other. None of the legendary sleepers mentioned earlier have yet awakened to action, and the destructive sleeper's gift is to conceal his awakening until it is too late to stop him. But what interests a polity most urgently is that very moment of awakening – precisely so as to prevent it or diffuse its impact. When we recognize the profusion, indeed the very normalcy, of secret, hidden, or suppressed identifications in heterogeneous societies, however, we should also acknowledge how impossible it is to provide easy toolkits for sleeper spotting.[30] Comparison through time and space at the very least lays bare the multiplicity of sleeper configurations and hopefully can inform social and political actors in such ways as to not react rashly or give in to hysteria, but rather seek to understand and address the pressures that force sleepers to abandon their secrets and explode themselves into revelation.

Notes

1. The level of "adjustment" has since been cause for public debate and was also discussed at our conference. There were ample signals of difference that Mohammed Atta and others in his cell displayed. Yet a heterogeneous host society intent on tolerating diversity (and guided by a few stereotypical elements of "Arab" cultures such as clothing, prayer, and gender relations) emphasized such signals only once the deed was done, and after the actors had revealed themselves to be suicide flyers.
2. Simmel's statement remains eminently worth consulting. His thoughts have been elaborated and critiqued in sociology (Hahn 1997, Nedelmann 1985 and 1995) as well as in social psychology and communication (Westerbarkey 1991). The conference proceedings published in 1997 by Alaida and Jan Assmann *(Schleier und Schwelle. Band 1. Geheimnis und Öffentlichkeit)* provide a particularly wide ranging discussion that goes far beyond Simmel. A more popular survey of secret codes and their use in politics has been offered by Simon Sing (1999).
3. In this work, Taussig also critically reexamines Julien Pitt-Rivers' *People of the Sierra* (1969) as one of the early ethnographic studies to address lying and dissimulation.
4. Roy Wagener's work (1984) is an exception here.
5. Freemasons seem to have attracted the most attention (Berger and Grün 2002), but there are many wider investigations (see Reinalter 1983, Fischer 1982, Schreiber und Schreiber 1993).
6. The present assessment draws on English and German language use; further linguistic comparison would likely enrich the semantic scope.
7. See http://www.die-maus.de/sachgeschichten/ siebenschlaefer/ (consulted September 2003) for the seven month assertion; for scientific information on the dormouse see http:// www.glirarium.de/bilch/arten.html (consulted in September 2002). The Christian legend origin is given in the Duden, the standard German dictionary and source of German etymology.
8. See Martin (1993) and Sarasin (2002) for the discourse on illness, bacteria, immunity and the bodily defenses against it. I am indebted to Viola Armbrecht's seminar paper on "The Terror of Viruses" in my "Sleeper" seminar, held during the summer semester of 2002 in Göttingen.
9. This is advertised as: "Like the Cherry Bomb, the Grim Sleeper is equipped with a high-quality ABEC 3 ball bearing and an adjustable string gap enabling incredibly long sleep times or quick returns. Available in a deep purple color for only $14.99" ("Team Losi YoYo's" http:// www.yoyopro.com/teamlosi.htm, consulted September 2002). The association with death (as in the 'Grim Reaper') may come about because earlier yoyos stopped spinning when they reached the end of their line…
10. Sleeper yoyos are not available in Europe and I only learned about them from a story (in the *Göttinger Tageblatt*, July 31, 2002, p. 6) about Dennis Schleußner, the only German to participate in the World Yoyo Championships in Orlando, Florida in 2002. Only fifty Germans "seriously" train with yoyos, a hidden – though not sinister – group of aficionados…
11. Source: "Das Freilauf Yoyo": http://www.andreas-gym.de/projekt/www/yoyo/freiyo.htm (consulted September 2003).
12. Originally, the legend featured Friedrich II, but as he had died abroad his death seemed uncertain. After a few centuries the legend inserted Friedrich I or Barbarossa in his stead; cf. "Kyffhäuser" http://roskothen.com/kyff/index1.htm (consulted August 2002). Koch's study contains many sources as well as poems and songs about Barbarossa's hoped-for return (1880). This theme persists in our time as well, as one can hear claims that John F. Kennedy never died; in 1998 I saw a newspaper headline in Vienna that proclaimed Rudolf von Habsburg, the Austro-Hungarian Crown Prince (around whom so much hope had gathered for a peaceful transformation of the decaying empire) was still living, some 109 years after his suicide.
13. Stammler, 1927. For a Charlemagne text, see Bechstein (1930), p. 635; on pp. 178–179 the same motif without royal association appears. A similar legend exists in Switzerland, surrounding the three Tells (for a representative text, see Bechstein (1930), p. 21, for commentary Schenda (1985)). King Arthur is another figure whose return was awaited (Brogsitter 1977:830). Van Gennep (1920: 189–200) treated the subject in more general terms.
14. In H.G. Wells's novel *The Sleeper Awakens* (1899), this theme is developed and shown to work against the sleeper himself, as his awakening disturbs the plans of those who rule in his stead.
15. Our conference discussion initially turned on the question of differentiating between harmless sleepers and not-so-harmless spies and terrorists in our vocabulary. Alas, that everyday discourse liberally brings these connotations together, relishing in mixing the harmless with the dangerous, rather complicates such an endeavor. The examples given here demonstrate the

16. constant potential of the dangerous inside the harmless, and the harmless inside the dangerous – which is how we address sleep itself as well.
16. The title of the successful Austrian novel *Schlafes Bruder* ("Brother of Sleep", Schneider, 1992) alludes to the popular equating of death with sleep; one English expression for sleep – "in the arms of Morpheus" – is a similar allusion.
17. See Schlafwandeln: http://www.medizinfo.de/kopfundseele/schlafen/schwandeln.htm (consulted September 2002). Stockinger (2003:130–131) reports on a violent variant of sleep-walking: some individuals who dream of imaginary monsters, wild animals, or powerful individuals in their everyday life may attack those nearest and dearest to them in their sleep, mistaking them for these sources of danger.
18. Vernacular narrative as well as science fiction give further shape to such suspicion and fear: the sleeper may be invaded by a ghostly or alien force and removed to another place and time; on awakening, she finds herself possessed by an alien force or even has alien implants. The X-Files TV series repeatedly offered such plots, but one can find themes of this kind in the type and motif registers of folk narrative research as well.
19. Sadly, one has to hasten to add that such rights to privacy often do not exist even in a democratic state's constitutional language; constitutions are rather at pains to spell out in which instances the representatives of a state have the right to invade our privacy.
20. Canetti's choice of locating secrets somatically links back to the topic of darkness and sleepers: "The mouth is dark, and gloomy are stomach and intestines. No one knows and no one thinks about what is happening, incessantly, in his innermost" (1992:335).
21. This is not the place to explore the different usage of terms such as assimilation, acculturation and integration in different disciplines and in different national discourses. For a cogent discussion on this, see Mintzel (1997). It is clear, however, that there is a spectrum of divergent expectations of what assimilation entails, with a one-sided model on one end (the immigrants assimilate completely to the receiver society) and a more interchangeable, mutual process of assimilating to each other between hosts and immigrants.
22. At the Reinhausen conference, Ned Lebow characterized the situation of Jews in Germany in these terms, with Fritz Kratochwil summarizing it as: "Damned if you do and damned if you don't".
23. "Men in Black", the secret agent movies of the present fin-de-siècle, exaggerate matters to the point where agents have the power to change the perceptions of those who know too much about the aliens among us back to a state of "not-knowing", thus permitting them to lead a life in ignorance again.
24. Marianne Gullestad's contribution to the Reinhausen meeting (published elsewhere, cf. Gullestad 2003) beautifully analysed precisely this dilemma as formulated by an Pashtun/Afghan woman residing in Norway.
25. The classic autobiography in this regard is Richard Rodriguez' *Hunger of Memory*, in which a Chicano immigrant son who becomes a university English professor laments what he has lost in terms of family and culture.
26. "Why a carnival of cultures in Berlin"? is answered at http://www.karneval-berlin.de/#text (for 2003) as: "It is a festival for all generations and social groups that is open to new trends and styles in youth and minority cultures. It demonstrates the overwhelming variety of traditional and modern cultures in our city. For many of the 440,000 migrants from 180 countries who live in Berlin, the carnival of cultures is a unique opportunity to express their cultural identity and show their colorful cultural presence through music and dance, and thereby allow Berlin to more consciously and deeply experience its internationalism."
27. On the notion of the "holocultural" and its critique, see Gingrich and Fox (2000:12), on the suggestion to abandon "singular identity" frameworks in the study of culture, see Bendix (2000).
28. This might be said of Hezbollah or other groups pursuing an agenda of liberation but using lethal methods that in turn incite others to try to get rid of them.
29. Cf.: http://victorian.fortunecity.com/literary/518/jeannetv.html (Aug. 26, 2002), or http://www.tcp.com/doi/jeanne/ (Aug. 26, 2002).
30. Germany revived Rasterfahndung soon after 911. This method, first developed during the days of the Red Army Faction in the 1970s, tries to systematically match different lists of data (say, one of foreign students studying engineering and another of Muslims living in Hamburg) to find potential sleepers (Graf 1997, Siebrecht 1997, Simon und Taeger, 1981). Wanner (1985) early on demonstrated the repressive potential of this type of prevention. That it infringes on democratic rights has also been amply evident in post 9/11 America. That it is a very fallible, imprecise tool with grave implications for the protection of individual rights, particularly in countries like Germany that have enacted stringent data privacy laws, goes without saying.

References

Abrahams, Roger D. 1992: *Singing the Master. The Emergence of African-American Culture in the Plantation South*. New York.

Assmann, Aleida/Jan Assmann (eds.) 1997: *Geheimnis und Öffentlichkeit. Schleier und Schwelle*. Bd. 1. München.

Bechstein, Ludwig 1930 (or. 1832): *Deutsches Sagenbuch*. Leipzig.

Bendix, Regina 2000: After Identity: Ethnicity between Commodification and Cultural Commentary. In: R. Bendix & H. Roodenburg (eds.): *Managing Ethnicity. Perspectives from Folklore Studies, History and Anthropology*. Amsterdam: 77–95.

Berger, Joachim and Klaus-Jürgen Grün (eds.) 2002: *Geheime Gesellschaft. Weimar und die deutsche Freimaurerei*. München.

Brogsitter, Karl Otto 1977: Artustradition. In: *Enzyklopädie des Märchens*, Vol. 1. Berlin: 828–849.

Canetti, Elias 1991(1960): *Masse und Macht*. Hildesheim.

Fischer, Michael W. 1982: *Die Aufklärung und ihr Gegenteil: Die Rolle der Geheimbünde in Wissenschaft und Politik*. Berlin.

Fox, Richard and Andre Gingrich 2002: Introduction. In: A. Gingrich and R. Fox (eds.): *Anthropology, by Comparison*. London.

Goffman, Erving 1959: *The Presentation of Self in Everyday Life*. Garden City.

Graf, Walther 1997: *Rasterfahndung und organisierte Kriminalität*. Mönchengladbach.

Grimm, Jakob and Wilhelm Grimm (eds.) 1899: *Deutsches Wörterbuch*. Vol. 9. Leipzig: 263–290.

Gullestad, Marianne 2003 (in press): Mohammed Atta and I: Identification, discrimination and the formation of sleepers. In: *European Journal of Cultural Studies*: No. 4.

Halm, Heinz 1994: *Der schiitische Islam. Von der Religion zur Revolution*. München.

Hahn, Alois 1997: Soziologische Aspekte von Geheimnissen und ihren Äquivalenten. In: Assmann, Aleida & Jan Assmann (eds.): *Geheimnis und Öffentlichkeit. Schleier und Schwelle*. Bd. 1. München: 23–39.

Israeli, Raphael 1997: Islamikaze and their Significance. In: *Terrorism and Political Violence* 9(3): 96–121.

Jaspers, Karl 1909: *Heimweh und Verbrechen*. Leipzig.

Koch, Ernst 1880: *Die Sage vom Kaiser Friedrich im Kiffhäuser nach ihrer mythischen, historischen und poetisch-nationalen Bedeutung*. Grimma.

Levine, Lawrence 1977: *Black Culture and Black Consciousness. Afro-American Folk Thought from Slavery to Freedom*. New York.

Martin, Emily 1993: Histories of Immune Systems. In: *Culture, Medicine and Psychiatry* 17:67–76.

Macfarlane, Alan 1985: The Root of all Evil. In: Parkin, David (ed.): *The Anthropology of Evil*. Oxford: 57–76.

Mintzel, Alf 1997: *Multikulturelle Gesellschaft in Europa und Nordamerika*. Passau.

Nedelmann, Birgitta 1985: Geheimnis – ein interaktionistisches Paradigma. In: *Vorgänge* 24(6): 38–48.

Nedelmann, Birgitta 1995: Geheimhaltung, Verheimlichung, Geheimnis – einige soziologische Vorüberlegungen. In: Kippenberg, Hans G. und Guy G. Strousma (eds.): *Secrecy and Concealment. Studies in the History of Mediterranean and Near Eastern Religions*. Leiden: 1–16.

Nedelmann, Birgitta 1999: Die Selbstmordbomber. Zur symbolischen Kommunikation extremer politischer Gewalt. In: Gerhards, J. & R. Hitzler (eds.): *Eigenwilligkeit und Rationalität sozialer Prozesse*. Opladen: 379–414.

Pitt-Rivers, Julian A. 1969: *The People of the Sierra*. Chicago.

Reinalter, H. (ed.) 1983: *Freimaurer und Geheimbünde im 18. Jh. in Mitteleuropa*. Frankfurt.

Rodriguez, Richard 1982: *Hunger of Memory*. Boston.

Sarasin, Philipp 2002. Politische Metaphern der Bakteriologie/Immunologie 1880–1959. On: http://www.fsw.unizh.ch/site.html (consulted July, 2002).

Schenda, Rudolf 1985: Die drei Teller im Modejournal. Bemerkungen zu einer Schweizer Sage bei den Brüdern Grimm. In: *New Zürcher Zeitung* Nr. 267, 16./17. November: 70.

Schindler, Norbert 1982: Der Geheimbund der Illuminaten-Aufklärung, Geheimnis, Politik. In: H. Reinalter, ed.: *Freimaurer und Geheimbünde im 18. Jh. in Mitteleurpa*. Frankfurt, pp. 284–318.

Schneider, Robert 1992: *Schlafes Bruder*. Leipzig.

Schreiber, Georg und Hermann Schreiber 1993: *Geheimbünde: Von der Antike bis heute*. Augsburg.

Scott, James 1990: *Domination and the Arts of Resistance: Hidden Transcripts*. New Haven.

Siebrecht, Michael 1997: *Rasterfahndung. Eine EDV-gestützte Massenfahndungsmethode im Spannungsfeld zwischen einer effektiven Strafverfolgung und dem Recht auf informationelle Selbstbestimmung*. Berlin.

Simmel, Georg 1999: Das Geheimnis und die geheime Gesellschaft. In: *Soziologie. Untersuchungen über Formen der Vergesellschaftung. Simmel Gesamtausgabe*. Vol. 2, Frankfurt: 383–455.

Simon, Jürgen & Jürgen Taeger (eds.) 1981: *Rasterfahndung: Entwicklung, Inhalt und Grenzen einer kriminalpolizeilichen Fahndungsmethode*. Baden-Baden.

Sing, Simon 1999: *The Code Book: The Evolution of Secrecy from Mary, Queen of Scots to Quantum Cryptography*. New York.

Sontag, Susan 2001: Untitled: "Talk of the Town". In: *The New Yorker*, September 24: 32.

Stammler, 1927: Bergrückt. In: *Handwörterbuch des dt. Aberglaubens*. Vol. 1. Berlin: 1056–1071.

Stockinger, Günther 2003: Jagdszenen im Schlafzimmer. In: *Der Spiegel* Nr. 32:30–31.

Taussig, Michael 1999: *Defacement. Public Secrecy and the Labor of the Negative*. Berkeley.

Wagener, Roy 1984: Ritual as Communication: Order, Meaning, and Secrecy in Melanesian Initiation Rites. In: *Annual Review of Anthropology* 13:145–155.

van Gennep, Arnold 1920: *La formation des legendes*. Paris: 189–200.

Wanner, Stephan 1985: *Die negative Rasterfahndung. Eine moderne und umstrittene Methode der repressiven Verbrechensbekämpfung*. München.

Wells, Herbert G. 2000 (or. 1899): *When the Sleeper Wakes*. New York.

Westerbarkey, Joachim 1991: *Das Geheimnis: Zur funktionalen Ambivalenz von Kommunikationsstrukturen*. Opladen.

Part II

Sense-making in Shadowy Contexts

The Nation and its Shadow
Imagining Subversion in Post-'911' Pakistan and Holland

Oskar Verkaaik

> Verkaaik, Oskar 2003: The Nation and its Shadow: Imagining Subersion in Post-'911' Pakistan and Holland. – Ethnologia Europaea 33:2: 45–56.
>
> The 11 September 2001 attacks on New York and Washington have led to renewed public debates on national identity in various countries. This contribution focuses on two of them: Pakistan and the Netherlands. Starting from the assumption that the nation is a project of liberation from a pre-nation past, it is argued that these debates necessarily imply an increased reflection on the nature of this pre-nation past, which is called the nation's shadow. In Pakistan, the nation is imagined as an Islamic liberation from feudalism, kinship solidarity, and ethnic loyalties. In Holland, the nation is imagined as secular and opposed to a Dutch history of pillarization in which religious authorities acted as intermediaries between the citizen and the state. What are considered the loyalties and sentiments of the past are allowed in private. However, they also inform the imagination of a subversive domain that encroaches upon the nation. Hence, subversion politics in Pakistan is imagined as a form of illicit kinship politics, whereas in Holland subversion is linked to religious – primarily Islamic – mentalities.
>
> *Prof. Dr. Oskar Verkaaik, Research Center Religion & Society, University of Amsterdam, Oudezijds Achterburgwal 185, NL-1012 DK Amsterdam. E-mail: O.G.A.Verkaaik@uva.nl*

If, as Richard Rubinstein (1987) suggests, the logic of modern-day terrorism lies in creating chaos and revealing the 'true face of naked power' lurking beneath state authority by provoking the state to take outrageously violent measures in retaliation for a spectacular attack on persons or buildings symbolizing the state, then Gavrilo Princip's killing of Archduke Franz Ferdinand of Austria in Sarajevo in June 1914 is still by far the most successful terrorist attack in history. The assassination was taken as an act of war by the Austrians and their handling of this attack eventually led to the First World War, which not only set Europe on fire, but also destroyed the Austro-Hungarian Empire, leading to the establishment of new nation states in Southeast Europe. It was an unprecedented success for a small group of Serbian nationalists known as the *Narodna Odbrana*, who would not have stood a chance, had they tried to reach their goals in some other way.

The attacks on the World Trade Center and the Pentagon on 11 September 2001 have as yet not been so successful. Their impact has nonetheless been remarkable, primarily of course in the US, where the new *Patriot Act* has affected the life of US citizens of Muslim, Arab or South Asian background (e.g. Feldman 2002; Mohammad-Arif 2002), and also for the Taliban regime in Afghanistan, which was held responsible for the attacks. But also in countries not directly related to the conflict, '911' has had considerable consequences. In this chapter, I want to focus on two such countries: Pakistan and the Netherlands. In both countries, domestic political affairs have been drastically affected by the attacks of 11 September. In Pakistan, the position of the military regime of General Parveez Musharraf has become much stronger. Isolated both domestically and internationally prior to '911', the military regime has become a major ally of the US since then, with the result that the undemocratic status of the regime is no longer questioned internationally. In that sense, Pakistan is back to where it was in the 1960s and 1980s, when the authority of the military regimes led by General Ayub Khan and General Zia-ul Haq respectively relied heavily on US support. Since the renewed importance of Pakistan for the US, General Musharraf has tried to present Pakistan to the world as a modern and liberal Muslim state, a far cry from supposedly aggressive or 'fundamentalist' Islamic states such as Taliban Afghanistan, Iran, Iraq, Syria, Saudi Arabia, or Sudan. As a result of this, '911' has led to an increased debate on the nature or essence of the Pakistani nation.

The relation between the Netherlands and the '911' attacks is less clear. Apart from the fact that Osama bin Laden in a video broadcast by Al Jazeera claimed that many copies of the Qur'an had been sold in Holland after the Al Qaeda attacks on the US, Holland was in no way directly involved. Nonetheless, in an almost unprecedented way the question of national identity has become a matter of fierce debate in Holland, too. In the first weeks or months after the attacks, the most popular explanation in the press and media was a culturalist or civilizationalist argument, which looked for reasons and motives in Islam, subsequently contrasted with modernity or Western civilization. Before long the public debate focused on the integration and assimilation of recent Muslim migrants in Dutch society, as Muslims were at best believed to live between two – supposedly incongruous – cultures. It was the up-and-coming populist political leader Pim Fortuyn, who used the prevalent anti-Islam sentiments in his campaign for the national elections in May 2002 in a way that many people felt was unthinkable prior to the Al Qaeda attacks of 2001. Fortuyn's campaign dramatically came to an end when he was shot dead nine days before the national elections.

What I want to argue here is that both in Pakistan and in the Netherlands, '911' not only led to increased reflection on the nation, but also on what I would like to call the nation's shadow. That is not the same as the nation's 'Other', although the nation's shadow may be projected onto the nation's 'Other'. More often the nation's shadow is projected onto the past. I take the nation as a project of liberation from a pre-nation past. In the case of Holland, for instance, the nation portrays itself as liberated from the clutches of community-based religion. Holland prides itself on being a rational, tolerant, and above all secular country. In Pakistan, the nation is often conceived as a liberation of kinship, tribal, ethnic, or otherwise 'particularistic' loyalties. Pakistan likes to see itself as a Muslim society true to the universal message of Islam. In the ideal situation – when the project of liberation has successfully come to an end, so to speak – the past has become a private matter. When restricted to the private sphere, religion in Holland and family or ethnic ties in Pakistan do not threaten the unity of the nation.

That, however, is a utopia, since the nation constantly defines itself in relation to the past it is about to free itself from. As Talal Asad (1999) has argued in a critique of secularism, religion is a lot more than a private conviction even in a secular society. It is rather the significant other by which the secular defines itself, and in that sense it is essentially public. A similar argument can be made for Pakistan, where the importance of Islam in the national project cannot be understood without taking into account how Islam has often been defined in opposition to ethnic or kinship (*biradari*) loyalties. The nation and its shadow – the past out of which the nation has sprung and from which it has freed itself – go together, just like in Freud's words modern civilization evokes its own discontents, or in Edward Said's words, the West only knows itself in relation to its imagined antithesis known as the Orient.

To some extent I use the term shadow the way it was used by Carl Gustav Jung. As Jung proposed, we can suppress whatever we do not like, but that does not mean it will go away. It finds refuge in our shadow, where it sticks with us and grows like mould in dark places. It continues to influence our behavior, but since we do not face and recognize it, we cannot effectively deal with it. Similarly, certain loyalties and identities are suppressed in the national project. They are at best tolerated within the private. But that does not mean they become unimportant. Rather, they are believed to be the forces that secretly and invisibly undermine the unity and purity of the nation. Part of the imagination of the nation is the idea that the nation's past grows rampant in a dark, shadowy place, from where it clandestinely encroaches upon the nation. Insofar as the nation is an imagined community (Anderson 1991), it is in part imagined in opposition to the loyalties and identities it has only partially and incompletely left behind. In other words, religion – increasingly in the form of Islam – is conceived as the biggest threat to the Dutch nation, which was firmly linked to Christianity and a history of religious 'pillarization' until the 1960s, when it radically embraced secularism. In contrast, the Pakistani nation is imagined in opposition to particularistic loyalties that undermine Muslim equality that forms the basis of the Pakistani nation.

The way I use the metaphor of the shadow is thus somewhat different from the way the metaphor has been used more often in subversive politics. More common is the concept of the shadow state. As Ranajit Guha (1999) has argued for rural India, revolts and revolutions usually reproduce the prevailing notions and symbols of authority while trying to change them. This is also often true for modern left-wing activities. Perhaps the most paradoxical example is the 19th century founder of Russian terrorism, Sergey Nechayev, who wrote a *Catechism of the Revolutionist* while promoting anarchist atheism. He had apparently no other model than a catechism to spread his anti-Church – and anti-state – message. In the 20th century, various left-wing groups have established 'shadow states' – parallel states or counter-republics that copied the organization of the state while combating it (Hansen & Stepputat 2001: 35). In addition to this, the modern state, while priding itself for its bureaucratic and democratic transparency, also maintains a 'shadow' or 'secret' domain in the form of secret services fighting subversive political activities and organizations. The existence of such secret organizations has given rise to collective fear, fascination and even admiration for such figures as spies and sleepers, moles and terrorists – a fascination that has most superbly been described by Joseph Brodsky (1995) in an essay on master-spy Kim Philby. During the Cold War period, the struggle going on in this secret sphere was one framed in terms of ideology: Marxism versus Capitalism. Today, however, the threat is rather perceived as a threat of culture or even civilization. That implies that not only the state is perceived to be in danger, but the nation – or civilization – as well. I suggest, however, that this cultural danger threatening the nation from a dark and less than transparent domain in fact reflects the insecurities of national identity defined in terms of what it rejects and represses. It is this perceived cultural threat that I call the nation's shadow.

I suggest, then, that this domain of the nation's shadow is a good place to look for present-day political scandals and rumors. Here we find the moles and maniacs who refuse to keep their private beliefs and preferences to themselves. Instead they engage in all kinds of secret activities that spoil the nation from within – that is, from its shadow or repressed past. To shed some light on these shadows I will in the remaining part of this essay examine the public debates in Pakistan and the Netherlands since September 2001. As for Pakistan, the focus will not only be on Musharraf's reformulation of Pakistan as a liberal, modern, progressive Muslim nation, but also on corruption as an ongoing national scandal that undermines the purity of the nation. In the case of the Netherlands, I will argue that sexual identities and lifestyles have been replaced by religious, mainly Islamic, identities and lifestyles as the main form of social critique and political protest. This indicates that tolerance of sexual identities and lifestyles has become the dominant norm taking prevalence over tolerance of religious identities and lifestyles. As a result, religion rather than sex has become the domain of the dark and scandalous, undermining the purity of the nation.

Pakistan

The argument I want to make here is an elaboration of earlier work on the state, nation building, and the role of the secret intelligence agencies within Pakistan society (Verkaaik 2001). Secret intelligence services, in the local vernacular known as *agencies*, play an important role in public discourse. There is no doubt that various of such agencies are active in Pakistan. During my research on an ethnic-religious movement in the south of Pakistan, known as the Muhajir Qaumi Movement (MQM), I noticed that various state forces infiltrated in neighborhoods to spy on the local members of this movement. The most well known is the ISI, the Inter Services Intelligence, which is the army-run agency and generally considered to be the most efficient and dangerous of all, but other agencies run by the paramilitary Rangers and local police forces are also active. Since these state forces are to a large extent politicized, they also spy on each other. To some extent, then, Pakistan is comparable to the state of Rumania prior to the fall of Ceaucescu in 1989, where, as Katherine Verdery (1996) has described, the Securitate managed to keep the Rumanian population under control by way of its secret manipulation and fearful reputation. However, there are also differences. Because the agencies are fragmented and often busy with each other, state control through covert activities is far from complete. Few people have personal experience with people working for one of the agencies. Nonetheless, there is general consensus in Pakistan that the influence of the agencies is enormous. Ethnic riots, sectarian terrorist attacks, and even the rise of successful popular movements are seen as the work of the agencies, primarily the ISI. More generally, there is a collective suspicion that there exists a secret and invisible domain of political activities that because of its very invisibility is considered more real and more powerful than the public sphere. Drawing on the work of Philip Abrams (1988), Timothy Mitchell (1991 & 1999) and others on the reification of the state as a cultural concept of hegemonic power that exists apart from and beyond society, I have suggested that this domain of secret activities is important in imagining the state. On the one hand, the state institutions that are visible are perceived by the public as notoriously inadequate, ineffective, corrupt, and fragmented. Many commentators have written about the lack of authority and the crisis of governability because of this. On the other hand, however, the Pakistani state is not a weak state. Its authority depends on the notion of a secret state that is everything the visible state is not: unified, efficient, disciplined, and ruthless. Insofar as the state in its reified form is believed to be simultaneously invisible and omnipresent, this secret domain with the agencies as its main actors is its perfect symbol.

This notion of the secret state is linked with another crucial aspect of the public debate in Pakistan since the 1990s, which is corruption or lack of accountability (*ehtasab*). Again, what we have here is as much, if not more, a product of the collective imagination as a fact of social life. It is doubtful whether practices deemed as corrupt – such as nepotism, bribery, or returning favors – take place more often now than in previous time, but the *talk of* corruption has certainly multiplied. This is to a large extent the result of the fact that the five prime ministers who have been in office since 1985 have been dismissed by the president on charges of corruption. These prime ministers include Muhammad Khan Junejo in 1988, Benazir Bhutto in 1990, Nawaz Sharif in 1993, Benazir Bhutto a second time in 1996, and finally Nawaz Sharif again in 1999. Time and again, the military – either directly or via the president – has called for a nation-wide campaign to get rid of corruption. In 1997, Prime Minister Nawaz Sharif even made this into the most important goal for his government, setting up special courts known as accountability or *ehtasah* branches that would investigate the bank accounts of all major politicians and bureaucrats. Before long, however, these branches were themselves accused of corruption. When in 1999 General Musharraf took over power by way of a coup, he mentioned this to argue that democratic politics had gone morally bankrupt, which indeed gave the military take-over some, albeit not much, credibility. In other words, although the military has been in the barracks between 1988 and 1999 and has not directly been involved in politics, it has successfully managed to discredit the main political parties as corrupt and not worthy of the mandate given to them by the people. Moreover, it was supported in this by various international development agencies and Western aid donors, which also regularly blamed the Pakistani government for insufficient transparency and a lack of good governance. As corruption had become a news item, journalists often reported on such statements, even if they came from representatives of obscure – from a Pakistani point of view – countries like the Netherlands. Given all this, General Musharraf met with little popular or international opposition when he exiled or jailed a large number of politicians from the established political parties, successfully creating a political vacuum, which in the short run strengthened his position as the country's strong leader, while in the long run potentially paving the way for radical Islamist parties that largely escaped persecution, legitimized as an operation against the national disease number one, namely corruption.

The popular explanation for corruption is also to be found in the same secret domain in which the intelligence agencies operate. It is also here where the notion of the nation's unresolved relation with its past come in play. In popular perception, corruption is the result of a mental deficit of discipline necessary to control loyalties, sentiments, and tendencies that are considered unpatriotic and un-Islamic. Such loyalties, sentiments, and tendencies are rooted in backwardness. In passing, I would like to ask the reader to make a mental note of this notion of backwardness, which will return in the discussion on Fortuyn in Holland. But first I will explain the role of backwardness in Pakistan.

To do this, it is important to realize that the imagination of the Pakistani nation is firmly rooted in 19th century South Asian, Islamic reformist movements of various kinds (Metcalf 1982). All these intellectual movements shared a renewed interest in the message of Islam in relation to British colonialism and the decline of Muslim dominance in North India. These movements were culturalist movements in the sense that they searched for reasons for Muslim decline in Muslim mentalities. Islam as such was of course not blamed. Instead it was argued that the Muslims of India had neglected the liberating and empowering message of Islam, corrupting it with 'innovations' (*bid'at*), that is, un-Islamic influences from other – mainly Hindu or Western – cultures. Muslim reform became the basis for Pakistani nationalism through the works of Muhammad Iqbal, poet, philosopher, politician, and widely revered in Pakistan as the intellectual founder of the nation – the most prestigious university of the country is named after him. For Iqbal, Pakistan was not merely a way to free the Muslims from Hindu dominance, but also a project to restore true Islam. According to Iqbal, Islam had become invaded with debilitating passivity and world-renouncing mysticism, which had cut the Muslims off from modernity. Local saints and mullahs symbolized the mental backwardness of the Muslims and they were therefore often the target of his sarcasm and scorn. The Muslims needed to return to the tradition of rational investigation or *ijtehad* – a term akin to *jihad*, but without the connotation of either mystical or military purification of temptation and infidelity. He therefore deemed education of the utmost importance to free the Muslims of local, folk, fake Islam and bring them back to the world of things.

As regional loyalties were the largest hindrance to nation building in the early years of Pakistan, the political and cultural elite soon translated Iqbal's disdain for folk Muslim traditions into a rejection of regional or ethnic culture, which was deemed un-Islamic and perverted by Hindu influences. A well-known example of this can be found in the autobiography of General Ayub Khan, who wrote about the Bengalis of former East Pakistan that they 'belong to the very original Indian races', 'have been and still are under considerable Hindu cultural and linguistic influence', and 'have not yet found it possible to adjust psychologically to the requirements of the new-born freedom' (Ayub Khan 1967: 187). Other ethnic groups were asked to leave behind their traditions and join progress. Moreover, every ethnic group was considered to have its own unique form of backwardness that stood in the way of true Islam and true patriotism. The Sindhis had feudalism and believed in the miraculous powers of local holy men. The Pathans or Pakhtun from the north had their tribal laws and codes of honor. The Punjabis were generally believed to be prone to kinship or *biradari* loyalties. As the last and smallest officially recognized ethnic group, the Baluchis were mainly too insignificant to be entitled to their own ethnic form of backwardness.

Corruption, then, is basically explained from the continuing covert influence of these ethnic forms of backwardness. The corruption of a Sindhi politician will typically be attributed to the fact that he belongs to a traditionally feudal society, where arrangements of power are not made rationally and bureaucratically on the basis of social equality as confirmed by both Islam and nationalism, but according to vertical and hierarchical bonds of birth. Hence, it is always pointed out that the Bhutto family – as the most well-known and, to some, most corrupt Sindhi clan – belong to the largest landowning families in the province. The Punjabi politician's corruption, however, will rather be explained from kinship or even caste politics, in which the *biradari* operates as a political unit on its own with no room for outsiders. Likewise, the Pathan is considered as an essentially tribal person, who may fight infidelity under the banner of jihad, but who eventually will let tribal loyalty prevail over Muslim brotherhood. Moreover, as all these loyalties have been discredited over the years as un-Islamic and unpatriotic, they are widely believed to have gone underground. They have been pushed into that secret domain that exists under the surface of Muslim brotherhood, national solidarity, democracy, and bureaucratic transparency. These are, in other words, the loyalties, sentiments, and tendencies that inform the secret politics of the agencies.

It is against this background that the post-'911' public debates in Pakistan have to be understood. Over the last few decades, the Pakistani nation has been defined less in opposition to the external 'Other' – primarily India – than to its own past of ethnic, tribal, or kinship backwardness. This is an aspect of Pakistani politics that many foreign analysts, focusing on international relations rather than domestic public debate, have failed to recognize. General Musharraf's contention that Pakistan is essentially a modern, liberal, and progressive nation may seem peculiar and opportunistic to those who primarily associate Pakistan with recent radical Muslim groups and the state-sponsored 'Islamization program' of the 1980s, but it rather is a neither illogical nor unpredictable return to the intellectual tradition of Muhammad Iqbal, subsequently turned into an authoritarian, progressive modernism by the military regime of General Ayub Khan. Musharraf has not only mentioned his predecessor from the 1960s as one of his role models, but has also declared to be inspired by other Muslim modernists from the past such as Gamal Nasser of Egypt. Naturally, Musharraf has been wise not to mention similar Muslim progressive modernists from the Ba`ath Party in Syria and Iraq. On the other hand, the continuity that lies behind this recent reformulation of national identity may be logical and consistent, it is another question whether it works or whether it will be successful. The return to Pakistan's intellectual tradition of its early decades can also be interpreted as a sign of ideological poverty. After all, from the military establishment's point of view, the moles undermining the unity of the nation are no longer protest movements organized along ethnic or tribal lines, but Islamist groups calling for jihad and the implementation of the Islamic law (*shar'at*). Although Musharraf has banned some of these groups after September 2001, which is in itself a break with the recent past when the government rather tried to pacify them and collaborate with them, it is questionable whether the discourse of Muslim liberal modernism will prove to be powerful enough as an alternative to a popular-based Islamism disseminated through Quranic schools, political parties, and some of the media. For the military, the social groups depending on them, as well as the US, it may be a matter of concern to see that General Musharraf cannot do better than to fall back on an ideology of the 1950s and 1960s that has been tried before but may be outdated today. On the other hand, it is in line with a more general revival of authoritarian modernism since '911', that can also be witnessed in for instance the US and also the Netherlands, the latter being the topic of the following section.

The Netherlands

Halfway, the short but dramatic political career of Pim Fortuyn, his ambitions to become the leader of a new populist party that would change the Dutch political spectrum, seemed to come to an end. This happened in the winter of 2001–2002, a couple of months after September 11. During the summer of 2001 he had joined a new party called *Leefbaar Nederland* ('Liveable Netherlands'), which had done well in local elections challenging established parties with an aggressively no-nonsense approach to local issues. A former sociologist teaching Leninist-Marxism at the University of Groningen who failed to make a career in the labor party (*Partij van de Arbeid*), Fortuyn was already a controversial figure because of the sarcastic and unorthodox columns he used to write for a right-wing weekly magazine. He was, however, also a gifted speaker and he had wealthy friends in the real estate and construction branch who were willing to support him financially, which made him acceptable as a leader for the Leefbaar Nederland party. Shortly after '911', however, a television news show called *Nova* reported on an imam in Rotterdam who had branded homosexuality a disease. This attracted some media attention, partly because everything on Islam was considered a hot issue after '911', partly because it raised the question whether the freedom of speech act can be reconciled with the anti-discrimination laws on sexual preferences, race, and religion. In an interview in a national newspaper, commenting on this affair, Fortuyn called Islam a 'backward culture'. This created a stir, Fortuyn was accused of Islam phobia, and the party he was supposed to lead in the coming elections decided to dismiss him. Everyone expected Fortuyn to go back to writing columns, but instead he started his own party, bluntly called List Pim Fortuyn (LPF), which subsequently became the media darling in the 2002 election campaign.

The fact that Fortuyn was so widely criticized for calling Islam a backward culture seems to indicate that he was saying something most people considered unacceptable and intolerable. To some extent this was true, but at the same time he was only saying too directly and too crudely what many established politicians, media experts, and newspaper columnists from conservative, liberal, and progressive background had been saying more elegantly in the aftermath of '911'. Moreover, although his bluntness may have been new and revolting, the idea that religion – Islam in this case – has something to do with backwardness is a central notion in the Dutch self-image since the 1960s. Since '911' I have been to many panel discussions where otherwise reasonable speakers insisted that there was inherently nothing wrong with the Dutch Muslims other than that they had not yet been through a process of secularization, like the Protestants and Catholics had been since the 1960s. In discussions on the position of Muslim women in Holland, it was similarly stated that all problems would come to an end as soon as the Dutch Muslim women would liberate themselves from patriarchal religious values just as non-Muslim women had done in the feminist wave of the 1970s. In other words, although few people would call Islam a backward culture, the notion that Muslims are lagging behind is widespread and linked to the Dutch experience of secularization in a not so distant past.

Since the 1960s and 1970s, religion is at best considered a private matter, or otherwise condemned and ridiculed as irrational and backward. Part of the cultural transition that took place in those years was a so-called process of 'deconfessionalization', in which many people left the religious community – Protestant, Catholic, and, one may add, socialist – in which they had spent most of their social, economic, recreational, and political life. This breaking away from religion was often a traumatic affair, considering the huge pile of novels written in those years by young authors who broke with their religious upbringing, discovering a world of free cultural, spiritual, and sexual expression. Insofar as they exist, spiritual wishes are now generally met by a range of new practices from New Age, Buddhism, Shamanism, Sufism, etc. The role of the established religions in public and political life, however, is often considered a thing of the past, in particular by the 1960s and 1970s generation. All the same, their freedom from religion is also considered a delicate achievement that can easily be threatened and taken away. In that sense, recent Muslim migrants in Holland not only struggle with language problems, unemployment, and bad housing conditions, but also with a dominant public discourse that project traumatic past experiences with a hierarchical, community-based, sexually repressive, women-unfriendly form of Calvinism onto Islam.

Dutch radical secularization can be explained from a pre-1960s past of *pillarization*. Starting in the 19th century up to the 1950s, the various churches played a crucial role in the centralizing project that turned peasants, merchants, and fishermen into Dutchmen (Van Rooden 1999). This was done by way of so-called pillars (*zuilen*) or 'own worlds'. *Zuilen* were configurations of organizations – political, educational, social, recreational, and to some extent economic – based on religious affiliation. Apart from a cultural and political elite, most people lived and raised their children within those pillars. The religious organizations at the head of those pillars functioned as intermediaries between citizens and the state, so much so that politics was to a very large extent first and foremost church politics. This came to a rather abrupt end in the 1960s and 1970s, when a process of depillarization (*ontzuiling*) was set in motion, which forced the churches into a more ecumenical spirit leading to the joining together of various Catholic and Protestant political parties into one Christian Democrat Alliance (CDA) in the late 1970s. For the then young generation breaking out of their pillars, religion seemed outdated, petty bourgeois, oppressive, and on the decline. Perhaps the most articulate expression of this trend is a party called *Democrats '66* (*D66*), a left-of-center, liberal, modernist party, established in 1966, which became the fourth-biggest party in Holland and the initiator in 1994 of the *purple coalition* of Labor and Liberals, which sent the Christian Democrats into the opposition for the first time in Dutch parliamentary history.

However, there was another element to pillarization – a more elusive way or tradition of dealing with difference and diversity – that was not so easily thrown overboard. I am alluding here to a culture of tolerance or indifference, beautifully analyzed by Halleh Ghorashi in a study on the encounter of Iranian refugees with Dutch society. According to Ghorashi (2001: chapter 11), depillarization has indeed led to a strong dislike or distrust of religion-based political identities, but depillarization has not eroded the concept of 'minding your own business', that was at the root of the more or less peaceful coexistence of various religious communities. Difference was accepted as long as its expression remained limited within the boundaries of the pillars. Within your own church, so to speak, you were free to do everything that would not be tolerated in broad daylight. This went with a certain degree of suspicion about possibly peculiar practices going on in somebody else's church or religious community. However, Dutch tolerance – a central feature of national self-image in recent years – primarily meant not probing into these potentially funny businesses of the other. This informed and influenced the way Dutch society dealt with the emerging multicultural society in the 1980s and 1990s. Tolerance toward minorities translated as respect for boundaries of identity rather than cultural interaction. Minorities were for instance allowed education in their own language and 'with respect for their own culture'. In this way, Dutch-style multiculturalism promoted and strengthened cultural boundaries in order to be better able to respect and tolerate them. Much less attention was given to social-economic and political aspects of migration and integration. As a result, minorities tend to have a weak social-economic position, are poorly integrated in the political process, and have a strong sense of cultural difference. The attitude toward minorities that led to these results has been characterized as 'hugging them to death', meaning that minorities were pampered because of cultural differences, but not allowed an equal position politically and socio-economically (cf. Kaschuba 1995).

'September 11' of course led to a public debate on possible explanations and interpretations of the attacks. For a long time, there was no attention at all for factors such as the ambivalent strategic relations between the US, its allies, and political Islam; the internal dynamics within a heavily-armed modern mercenary army with no cause and under threat of losing its main sponsors; or the poor and often violent experiences young, ambitious, and desperate men have with authoritarian states in the Middle East and Asia oppressing political parties and social movements in the name of democracy and free speech. Instead one looked for reasons within Islam and its history. Headlines in national newspapers and weeklies stating that 'there is something wrong with Islam' (e.g. Frentrop 2001) articulated a wider sentiment that Islam lacked a tradition of tolerance and secularization. A D66 member of parliament suggested that an Islamic Voltaire was needed. Others proposed that a Muslim Kant or Tocqueville would be more appropriate. In other words, no distinctions was made between Islam and a rather recent line of political philosophy known as political Islam, let alone between various forms of political Islam. One looked for explanations in tradition instead of present-day power conflicts. And by juxtaposing Islam and Western civilization, one also retreated into a hard-line modernist notion of the West as the product of the Enlightenment in which colonialism, the World Wars, the Holocaust, etc., have no place. Small wonder that Samuel Huntington's *The Clash of Civilizations and the Remaking of World Order* (1997) became a bestseller and was translated in Dutch under a title that left out the second part of the original title. In this climate, Pim Fortuyn's remarks on Islam's backwardness only stood out for its rude and unsophisticated use of language.

This soon had ramifications for the way the Dutch Muslims were looked at. For if indeed something was wrong with Islam, then how could one expect Muslims to be part of a modern, secular society, playing the game according to the rules of "minding your own business"? A clear example of this line of thought was given when Ayaan Hirsi Ali, a member of parliament for the right-wing liberal party and a migrant from Somalia, said that to modern, Western standards, the Prophet Muhammad was a pervert, suggesting that the sexual oppression of female Muslim migrants was essentially a problem of Islam that could not be solved as long as one remained a Muslim. Moreover, not only Islam was attacked, but also the policy of tolerance (*gedoogbeleid*) of the 1980s and 1990s. As initially one of his most provocative and "mediagenic" demands, Pim Fortuyn asked for a much more stringent policy of assimilation – a point that was later adopted in a more disguised form by mainstream parties such as the Christian Democrats when they stressed the importance of social cohesion and sharing a set of norms and values that remained unspecified.

Since '911', problems of migration, integration, and social inequality have been defined primarily as a cultural problem. At the root lie particular religious mentalities. Moderates take this as Muslims lagging behind – a problem that can be dealt with by education and possibly affirmative action programmes. Hardliners instead see it as a problem of contrasting and clashing cultures, and they are therefore no longer willing to accept the old concept of minding your own business within your own community.

The old Dutch embarrassment of wanting to know what goes on in somebody else's church but not daring to satisfy this desire out of considerations of decency is turned into a more aggressive suspicion about possible anti-social and subversive activities taking place in culturally exclusive spaces such as mosques or Muslim schools. This takes a radical form in the fear for militant groups recruiting large numbers of young Dutch Muslim males for jihad – a fear fostered by ill-researched reports of the Dutch secret intelligence service (AIVD) on Muslim terrorist activities in the Netherlands, resulting in court cases against accused terrorists which the public prosecutor fails to win because of insufficient evidence. The same fear is also evident in the hostile reactions against the Arab European League (AEL), established in Belgium by the young and charismatic Abu Jahjah and possibly becoming a political platform for angry young Muslims in the Netherlands too. Politicians from right wing and conservative parties, however, see it as a movement engaged in undermining and subversive activities and therefore demanded that the AEL be banned before the Dutch branch was even established.

Insofar as problems of multiculturalism can be explained in cultural terms, it is clear that the dominant Dutch discourse on cultural and religious differences is as much at stake as the cultural and religious mentalities of the migrants. What has clashed in Holland since '911' is not Islam versus Western civilization, but an ideology of secularism and personal freedom that came of age in the 1960s versus its shadow that is projected onto Islam. Increasingly, Islam is defined as the exact opposite of everything people in Holland have fought for since the 1960s: free sexual expression, gender equality, individualism. To some extent, these struggles have been won. The best evidence for this is of course the extreme popularity of Pim Fortuyn, an openly homosexual dandy, among male supporters of Feijenoord, a working class soccer team in Rotterdam, and other groups otherwise prone to homophobia. Another example: during the 2003 election campaign, Jan Peter Balkenende, prime minister and leader of the Christian Democrats, let himself be interviewed daily by two young female TV reporters, one of whom is the anchorwoman of a TV show called *Neuken doe je zo* ('This is how to fuck'), and the other one being sex symbol number one among Dutch male teenagers. Apart from the sexual abuse of children, sex has lost its potential for scandal. But while the pre-1960s generation was obsessed with sexual mores, today's generation is preoccupied with religion. Islam in particular is seen as a threat to the newly won freedom. The editor of the main feminist magazine *Opzij*, for instance, obstinately refuses to employ Muslim journalists wearing headscarves, saying that she will not allow the achievements of her generation to be destroyed by Muslim migrants, and thus bringing the almost defeated impact of religion in through the backdoor. In sum, the progressive elite has more in common with Pim Fortuyn then it is willing to admit.

Conclusion

In the cases I have described, we see renewed debate on national identity after the suicide attacks of '911'. This reflection on the nation brings to the surface at least two observations. First, there is a reaffirmation of the ideological pillars of the nation. In Pakistan, it is reformist and modernist Islam in the tradition of Muhammad Iqbal. In the Netherlands, it is secularism and personal freedom of lifestyle and sexual preferences. Second, while re-emphasising the nation's ideological foundations, it also stresses what the nation is not. I have called the flipside of this national identity the nation's shadow, indicating that it sticks with the nation whatever moves it makes. Hence, the more Islam is stressed as the unifying force of the Pakistani nation, the greater the suspicion that ethnic, tribal, or kinship loyalties and sentiments will undermine the nation. The more it is argued that secularism is the basis of the modern Dutch nation, the greater the fear that new religious mentalities in the form of Muslim migrants will bring back a traumatic national past.

Ideological conflicts thus become more polarized and charged, but these conflicts are more specific and concrete than the much-discussed clashes of civilizations – even though it is clear that more global discourses are at play in both cases. In Holland, renewed and crudely popularized Orientalist stereotypes about Muslims clearly affect the public debate on multicultural society, whereas in Pakistan we see the impact of global discourses on good governance and transparency in the debate about corruption. Nonetheless, these global notions, images, and fantasies are shaped and translated in national contexts to come to a starker contrast between the nation and its shadow. Part of this polarization is the increasing fear of subversive, undermining activities, symbolized by such figures as moles, spies, and sleeper-terrorists. Similarly, the stark juxtaposition of the nation against its shadow increases the number of scandals and rumors, the nature of which also indicates the central aspects of the nation's self-image. Thus, we have seen an unprecedented number of scandals and rumors connected to the renewed reflection on the place of Muslim migrants in Dutch society over the last two years. In Pakistan, scandals and rumors are about corruption caused by a range of unpatriotic and un-Islamic loyalties. As a hypothesis for further research, then, I conclude by suggesting that the bigger the political scandals and the more fearful the rumors about subversive, undermining activities, the more intense the debate on national identity.

References

Abrams, Philip 1988: Notes on the Difficulty of Studying the State. In: *Journal of Historical Sociology* 1(1): 58–89.

Anderson, Benedict 1991: *Imagined Communities: Reflections on the Origin and Spread of Nationalism.* Revised edition. London.

Asad, Talal 1999: Religion, Nation-State, Secularism. In: Peter van der Veer & Helmut Lehmann (eds): *Nation and Religion: Perspectives on Europe and Asia.* Princeton: 178–196.

Ayub Khan, Muhammad 1967: *Friends, Not Masters: a Political Autobiography.* Lahore.

Brodsky, Joseph 1995: *On Grief and Reason.* New York: Farrar Strauss Giroux.

Feldman, Allen 2002: Ground Zero Point One: On the Cinematics of History. In: *Social Analysis* 46/1: 110–117.

Frentrop, Paul 2001: Er is iets mis met de islam. In: *HP/De Tijd*, 5 Oktober.

Ghorashi, Halleh 2001: *Ways to Survive, Battles to Win: Iranian women exiles in the Netherlands and the US.* University of Nijmegen: doctoral thesis.

Guha, Ranajit 1999: *Elementary Aspects of Peasant Insurgency in Colonial India.* Durham, NC: Duke University Press.

Hansen, Thomas Blom & Stepputat, Finn (eds.) 2001: *States of Imagination: Ethnographic Explorations of the Postcolonial State.* Durham: Duke University Press.

Huntington, Samuel 1997: *The Clash of Civilizations and the Remaking of World Order.* London: Simon & Schuster.

Kaschuba, Wolfgang 1995: Kulturalism: Vom Verschwinden des Sozialen im gesellschaftlichen Diskurs. In: *Zeitschrift für Volkskunde* 91:27–46.

Metcalf, Barbara Dale 1982: *Islamic Revival in British India: Deoband, 1860–1900.* Princeton: Princeton University Press.

Mitchell, Timothy 1991: The Limits of the State: Beyond Statist Approaches and their Critics. *American Political Science Review*, 85/1: 77–96.

Mitchell, Timothy 1999: Society, Economy, and the State Effect. In: G. Steinmetz (ed.): *State/Culture: State Formation after the Cultural Turn.* Ithaca: Cornell University Press: 76–97.

Mohammad-Arif 2002: The Impact of September 11 on the Muslims from the Indian Sub-Continent in New York. In: Frédéric Grare (ed.): *The Muslims of the Indian Sub-Continent after the 11th September Attacks.* New Delhi: India Research Press: 39–72.

Rubinstein, Richard E. 1987: *Alchemists of Revolution: Terrorism in the Modern World.* London: I.B. Tauris.

Van Rooden, Peter 1999: History, the Nation, and Religion: the Transformations of the Dutch Religious Past. In: Peter van der Veer & Helmut Lehmann (eds.): *Nation and Religion: Perspectives on Europe and Asia*, 96–111.

Verdery, Katherine 1996: *What Was Socialism, and What Comes Next?* Princeton.

Verkaaik, Oskar 2001: The Captive State: Corruption, Intelligence Agencies, and Ethnicity in Pakistan. In: Thomas Blom Hansen & Finn Stepputat (eds.): *States of Imagination: Ethnographic Explorations of the Postcolonial State.* Durham: Duke University Press: 345–364.

Moles, Martyrs and Sleepers
The End of the Hobbesian Project?

Friedrich Kratochwil

Kratochwil, Friedrich 2003: Moles, Martyrs and Sleepers. The End of the Hobbesian Project? – Ethnologia Europaea 33:2: 57–68.

The paper addresses two issues: the events of September 11 in terms of the traditional vocabulary of terrorism, and the implications of these acts for the modern political project. I argue that the traditional vocabulary of the law of war, adapted to the circumstances of armed conflict, remains useful. In appraising the effect of these actions on the realization of the political project of modernity, I look to Hobbes, as he suggested peace was possible only when "fundamentalist" questions were eliminated from the political agenda. Only under a secular version of political rule can the sovereign become an effective guarantor of law. Hobbes's arguments resulted in a new vision of politics based on fear and its manipulation, but also on a certain rationality allowing individuals (and sovereign states) to pursue their own interests. Insofar as both the domestic and international social order is based on such notions, the emergence of fundamentalist-inspired terrorism decisively challenges the modern political project.

Prof. Friedrich Kratochwil, European University Institute, Via dei Roccettini 9, I-50016 San Domenico die Fiesole (Fi). E-Mail: Friedrich.Kratochwil@IUE.it

Introduction

Whatever the long term consequences of the September 11 attack will be, one thing seems certain: this event has not only victimized the US but has challenged some of the most basic assumptions underlying our social life. We are accustomed to think that conflict is above all a result of poverty and ignorance, yet the attackers of the World Trade Center and their fellow travelers were neither exemplars of the downtrodden of the earth, nor were they people who did not understand the modern world. Well at home in our midst, they chose to reject our way of life with a decisiveness, characteristic of fanaticism, that is seldom encountered.

But beyond the wanton thirst for fame these deeds reflect, we feel there is a wider danger that issues from a political "project" so alien to us that we hardly can find a way to comprehend it. Gone are our familiar notions of the inevitable secularization of modern life; gone is the idea that political projects have to be based on the largely "private" pursuit of happiness; gone is the idea that in politics the "right" somehow has to take precedence over the "good"; gone is the notion that "politics" has to take place in or among demarcated spaces by citizens or their authorized agents

In a way, this act of fanaticism might have borne out the fear that the pursuit of the "good life," if at the expense of individual rights, can end in disaster. Yet the self-evidence of this position has been shattered. Precisely because we can no longer take this political ideal for granted, new threats emerge: traditional institutions such as the state, or even the practices of "war," no longer bind violence. Governments past and present have been repressive, and wars have taken on horrendous proportions, but there was always some understanding, and hope, that the spread of human rights, or the stabilization of the balance of terror, might mitigate or even prevent violent conflagrations. Perhaps we even adhered to the Kantian idea that despite breakdowns in civilized conduct, "humanity" was advancing along a path that, whether through the cunning of nature or of history, would eventually result in the emancipation of humankind. After September 11, nothing seems farther from those hopes: for the first time in memory all aspects our way of life seem to be threatened.

What we need in such a situation are proper diagnostic tools to allow us to appraise where we are and what has changed, now that our conventional understandings and theories have failed us. It is therefore useful to take a step back and examine the concepts and vocabularies that constitute our political practice, and ascertain whether they still help us understand events or can help us (re)-orient our actions. Such an investigation necessarily leads us to identify the linkages between concepts and general vocabulary. Because the social and political world is not "natural" but is created by actors and their actions, we have to see how practices are part of a particular social and political project, and of its concomitant discipline. In other words, we need to both examine the cognitive framework that determines what can be said, and the set of "self-fashioning" prescriptions that link the individual to others, be they friends or foes.

Thus, in this paper I want to probe the origins of the political vocabulary of modernity, to show how it constitutes and frames the political project we usually identify with a liberal order, though that political project actually is more encompassing. It sets the "bounds of sense" in the political arena not just for liberals, in the classical sense, but also for traditionalists, communitarians, and even "nationalists." It provides the practices we use to fashion ourselves as individuals and as members of a community. By observing certain "do's" and "don'ts," which through practice become our ingrained habits, we can be "secure," or without worry (*sine cura*) because certain things are taken for granted. They are cared for by institutions, and certain otherwise problematic issues of social life are no longer focal points of political disputes, as they have been relegated to the "private" realm. Inequality is one of the crucial problems for any social order, for example, but because the political project of modernity has placed wealth differences, along with questions of moral "truth," into the "private" category, they have largely been eliminated from the public agenda. Likewise, the "economy" largely determines issues of distribution, and any truth claim based on revelation is sequestered into "private" religion.

For a number of reasons I will indicate below, this modern understanding of politics and how it is connected to the state, as well as the project of modernity, is thoroughly Hobbesian – though his particular solutions (establishing an "absolute" sovereign or church; having a supreme power (Leviathan) authorized to settle all disputes with finality) have not been followed. In this the crucial antecedent point, in founding a body politic, was to base the social order not on a shared notion of the common good but on a "negative" consensus based on avoiding the particular evil violent death represented. A secondary point was Hobbes's reformulation of happiness, not in the Aristotelian sense of a state of contemplative insight, but rather as the *pursuit* of pleasure (happiness could not be gained by a state of existence but only by fleeting moments of satisfaction).

Both moves created a thoroughly secular space that has been characteristic of modern politics since. That secular space is fundamentally challenged by a notion of politics as rule in the name of a creed, which is a concept of politics that in its turn eliminates the other conceptual distinctions that are part of the project of modernity, such as the distinction between state and society, or between public and private. Politics in the name of a creed also dispenses with a further (though not necessary) move of modernity, namely the prohibitions against using violent means, due to alleged exceptional circumstances.

Hobbes thus stands, in my view, as a modern antithesis to the Aristotelian "political project," which had an idea of the good life that encompassed both the individual and politics. Hobbes also articulated ideas about establishing a state and steering it, laying the groundwork of what became an international system. In both cases, his political notions were thoroughly secular. Indeed, the modern international system is based on secular ideas that it is the public authority that determines what is public and what is private (and not an individual's conscience), that individuals in nation-states are ultimately subject to and loyal to political authority (even if they follow religious authorities in matters of faith or belong to a community of believers), that war and intervention are political decisions (and not questions of faith), and so on. Later elaborations about civil liberties, the neutrality of states, the balance of power and the like derive from Hobbes's "moves."

In this context, I want to focus in particular on how one deals with incommensurable moral claims if they appear as "the truth" demanding recognition and obedience, and thereby engender conflicts. Hobbes suggested that in such a case, political order could no longer be based on a common ontological understanding, or on some universally accepted revealed truth, because these mutually exclusive truth claims sooner rather than later engendered the jurisdictional issue of *quis judicabit*. Yet to enable the sovereign to settle such questions, the sovereign had to be buttressed by newly articulated common understandings that did not contain justifications based on a revelation. Hobbes, not wanting to dispense with the foundational notion of the existence of some form of a transcendental authority, resorted to the Laws of Nature, which he construed as commands of universal human "reason".

Thus, we can see why Hobbes's two conceptual moves were more important in structuring the political project of modernity than the particular solution he himself advocated (the creation of the Leviathan), a theme upon which I elaborate in the second section. In the third section, I adduce the conceptual apparatus of the classical Laws of War, and their more recent elaborations, in order to analyze in greater detail the problem of "terrorism" and appraise the threats posed by sleepers, moles and martyrs. A brief summary of the main lines of the argument concludes the paper.

The Hobbesian Project

Though it is common to interpret Hobbes as a theorist who took a mechanical and naturalist approach to politics, given what his emphasis on power and on the fear of violent death seems to indicate, his analysis is far subtler. For despite Hobbes's insistence on power and sanctions, it is the complementarity of expectations among actors that makes social order possible, even if power and punishment may be the most important means to structure expectations. Thus, unlike the "realists" in international relations today who focus on "power" and capabilities, Hobbes is well aware a sovereign's effectiveness cannot rest primarily on his capacity to exert sanctions: "actions of men proceed from their opinions; and in the well governing of opinions consisteth the well governing of men's actions, in order to their peace and concord" (Hobbes 1983: 223).

After all, the Hobbesian sovereign is not by accident the "fixer of signs." Most of Hobbes's *Leviathan* is devoted to definitions and arguments about proper names and instructions that will permit sedition to be nipped in the bud (Hobbes 1983, chapts. 5–9 and 30), and some of the most telling passages of *Behemoth* are devoted to the power of imagination, prophecy, fantasy and folly. Despite his alleged materialism, Hobbes pays particular attention to the role of ideas and emphasizes the powerful force of "names" for politics, including whom to call a "traitor," for example (Hobbes 1990: 37). He is also well aware that norms such as traditional legitimacy engender loyalty and have to be overcome by appeals to other sources of legitimation.[1]

In this context, Hobbes is particularly suspicious of teachings that are promulgated by a clergy who rely on personal revelations or on alleged divine authority. As Hobbes himself suggests in his *Elements of Law*, the fundamental disagreement between sacred and secular authority creates a radically different situation for which neither Biblical examples nor those of the classical *polis* provide any templates. Hobbes writes:

"This difficulty hath not been of very great antiquity in the world. There was no such dilemma amongst the Jews: for there civil law, and divine law was one and the same Law of Moses. Nor is it a controversy that is ever taken notice of amongst the Grecians, Romans, or other Gentiles. Also those Christians that dwell under the temporal dominion of the bishop of Rome are free from this question... This difficulty, therefore, remaineth amongst and troubleth those Christians only to whom it is allowed to take for the sense of the Scripture that which they make thereof, either by their own private interpretation, or by the interpretation of such as are not called thereunto by public authority" (Hobbes 1994:141f).

To that extent, the Hobbesian problem of order is one in which the individual's free conscience no longer interferes with the exercise of authority by the secular sovereign, because individuals need no longer fear that there is *"the danger of eternal damnation from simple obedience to human laws"* (152f).

As Hobbes well knew, belief cannot be enforced. Yet men may believe whatever they want as long as it is a "private" belief that keeps its prescriptions for personal conduct in tune with the requirements of public order, as well as within the "natural law" to seek peace. The demand for the sovereign to publicly display his adherence to a particular religion is not incompatible with freedom of conscience. As he points out, it cannot be considered as a voluntary act: *it is not attributable to the individual but to the sovereign* "nor is it he that in this case denied Christ before men, but his Governor, and the law of his country" (Hobbes 1985: 528).

Yet it is also an order in which individual beliefs can no longer be used for the de-legitimization of the public authority on the basis of conscientious objections either.[2] Much of *Leviathan* is therefore devoted to demonstrating that it is the sovereign who has the right to determine which interpretations are to be admitted, as they are the ones conducive to peace and stability in a society.

Thus, an entirely new picture of the Hobbesian project emerges when we read his texts at the level of the controversies Hobbes was observing and participating in. Far from postulating some "natural" foundation, Hobbes knows that even the passions are powerfully formed by cultural factors and ideals. They give rise to "ways of life" that can powerfully counteract the "law of nature" that seeks peace. Even our emotions are not "natural" or pristine in their immediacy but are instead part of a specific cultural milieu whose influence becomes visible only when we reflect upon it.

So even in the case of the "fear of violent death," Hobbes is again not referring to something that is un-problematically given. Rather, he is engaged in a deeper political struggle over public authority and the effectiveness of "secular" sanctions that buttress political order. After all, St. Augustine already had remarked that it was eternal *damnation*, and not the *fear of violent death*, that represents the *summum malum*. Such a belief, if accepted, tends, however, to weaken the deterrent power of secular punishment, as Hobbes was quick to point out. In drawing the clear lessons with respect to the English Civil War, Hobbes argues that: "As much as eternal torture is more terrible than death", so much more (the people) would fear the *"clergy more than they would the King"* if such a belief was prevalent in society (Hobbes 1990: 14f).

Seen in this light, some recent interpretations of Hobbes become more plausible as they stress the "rhetorical" character of his work and view it as an attempt to persuade his audience, rent at the time by civil strife and a ruinous competition for honor. Far better to "seek peace" (Hobbes 1985: 190) and pursue happiness by following their "interests" rather than risk life and limb for ultimate truths, or reputation, or prestige. Only with such a reformulation of the project of individualism – a change that requires an individual to coolly calculate his advantage rather than pursue glory and honor – can the political project of securing peace succeed.

In addition, important elements of power are "privatized" in this project, since property is largely exempted from public intervention (other than for reasons of eminent domain). Later, in the Lockean version of the liberal project, government is viewed as the trustee of civil society, and is created to perfect it: by guaranteeing property rights and by preventing disputes among its members who recognize each other primarily as property owners (Locke 1965:361ff) rather than as members of an estate or a community of co-religionists. Yet even the moderate liberal individual pursuing his self-interest had to be fashioned and "normalized," and was far from a "natural" person.

We also can now see why the Hobbesian

project became so fundamental for our modern political order – it relied essentially on deterrence or the manipulation of fear. Sanction and punishment became a characteristic of law, and for theorists of the state, even the characteristic that distinguished the public order from "private" notions of the good.[3] The tender reeds of the international order are the result of "deterrence" as well, not of some Aristotelian idea of a substantive "good" as the foundation for societies.

Hobbes himself suggested that by creating the sovereign most of the security problems for individuals had been solved. While a type of radical equality exists among individual men, as even the strongest can be overpowered when he sleeps or is not mindful of his security, social organizations can take care of these problems. No equal strength is required between societies, as a weak nation must only make it unlikely it can be overrun by another nation in order to possess a viable deterrence. Such a calculation is based on common standards of acceptable risks, however, which in turn presuppose a certain "normalcy" of politics in which excessive goals are ruled out and "survival," not only in the physical sense but as a way of life, is taken as the guiding maxim and is enshrined in "reasons of state." Intervention and war for religious purposes are ruled out, as are acts of war involving excessive indiscriminate force, cruelty, or measures against "civilians." War, as Rousseau will later remind us, is a relationship between states, not individual persons.[4]

These notions could not be farther from those inspiring the terrorist violence of recent times. It is not states but believers who have to be organized; it is not a political project that safeguards rights and "privacy" in pursuit of the good life, but instead fundamentalist and radical notions of the good that are being pursued. The ideal is not to ensure a "civilized" life, but rather to pursue a life of glory and eternal reward – that "believers" are to devote themselves to, irrespective of the costs to life and limb.

Against such a background, the foundationalist attempts of much of our contemporary political theory seem downright quaint (Rawls 1971; Habermas 1981). Having forgotten the heavy conditioning that is part of becoming a "normal" person in our society, our only worry now seems to consist in demonstrating that the rules and practices we utilize in our political life are those which stand to reason, i.e. would be chosen by all. Or that all of our political problems can be talked out in an ideal speech situation from which consensus will emerge. The last flickers of the Enlightenment combine here with a political project in which privacy and consumption have become paramount, and in which most politics seems to revolve around how both can be reached in an efficient and conflict-free way.

To that extent, September 11 is a ghastly reminder that the Hobbesian project is not only not universally shared but also downright fragile. It can be challenged by reopening questions which have long been silenced, and since the old answers do not seem to be convincing, at least to some, the Hobbesian project is in danger: with it, our basic understanding of the social order is also endangered. That helps explain the prevailing feeling of insecurity (noticeable particularly in the US), a fear that can easily be misdirected and create still more problems. It is not clear what can be done, other than efforts at greater surveillance, which themselves may subvert the goals of "privacy" and individual rights that are part of the Hobbesian project. It is therefore important to take stock and see to what extent the events of September 11 defy our assessments and necessitate new departures in thinking and acting. Here the traditional Laws of War provide useful instruments for assessment.

The Phenomenon of Terrorism and the Traditional Laws of War

Despite the shock of September 11 and the use of high tech "weapons," using extreme violence against indiscriminate targets is not without historical precedent. Even the self-immolation of perpetrators in the course of attacking has well-known parallels, both of individuals and of groups. The *sicarrii* zealots of biblical times,[5] who used personal assassination to eliminate opponents and instill terror, come to mind, as do the sect of Assassins who operated out of Persia.

Genghis Khan's war conduct, which often seemed more like extermination campaigns than "normal" wars, is also a case in point. And we should also remember the Japanese kamikaze pilots in World War II who tried to force a decision by their suicidal attacks. Despite these similarities – which basically consist of the unconventional ways force was used – significant differences exist among such cases. The kamikaze pilots may be closest to our conception of warfare, since we are dealing with soldiers used against an enemy's armed forces, although their acceptance of death in completing their mission was unusual and led to higher than usual casualties in the conduct of hostilities. On the other hand, the massacre and deportation of the civilian population, as practiced by the Assyrians or Genghis Khan, come much closer to our notion of terrorism, in that the violence is no longer addressed to the agents of the opposing power.

Since the attackers of the World Trade Center chose this target because of its highly significant symbolic character, well aware that numerous civilians not only of the enemy but also of *other groups and nations* would be among the victims, the September 11 attacks reflect a further important rupture of certain traditionally accepted limits. In addition, the "private" character of Al-Qaeda's attacks distinguishes these events from attempts by Mongols to extend their rule, for no ruler is here trying to extend his realm. Rather, as with the sect of the assassins, we are dealing here with a group assembled by a self-appointed leader, or prophet, who has no political legitimacy or apparatus of a traditional society. Despite the astonishing submission of individual followers to this prophet, even to the point of self-extinction, the model that seems best for categorizing this phenomenon is not that of the maladjusted individual personality – a favorite defensive mechanism when we encounter the unusual – but Weber's charismatic ruler or prophet.

Weber argued that such a ruler unites the group by proclaiming a "truth" that radically contradicts the projects and ideals of the surrounding society. In this way, Weber draws our attention to the social dimension of the phenomenon and the crucial role of shared beliefs among the members of the group. It has been observed that Weber himself dealt with the phenomenon of charisma largely in negative terms, by contrasting it with the other two forms of legitimate domination, traditional authority and legal authority. But since charisma sooner or later gets "routinized," and since claims to traditional rule are hard to sustain under the onslaught of modernity, and result in the demystification of the world (*Entzauberung*), Weber suggests charisma largely belongs to "prerationalistic periods." True, he is aware that with the advent of mass democracy, populist leaders may come close to charismatic figures – his remarks about Napoleon III are significant in this respect – but the role of charisma under conditions of modernity remains a largely unexplored problem within his magisterial work *Economy and Society*.

It is only in the later debates about political religions[6] and the attempts to come to terms with "totalitarianism" that add some insights by identifying the abolition of law in the name of an ultimate goal as the decisive element of the totalitarian project. For it is, as Arendt cites Cicero, the *consensus juris* that constitutes not just a people but the civilized world, "insofar as it remains the foundation-stone of international relations even under the conditions of war." Totalitarians, on the other hand, believe they can dispense with this basic consent by making mankind itself the embodiment of law, and on the other hand believe they will not fall into tyranny, lawlessness, arbitrariness, and fear (Arendt 1973: 462). Weber's discussion of values and of an ethics of responsibility, as well as the problem of existential choices, strikingly prefigures these observations. Responsibility is not owed to a definite group or audience, not responding to some legally constituted authority, but instead the individual and his or her conscience as ultimate judge and ultimate court of appeal (Weber 1958: 493–548). This notion stands in strange tension with Weber's own emphasis on shared meanings and the importance of historically formed collective representations.

As some critics have noted, Weber's emphasis on the prophet – and by extension, on individual conscience as a secularized version of the demands made by a charismatic leader – leaves the social interaction between leader and followers strangely opaque, as all influence seems to radiate only from the prophet. But as Alberoni suggests, the prophet can become this central figure only when he is part of a group that is ready for his message (Alberoni 1984). The "group" is thus important for the formulation of the message itself, and its role is not limited to a later period after the death of the prophet when questions of succession and the routinization of charisma have to be addressed.

As social psychologists have remarked with respect to radical groups that confront society with a new way of life, the power of the group, and loyalty to it, may be more important for explaining its internal and external dynamics than its message, for "the cause is long term, [but] the group is tangible" (Paz 2001: 4). Though we do not well understand this internal process of identity formation, two problems attain to it: how do terrorists become convinced that their deed is not a simple suicide but a sacrifice for a higher cause? And how *in general* are the process of individuation and cultural forms linked?

The first issue is usually debated in terms of brainwashing techniques in sects and of induced dependency. The acolyte is usually rigidly separated from all familiar interactions with friends or family in order to transform his or her personality and to instill a new discipline based on absolute obedience. Point 4 of the instructions found among Atta's belongings after the September 11 attack, for example, emphasized nearly pedantically that it was not only obedience but "100% obedience" that was required. The second issue points to the seemingly counterintuitive notion that an individual is not simply a "given" element of a society that comes into being by the aggregation of such persons. Rather, the individual is the *product of certain social and political ideals and strategies*.

One can examine this second point with reference to the perpetrators of the September 11 attacks, as one can roughly reconstruct the formation of their group from documents left behind and from various *Manuals of Jihad* in pamphlet form. All of these share a religious idiom that is familiar to all Muslims, though the pamphlets are usually written in the idiolect of a specific group devoted to a specific, radical, and "fundamentalist" interpretation of the Koran. The contemporary situation of Muslims in the world is depicted as one of shame and degradation in all such writings, and that is in turn blamed on the activities of "Satanic" forces. A Hamas script published before the start of the *Intifada* suicide attacks states:

"The whole world is persecuting you and the satanic powers ambush you. The whole world is your front, and do not exclude yourself from the confrontation... The life of misery prevents you from grasping the meaning of life and turns life into death. You live as a dead man... We stand today at a crossroads: life or death, but life without martyrdom is death. Look for death and you are given life" (*Filastin al Muslima* 1991: 63 – as quoted in Paz 2001: 5).

The universal scope of the mission is outlined, after this invocation of the general threat, so that martyrdom can be seen as the glorious way out of individual and collective misery. Future suicide attackers are not only exhorted to not fear death but to submit to it and accept it as a duty. This "allegiance to death" that was introduced into the discourse by the chief ideologue of the Egyptian Islamic Jihad in his book *The Forgotten Duty* was also listed as Point 11 in Atta's instructions. The cowardliness of enemies is shown by the defiance of death attackers, and the "72 beauties" waiting for the suicide attackers in paradise can then reward the martyrs for their rejection of a normal life. It is significant that this marriage in heaven is mentioned no less than three times in Atta's instructions – it is apparently an element considered important for counteracting self-doubts and the weakness of will problem among the attackers. To minimize pity with the victims, the instructions also depict them as representatives of evil rather than as persons, enabling their death to be compared with the butchering of animals. The demand that one check one's weapons again shortly before an attack is thereby linked to a Koran verse: "let every one of you sharpen his knife and kill his animal and bring about comfort and relief to his slaughter."[7]

Such strategies for desensitizing the attacker to the suffering of his victims and of demonizing the "enemy" are well known and part of the (de)formation of the terrorist personality. The strategy is powerfully reinforced by two further gambits: the claim of an extraordinary threat, suspending for the believer the stringent restraints placed on pursuing even the most worthwhile goals, and the idea that the fighter is not fighting for a specific purpose, whose value he would then have to consider in the context of other values, but that he is fighting *evil itself*. To that extent, the impact of religiously inspired terrorism is powerfully heightened as it goes far beyond the limits of both unconventional warfare and simple terrorism. It shares with all forms of terrorism that its main targets are not the state or its apparatus as such, but targets with symbolic significance whose destruction will likely strike terror in the hearts of the population.

In selecting targets this way, terrorists try to undermine the general societal sense of security and confidence, one that is necessary for the reproduction of the social order *and* of the individual personality, and thereby disorient individual and public officials alike. A maximal psychological effect is expected from the use of relatively minimal means, at least when compared to the resources expended. One of the implications of this terrorist calculus is to erase the distinction between war and crime: rape, murder, arson, and kidnapping[8] can all become tactics in this "struggle," in addition to the more familiar, spectacular acts of destruction. Even classically constituted military detachments may resort to such terrorist tactics, as the events in Bosnia-Herzegovina and Kosovo amply demonstrated.

Relative to the patterns of classical warfare, there also seems to be a strange reversal of the relationship between power and resources, or between cause and effect. If the use of force through war is Clausewitzian ("war is the continuation of politics by other means" [Clausewitz 1984]), then two corollaries follow. First, the use of force is subordinated to politics, and thus the military is subject to civilian control, and second, that political goals are themselves limited because "total" victory is hardly ever possible, or so costly, that pursuing such a strategy becomes self-defeating. "Unconditional surrender" is then the exception rather than the rule, even when a decision to do so is aided by the great decisive battle, on which Clausewitz focused his attention.[9] The capitulation point of one of the parties is usually reached long before the decisive battle degenerates into a slaughter "to the last man," particularly so when the terms of surrender offered are lenient and open the possibility of influencing the outcome through negotiation. The point in classical wars, in most cases, is less to "break" the will of the opponent than to "bend" it.

But in unconventional or guerrilla war, as well as in terrorist attacks, the logic seems reversed. Through the use of limited means, virtually unlimited goals are pursued and without compromise. Yet if guerrillas want to be successful, they have to concern themselves with building parallel political structures that can take over when the old regime's structures collapse. Guerrilla tactics cannot themselves force a decision, so a guerrilla movement can only succeed if it can become powerful enough to change its tactics from hit and run to a form that will overpower the enemy (Giap 1970). Here conventional battle and psychological disintegration of the enemy play an important part, and are manifested in the disloyalty of the troops and in paralysis of the decision-making apparatus. Thus, the crises in the aftermath of the collapse of Japanese rule in China led entire Kuomintang military units to switch sides, and the pitched battle North Vietnam waged to subdue Saigon was similarly important.

All this requires at least a modicum of political responsibility, or observation of traditional rules, on the part of the guerrillas, despite whatever brutalities they perpetrate in their march to power. The "enemy" to the guerrilla is the regime and its structures, so the civilian population cannot, other than incidentally, become the target of attacks. This not only limits the scope of targets drastically but it makes a guerilla conflict quite different from terrorism. Furthermore, because guerrillas seek to "liberate" a given society, and to become "free" to work out its political destiny, it entails claims made in the context of the claims of other peoples and states. That makes it imperative in turn to be recognized by others, which itself means a modicum of the conventions and institutions that constitute the fabric of international life must be observed, including those that regulate the use of force.

But in terrorism, and particularly among religiously motivated terrorists, the project is different. We are not dealing with a given society (run by an old regime) or a specific people (overrun by invaders) but rather with "believers." Their potential number is unlimited, and because of the alleged emergency situation (e.g., "the whole world is persecuting you") those addressed are simultaneously absolved from the otherwise stringent limits on the use of force. The goals of these groups are usually ill defined, since it is the "survival" of a particular way of life that is at stake, not the goals of a state.

Furthermore, since the religiously motivated way of life cuts across traditional boundaries between public and private, internal and external, economic and political, or state and society, "victory" by definition can only be achieved when Satan's grip on the world has been loosened. And that can come about only by dealing severe blows to all of Satan's collaborators and representatives, as the (Feb. 23, 1998) *fatwa* of Osama bin Laden and several Islamic spiritual leaders stated:

"The ruling to kill Americans and their allies – civilians and military – is an individual duty for every Muslim who can do it in any country in which it is possible ... in order to liberate the al Aqsa Mosque and the Holy Mosque from their grip, and ... for their armies to move out of all the lands of Islam, defeated and unable to threaten any Muslim. This is in accordance with the word of Almighty God: "and fight all the pagans all together as they fight you all together" and "fight them until there is no more tumult or oppression and there prevail justice and faith in God ... We, with God's help, call on every Muslim, who believes in God and wishes to be rewarded, to comply with God's order to kill the Americans and plunder their money wherever and whenever they find it. We also call on Muslim ulema, leaders, youth and soldiers to launch the raid on the Satan's US troops and the devil's supporters who ally with them."[10]

This clarion call to violence is a chilling reminder that the "normalcy" of international life could become a thing of the past.

Nevertheless, it is also clear that the conceptual distinctions based on an adapted version of the Laws of War, are still useful for finding our bearings. To that extent, the argument that efforts at "defining" terrorism are futile (we cannot agree on what a terrorist is, your terrorist is my freedom fighter, etc.) is clearly false. Thus, because in many modern conflicts it is no longer states that are the relevant actors, it has been necessary to clarify the rights and duties of combatants, and the 1977 Geneva Conventions have been extended to apply not just to "wars" but to other forms of armed conflict. As one student of terrorism has pointed out:

"The normative principle relating to a state of war between two countries can be extended without difficulty to a conflict between a non-governmental organization and a state. This extended version would thus differentiate between guerrilla warfare and terrorism. Exactly parallel with the distinction between military and civilian targets in war the extended version would designate as "guerrilla warfare" the deliberate use of violence against military and security personnel in order to attain political, ideological and religious goals. Terrorism, on the other hand, would be defined as "the deliberate use of violence against civilians in order to attain political, ideological, and religious aims." What is important in these definitions is the differentiation between goals and the means used to achieve these goals. The aims of terrorism and guerrilla warfare may well be identical; but they are distinguished from each other by the means used, or, more precisely, by the targets of their operation... By this definition, a terrorist organization can no longer claim to be "freedom fighters" because they are fighting for national liberation, or some otherworldly goal. Even if its declared ultimate goals are legitimate, an organization that deliberately targets civilians is a terrorist organization" (Ganor 2001:1).

With these distinctions in mind, we can see that the difference between terrorism and unconventional force no longer coincides with whether force is being wielded by a state. Traditionally, states enjoyed a virtually automatic presumption of legitimacy and "private actors" did not, but as the prosecution of Milosevic and Pinochet have shown, even those acting in an official capacity can now be charged with engaging in terrorist activities, particularly since personal responsibility for atrocities committed in war has been long acknowledged to imply personal criminal responsibility.

Conclusion

Still, confronted as we are virtually every day with reports of child warriors, massacres committed by fanatic mobs or suicide bombers, of marauding bands that have suspended the rule of law in entire regions of several countries across the globe or about ethnic cleansing that is carried out by "private" groups as well as by troops under official command and control, one is inclined to question the usefulness of such academic distinctions. Isn't it a case of hair-splitting, or the result of the tunnel vision that comes from hiding out for too long in ivory towers? What is the relevance of these seemingly ethereal discussions in view of the stark realities we face, and of the urgent need to find practical answers to these problems?

The reason for holding on to this vocabulary and these concepts is a belief that without them, we have great difficulty in orienting ourselves. Granted, such distinctions are not natural ones and cannot be justified by some reference to an independently existing reality. Their value derives instead from their heuristic power and connection to underlying political project. Rather than simply letting the debate continue on a superficial level (e.g., your terrorist is my freedom fighter) or arguing that new concepts are needed to understand allegedly new threats, the conceptually-oriented analysis here forces us to see that concepts are not simple descriptive labels of sociopolitical phenomena but instead a means of appraisal or signals for action within wider political projects.

As to the heuristic dimension, the above distinctions show their value by putting things in perspective, though important problems remain for which the traditional notions of the Laws of War provide little or no guidance. The enemy in a terrorist attack is virtually invisible, and also has no way to be present in order to sign a capitulation. So how long is the target society then entitled to "self defense"? Given that the eradication of all terrorist cells throughout the world is hardly possible or has no clear boundary set to it, how much countermeasure is enough? *Quis judicabit* is also a big problem here, and as with organized crime or "domestic" terrorism of the ETA variety, many states have little choice but to live with considerable insecurity. In other words, a convincing argument for self-defense can only properly be made if the asserted "threat" is imminent, patent, and very serious. In that context, the justificatory arguments put forward by US decision-makers seem to be suffering from a troubling degree of "mission creep."

The present wave of terrorist attacks is not a simple continuation of the "state terrorism" of former years either: they come from different sources and pose different dangers precisely because the threats have become *internationalized*. The target of this new terrorism is not simply the "West," despite the prominent place it is accorded in the vitriolic rhetoric of the terrorists, but also regimes in Muslim countries charged with corruption and deviation from an imagined standard of Islamic purity. These efforts have also always had the fight against the state as an autonomous center of secular power as a subtext.

The double strategy of many regimes in response has been to try on the one hand to suppress these fundamentalist movements, and on the other hand to pay "protection money" to them – as long as they took their business elsewhere. Thus, the "internationalization" of terrorist networks (and the development of ideological support systems through Koran schools, through the Taliban, through foreign "volunteers" arriving to help fight in Dagestan, Kashmir, Kosovo, Afghanistan) was to some degree the result of such response strategies by regimes. In some places, ethnic liberation movements have also been transformed into various kinds of universalistic armed struggles against "non-believers," thereby providing further fuel (and recruits) for the present wave of terrorist attacks.

The September 11 events fundamentally challenged our political order not just because they represented heinous acts of violence, but also because they violated some of our most deeply ingrained understandings about the nature of politics. Nevertheless, we are neither analytically nor practically helpless. In practical terms, the sharing of information and the tracking of funds and persons have enabled some planned attacks to be prevented, though events in Bali, Saudi Arabia, Djerba and elsewhere show the record is far from satisfactory.

Experience also suggests that every uncovered, and thereby foiled, plan chips away at the image of invincibility of the terrorist. Terrorists are endowed with a mystique when they are spectacularly successful in shaking our confidence, but the mystique clearly suffers when it becomes an everyday reality that planned missions fail. Even convinced terrorists leave the movement, or begin to "sing" when they have been nabbed; their special status can be called into question by their lack of success. Time will likely to lead to some internal organizational disintegration as well, because the high tension and motivation cannot be sustained forever. New recruits may also be difficult to find. But much will depend on whether we understand this challenge correctly.

In this vein, the present paper wanted to identify what the challenges to our political project were, in the belief that the first step to a successful cure is a correct diagnosis of the problem. The discussion of the Hobbesian project indicates the seriousness of the challenge, one that cannot be overcome by appeals to better communication precisely because what is lacking are aspects of a common life world that are taken for granted in every meaningful communication. The more detailed examination of the phenomena relative to the traditional vocabulary of the Laws of War indicated the continued usefulness of that vocabulary in providing perspective and pointing to the lacunae.

Both examinations seem more useful than the conventional discourse on progress and development, which sees in this religiously inspired terrorism some atavistic reflex on the part of losers in the globalization game, a reflex that could be countered by using traditional economic and military measures. While these will obviously play a role, a reasonable counter-strategy cannot rely on the typical "carrot and stick" approach of politics as usual. The challenge is not an economic one, but is one about the meaning of life, and about a vision of the "good" that is quite different from the one of Aristotle of that of Hobbes. The challenge is also not a simply military one, because as Napoleon once so aptly put it, you can do a lot of things with bayonets, save one: you cannot sit on them!

Notes

1. For a general discussion see Holmes 1990, chap. 7.
2. See the interpretation of Pasquino (1996).
3. See Kelsen (1966: 5): "Delict and sanction are the two fundamental data of the law, which is a set of norms to which a coercive act, the sanction, is attached to a conduct."
4. Cf. Rousseau (1967: 14): "In short each State can have as enemies only other States and not individual men."
5. On the *sicarrii*, a group of zealots who used terrorist tactics by hiding their daggers, killing people and disappearing in the crowd, as well as their role in seizing Masada and committing mass suicide when the Romans stormed that fortress, see Flavius (1989: 393ff).
6. See the discussion in Schmitt (1970).
7. See point 13 of the instructions to Atta, for a translation of the entire text see: http://observer.guardian.co.uk/international/story/0,6903,560773,00.html
8. See Skjelsbaek (2001: 211–238).
9. For a brief discussion of Clausewitz's doctrine see Paret 1986: Chap 7.
10. Osama bin Laden's Fatwa http://www.ict.org.il/articles/fatwah.htm (1998: 1).

References

Alberoni, Francesco 1984: *Movement and Institution*. New York.

Arendt, Hannah 1973: *The Origins of Totalitarianism* (new edition). New York.

Clausewitz, Carl von 1984: *On War* (translated and edited by Michael Howard and Peter Paret, revised ed.). Princeton.

Flavius, Josephus 1989: *The Jewish War* (translation by G.A.Williamson). New York.

Ganor, Boaz 2001: "Terrorism: No Prohibition without Definition". In: *International Policy Institute for Counter-Terrorism* (http://www.ict.org.il), October 7.

Giap,Vo Nguyen 1970: *The Military Art of People's War: Selected Writings* (ed. by Russell Stetler, Russell). New York.

Habermas, Jürgen 1981: *Theorie des kommunikativen Handelns*, 2 vols. Frankfurt.

Hobbes, Thomas 1983 (or. 1651): *Leviathan*. London.

Hobbes, Thomas 1990: *Behemoth or the Long Parliament* (ed. Stephen Holmes). Chicago.

Hobbes, Thomas 1994: *The Elements of Law*, Book 2 (ed. by J.C.A. Gaskin). New York.

Holmes, Stephen 1990: "Political Psychology in Hobbes's Behemoth". In: Dietz, Mary G. (ed.): *Thomas Hobbes and Political Theory*. Lawrence.

Kelsen, Hans 1966: *Principles of International Law* (2nd edition, ed. Robert W. Tucker). New York.

Locke, John 1965: The Second Treatise on Government. In: Locke, John: *Two Treatises on Government* (ed. Peter Laslett). New York.

Paret, Peter 1986: "Clausewitz". In: Paret, Peter (ed.): *Makers of Modern Strategy: From Machiavelli to the Nuclear Age*. Princeton, chapt. 7.

Pasquino, Pasquale 1996: "Political Theory, Order, And Threat". In: *Nomos* 38:19–41.

Paz, Reuven 2001: "Programmed Terrorists: An Analysis of the Letters Left Behind by the September 11 Hijackers" (http://www.ict.org.il), December 13.

Rawls, John 1971: *A Theory of Justice*. Cambridge.

Rousseau, Jean Jacques 1967: *The Social Contract*, Book I. (ed. by Lester Crocker). New York.

Schmitt, Carl 1970: *Politische Theologie II: Die Legende von der Erledigung jeder Politischen Theologie*. Berlin.

Skjelsbaek, Inger 2001: Sexual Violence and War. In: *European Journal of International Relations* 7:211–238.

Weber, Max 1958: "Politik als Beruf". In: Weber, Max: *Gesammelte Politische Schriften*. Tübingen: 493–548.

Alias 'Yusuf Galán'
Neighbors, Sleepers, and the Violence of Recognition in Urban Spain[1]

Dorothy Noyes

Noyes, Dorothy 2003: Alias 'Yusuf Galán'. Neighbors, Sleepers, and the Violence of Recognition in Urban Spain. – Ethnologia Europaea 33:2: 69–84.

The arrests of alleged Al-Qaeda members in Spain reactivated a longstanding local discourse on the insoluble tensions between individual, state, and community. In two 19th century fictions and two 21st century news stories, I show how the figure of the neighbor and the framing device of the façade are invoked to explore the limitations – both negative and positive – of the liberal project in Spain. In these façade narratives, the twin behaviors of secrecy and display call attention to an imbalance between the private space of the individual and the public space of the community. The state proving inadequate as a regulator of the commerce between these two spheres, equilibrium is restored through an act of violence across the façade that separates them. This violence is at the same time the means by which individuals are accorded social recognition.

Dorothy Noyes, Associate Professor of Folklore and English, The Ohio State University, Mershon Center, 1501 Neil Ave., Columbus OH 43201.
E-mail: noyes.10@osu.edu

"It is therefore important, just as in the apparently opposite sociological pole of the secret, to demonstrate an analogous structure of social meaning in adornment. It is the nature and purpose of adornment to draw the eyes of others towards its bearer, and it is thus far the antagonist of secrecy, which however also, for its part, does not evade the function of accentuating the person."
Georg Simmel, "Das Geheimnis und die geheime Gesellschaft".[2]

"If I had to locate…that which is most characteristic of Hispanic life, I would put it as a median between a kind of withdrawn inertia and the willful outburst through which the person reveals what there is…in the depths of his soul, as if he were his own theater."
Américo Castro, *The Spaniards*.

"Quien vive con vecinos, de cuanto hace tiene testigos." (One who lives with neighbors has witnesses to all that he does.)
Castilian proverb.

On November 13, 2001, the Spanish police in Madrid arrested eleven men said to be members of a "sleeper cell" providing logistical support to Al-Qaeda in the organization of the September 11 attacks. As it happened, one of the men lived nearly next door to some friends of mine in a middle-class neighborhood of 19th century apartment houses in central Madrid. Unlike the others arrested, naturalized Spaniards of Syrian or Maghrebin origin, he was a native Spaniard converted to Islam, with a Moroccan wife. In newspaper accounts he was presented as "Luis José Galán González, alias 'Yusuf Galán.'"

My friend remarked on the conspicuous incoherence of Galán's conduct prior to his arrest. Arab music often blared forth from Galán's open window, and he sometimes left the house in Saudi-style white robes, far more emphatic than the typical dress of Muslim men in Spain. At the same time, he was known for tossing his garbage out on the street, and it was "always full of vodka bottles." "It seemed both impossible that he was and impossible that he wasn't what he was."

Judicial investigation confirmed Galán's connections to Al-Qaeda: he had trained in an Indonesian camp, had arms and documents in his apartment, and was extensively networked with other members of the cell. But Galán was not a model "sleeper"; rather, as my friend had observed, he had a record of calling attention to himself. He shouted out agreement during sermons at his mosque in Madrid; shortly before his arrest he had grabbed the microphone to make speeches at demonstrations against the Afghan war. When CNN visited his mosque after September 11 to canvas Muslim opinion, he was one of those interviewed, praising the Taliban and saying nothing against the attacks. Polaroids were found showing Galán in the Indonesian camp, wearing mujahedeen garb, loaded down with arms, and surrounded by comrades, surprising evidence for a member of a terrorist cell to leave lying around his apartment. Moreover, Galán had participated to a lesser degree in a variety of movements: in 1989 he had served as an electoral monitor for the Basque radical nationalist party Herri Batusuna, and more recently he had participated in antiglobalization protests. He was an enthusiast for martial arts, studying karate in Madrid with an Indonesian aviation engineer who also joined Al-Qaeda, and Olympic shooting, practicing at the range of the military casino in central Madrid. The Barcelona newspaper *La Vanguardia* summed him up as "a curious character" (31 January 2002).

The flamboyant Spanish Catholic-born Galán seems like the inverse of most of the "sleepers" arrested since September 11, Muslim immigrant men living discreetly in Europe with all the outward signs of assimilation. But his case opens up the same questions. As Simmel suggests, secrecy and display both serve to enhance the value of the person, and both thus call for *Anerkennung*, acknowledgment from others – or what the current multicultural discussion in the U.S. calls "recognition."[3] More deeply, the question is one of how personhood is shaped by the eyes of others, a matter especially problematic for these interstitial men who were not certain who their others were.

Much ink has spilled in recent years over the panoptical gaze by which institutions discipline individuals into internalizing control (Foucault 1979). But despite the atrocities perpetrated by church and state in Spanish history, we should not forget that direct institutional surveillance is of less importance to most individuals and perhaps less influence in the overall national trajectory than the gaze of the neighbors. One can say the same, to be sure, for any state that is not outright Stalinist, and even then we should remember that the state generally lacks the resources to live up to its repressive ambitions.[4] Primary selfhood is formed and maintained, as symbolic interactionism teaches us, in the everyday gaze between equals.

Another scholarly account of the gaze has the virtue of reminding us of the material relations beneath social constructions: this is the levelling gaze of envy and social control, as described by Mediterranean anthropologists of the Anglo-American old school.[5] The most sophisticated critiques of this work have recognized that several themes of it – including, I would argue, the structural-functionalist emphasis on equilibrium – are not purely extrinsic impositions, but draw heavily upon prominent local metadiscourses (e.g. Herzfeld 1987). Its blind spots stem in part from insufficient reflexivity on this point: its real object is not community realities, but a certain body of collective representations.

Here I want to begin to explore one set of such representations in Spain (and I stress the preliminary, provisional character of the present article).[6] There is a Spanish tradition of narrative, iconography, and performance elaborated around the façades of private houses, churches, and government buildings, often symbolically equated as enclosures keeping goods out of public circulation (Noyes 1995). The enclosure is an enlargement of the person (individual or corporate), and its surface is similarly maintained and adorned to assert respectability before the neighbors.

In traditional Spanish ritual life, façade performances (balcony decoration, serenading, luck-visit, charivari, etc.) create occasions of exchange between interiors and the street. The owners of enclosures provide careful glimpses of their interiors, proclaiming that they have nothing to hide. On the other side of the façade, the gaze (and sometimes more violent penetration) of the street demands a share of what is enclosed: demands intensified by an excess of secrecy as by an excess of display. A labile membrane between the public and private realms, the façade regulates the equilibrium between them. Imbalances are addressed by forced entry from without, or fortification from within.[7]

Façade performances constitute part of the traditional public sphere in western societies, never entirely displaced by the Habermasian bourgeois variety (1989). In Spain the deficiencies of the latter have contributed to the continuing vitality of the former. Frequent political upheavals, long periods of de jure or de facto censorship, extreme social inequalities limiting access to education, and deep ideological divisions have all contributed to a fragmented civil society with many discontinuities. Encounters between different interests still occur most meaningfully within real public space – where difference cannot be forever evaded – and through symbolic performance, a safer vehicle for divisive messages than expository prose.

This local public sphere – which generally maps onto a neighborhood – is at once the framework in which political relationships can be worked out and the site at which they can be gauged and evaluated. And while façade performances appear to be transactions between the community and the individual, the state makes a constant and uneasy third. Identity is contested between the three. The community grants social personhood; the individual creates herself; the state makes the citizen. These three processes are deeply intertwined historically and in the present, but none can successfully be elided with the others. Jacobin modernity has failed to reduce the community to the state or the individual to the citizen. Liberal modernity has failed to reduce community to the aggregation of private individuals or the state to their guarantor. Fundamentalist modernity has as yet made no convincing effort to reduce the state or the individual to embodiments of "community values" (a.k.a. the voice of God).

In this paper I will look at the façade narrative as a space of Spanish reflection upon liberal modernity and thus on the status of the individual. Historically in Western thought, Spain stands for two extremes of the latter. The Black Legend credits Spain with the mother of all repressive regimes, the Inquisition in the service of empire. The Romantic reaction points to the Spanish love of individual independence – "liberalism" as a political ideology was, after all, a Spanish coinage, and anarchism became, as nowhere else in the world, a serious political project.[8] This second stereotype has a long history within Spain itself (cf. Castro 1971, 1:300), and is still current. But despite the routine complaint that no political project can get anywhere in the face of the kneejerk individualist "¡Abajo los de arriba!,"[9] partisan affiliation is for many an important component of personal identity and a means of self-distinction within community settings. And community is present too in a continuing sense of claustrophobia and constraint expressed by individuals.

Four narrations follow: two 19th century fictions, two 21st century news stories. Each dramatizes a different dynamic between community, state, and individual, mediated around an act of violence at the domestic façade. In each, the relationship between the householder and the neighbors is used to comment on the limitations of the liberal project in Spain.

The Neighbors Admire

My first narrative dates from 1833 and received a critical revision in 1878. It addresses the relationship of neighbors, individuals, and the state in Barcelona, taking as its historical moment the July 1833 swearing-in of the Infanta Isabel as heiress to the throne of the dying Fernando VII. The event was preceded by Queen María Cristina's accommodation with the moderate liberal faction at court, intended to secure support for her daughter's claim, and an amnesty granted to the 10,000 Spanish liberals who had been exiled during various phases of political reaction since the 1814 restoration of the Bourbon dynasty. Moderate royalists as much as moderate liberals welcomed these developments, which they saw as a means of fending off extremisms on both sides, and the urban bourgeoisie welcomed the prospect of peace after twenty-five years of instability and civil violence (Vicens Vives 1967:127). Nationwide festivities were declared and urgently promoted by the local authorities; in the liberal coastal cities, the more radical masses participated energetically in the celebration, which was thus ambiguously one of national reconciliation or one of liberal triumph. Not surprisingly, the show of reconciliation could not sustain itself, and immediately after the death of the king the conservatives inaugurated the seven-year First Carlist War to install their own claimant to the throne.

Josep Robrenyo, a popular liberal actor and author of artisanal background (Fàbregas 1975:127–131), wrote a comic *sainet* (a one-act play about contemporary life) on the Barcelona celebration of the *jura de la Infanta*.[10] "La Union ó la Tia Sacallona" (sic) was performed on September 3, two months after the celebration and one month before the first Carlist insurrection, and the timing explains both its political caution and its didactic character, intended "to intensify the civic attitude of citizens in a moment when the external signs of participation were important" (Romea Castro 1994: 55).

In a "very simple" household, neighbors are collecting money and material to decorate their street for the celebration. Although the modest artisan Sagimon and his wife Madrona indicate the neighborhood's sociological center of gravity, class boundaries are overcome for the festival. The rich neighbor Don Julián comes in to offer his assistance and ultimately pays for most of the decoration, while the two poorest neighbors, male and female, are reported as having each donated a day's wage. Sagimon's old comrade-in-arms brings his family from the country to see the festival, and goes touring every street of the city, reporting to the company on the beauty of the decorations and of the city itself, then undergoing extensive renovations to improve the hygiene, the legibility, and the visual dignity of its medieval infrastructure (Romea Castro 1994). All praise the restoration of "just laws" and the amnesty that has reunited families.

Two sources offer the potential to disrupt the social harmony promised by the new political order: one public and masculine, one private and feminine. Sagimon has had a political quarrel of ten year's standing with a neighbor. And domestically, Madrona's aunt Sacallona offers a litany of complaints that embody a longstanding stereotype of the calculating, individualist Catalan character. Everyone has stopped working to celebrate; the festival itself is a waste of money and the hospitality to visitors costs still more; outsiders are to be mistrusted; it is better to stay at home than go gaping around the streets; and so on.

But these two threats are resolved by the force of genre. Tia Sacallona's arguments are discredited by her structural position: comedy requires her to be expelled without mercy from the community of sympathy. In addition to the calculating class habits that make her a spoilsport, she is a typical duenna, talking endlessly of the decay of the times and universally disapproving the actions of the young. She is politely hated by everyone else in the play, who collectively ridicule her age, tell her to shut up and go to her room, and propose a variety of acts of violence to get rid of her. (To be sure, she takes up a prominent part of the action and gives the play the second half of its name.) As for the external threat, Don Julián forces the two warring neighbors together by appealing to their patriotism: "Cover the past with a veil, let us not remember parties and passions, but union and peace. Cristina forgets, and we cannot forget?" The queen's amnesty sets the example, and the reconciliation guaranteed by benevolent authority figures is celebrated in a collective patriotic song at the end. The play exploits the full machinery of comedy to show Catalans what they need to overcome if the new political order is to succeed: economic selfishness in private life and historical grudges in public.[11]

To be sure, economic individualism will have a lengthy afterlife in Catalan politics and is, after all, the whole point of liberalism. An 1878 rewrite of Robrenyo's normative exhortation points out this paradox and also notes the destructive persistence of memory. "Viva la llibertat!" by Joan Pons i Massaveu (1850–1918) is a "picture of customs," a genre of realist short fiction that was the mainstay of Spanish periodicals in the mid-19th century. Without any direct reference to Robrenyo's play, it reproduces its setting and format, while challenging its resolution.¹²

Speaking from the present of the reader, the narrator describes his father Mariano's participation in the street decoration for the 1833 festival. The *alcalde del barri* (district mayor) has orders to organize the neighborhood and is conferring with Mariano, the most enthusiastic of the local liberals. There is a contest for the best-adorned street in Barcelona, and a prize for the individual with the best façade; Mariano vows to win this and to spend the money on a feast for the neighborhood. Swearing to pawn even his shirt if necessary, he rents damask cloths, buys sacks of greenery, and appropriates his wife's best linens, topping off the decoration with his portrait of the queen's supporter General Espartero, framed by candles and topped with a wreath of laurel. Later, realizing that the display will be invisible at night, he spends all his remaining cash on lights and firecrackers and mounts a show to overcome, visually and sonorally, all conceivable competition.

The interpenetration of self and state is revealed by all kinds of slippage. The slogan "Viva la llibertat!," spelled out in lights on the façade, opens in the public language of Spanish and closes in the domestic one of Catalan. Mariano's façade is infinitely permeable and reversible, as he takes out on the balcony elements of the domestic environment, which in turn – notably the General's portrait – are drawn from the public realm. This permeability is emphasized by the importance of sound in the story, signalling the impinging of the state on the domestic interior. The narrator notes being awakened by the cathedral bells and the liberal "Hymn to Riego," hearing all day long the songs of the street musicians hired by the district mayor for the celebration, and the intrusion at dusk of the cannons of Barcelona's fortresses: it is these explosions that inspire Mariano to go out and buy fireworks. Mariano himself spends more time out of the house than in it: once his decorations are up, he spends most of the day going back and forth in the street to listen to the admiring comments of passers-by. He delights in the confirmation of his political identity ("That one is really a liberal!"), and this is his argument for the necessity of participation: "Everyone knows who Mariano is as a liberal."

As in the *sainet*, there are two points of interference with Mariano's integration of self, community, and state. The first is the feminine defender of the domestic interest: this time she is a rational voice, worried about the expense but more about the confusion of public and private spaces. Mariano's wife scolds him for the mess he is making and is horrified when he brings sacks of fireworks into the house. The narrator implicitly supports his mother's evaluation of misplaced priorities: he opens by saying that he never saw his father as delighted as on the day that Isabel was sworn, and lists a range of domestic occurrences, such as the birth of grandchildren, as paling by comparison. The domestic events are increasingly colored by politics as they rise in importance to his father: having his wife, after thirteen sons and seven years' wait, give birth at last to "little Isabel," who, however, does not live; or the last, winning the lottery after years of betting on "1833." Mariano's selfhood is invested entirely in his façade, and he neglects his interior, at a high cost to his domestic others – a strange position for a self-declared liberal. Rather than genuinely promoting the private sphere, Mariano shows a purely contrarian spirit: "Abajo los de arriba!"

For the façade is the site of masculine competition, and here we find again the neighbor of a different political opinion. The house opposite is inhabited by one Senyor Bruno, the sole declared member of the other party on the street. Throughout the story, the two men engage in shouting matches across their balconies,¹³ and the polarized symmetry of their political identities is clear. When his wife complains, an indignant Mariano demands, "Do you want the neighbors to point the finger at me like they will at that idiot across the street?" Mariano gloats that Senyor Bruno, had his side won, would have filled his balcony with candles and the image of the Virgin rather than that of Espartero, and Bruno agrees, declaring that he would pawn even his pants to do so. They shout reciprocal insults back and forth: "Apostolic!" "Mason!"¹⁴ Later, when Mariano is setting off his fireworks, a spark flies through Bruno's balcony and sets a carpet alight; Bruno puts out the fire but is transported in rage; Mariano lights still more rockets to drown out his shouting. The next day, Bruno has his revenge, using the neutrality of the state: he files a complaint with the *alcalde del barri*. The *alcalde* obliges his friend to pay the fine, preaching the necessity of compromise and coexistence. But the reconciliation is not final, as in "La Union": Mariano retires vowing to get his own back by leaving "Viva La Llibertat!" lit up on the balcony for the rest of the week for Senyor Bruno's exclusive benefit.

The reader of 1878 knows that this is not the end of the story either: Senyor Bruno's faction will shortly inaugurate seven years of civil war, and even that is not the end of the story: the Third Carlist War had just ended in 1875. Nor, indeed, was that to be the end: the polarization of Spanish politics in everyday public space would intensify in the 20th century into appalling face-to-face factional violence and culminate in the Civil War. Despite the satirical tone, repeated parallels are drawn between festival and war: the explosions of fireworks and the explosions of cannon, festival songs and military hymns, the fires of celebration with the arson of private enclosures in civil war (such as the church and factory burnings of 1834–36 in Barcelona). Mariano says at the beginning, "The show on my balcony…I want everyone to talk about it as if it were the burning of Moscow." Spanish men are seen here as so many would-be Napoleons, imposing themselves on the notice of others through acts of aggressive display.

The Napoleonic reference is not casual. Robrenyo's play had pointed to the Napoleonic invasion as the founding moment for the present political climate, since the solidarity between the protagonist and his country visitor depends on their shared experience as prisoners of the French; the suggestion is that liberal patriotism is the natural continuation of that shown by the entire population during the War of Independence (Fàbregas 1975, 173).[15] Both Robrenyo and Pons depict a founding moment of popular Spanish liberalism, in which a sense of proprietorship in the modern state is grafted on to older forms of civic and individual display. In the triumph of the moment, Robrenyo imagines the elision of person, citizen, and individual; Pons writes when such a vision can no longer be sustained.

The Neighbors Break In

The Catalan wife recovers her dignity completely in the next story. In Narcís Oller's "La Bufetada" (The Slap), it is 1888 and Tia Sacallona has become a lovely young woman named Anneta, whose commitment to hard work and privacy is now identified as admirable and modern in relation to the values of the street. The continued dominance of the latter is, however, clear from the opening sentence. "About five years ago, the neighbors of Canuda Street saw Anneta's ironing business open." The newcomer's sense of self-respect is evident from her immaculate windows, but she keeps her awnings closed until the day her shop opens, and does not come out to present herself to the neighborhood. The "women of the doorways," curious, send their children to peer under the awnings, and the boldest eventually goes to investigate directly. Seeing herself spied upon, Anneta comes out to present herself, and thereafter becomes the pride of the neighborhood for her handsome appearance and her industry in setting up, succeeding in, and rapidly expanding a business that is itself emblematic: supporting the starched respectability of, eventually, her entire urban district.

At the same time, she bothers the neighbors. She is a little too good for them: having been a servant of a local marchioness for ten years, her speech and manners are refined enough that "she could pass for a lady in reduced circumstances." She is reserved: she works constantly and concedes little to sociability. The neighbor reports to the others that she is "very much a woman of her house, and not given to crossing the threshold," and the neighbors agree, "She would certainly never be one of the club."

Finally, Anneta's marriage is unusual. Despite her own refinement, she has married a butcher whom the neighbors define as "savage." He helps her in her expanding business, which generates four times the income of his own labor, and is seen by the neighbors as under her thumb. Absorbed in each other at the beginning of the story, the two are content with their atypical relationship. In the course of the story, the neighbors undermine this self-sufficiency. Anneta is already vulnerable to external gazes: she has a fear of "scandals" and is also intensely jealous. The neighbors tease Llorenç and one of the shop workers provokes him sexually. With the voices of the critics in his head, he eventually has a half-hearted flirtation with the woman, who flaunts her position to her coworkers and Anneta herself. When Anneta sends her away, the couple confront each other in a quarrel over "who wears the pants," each entirely penetrated with a sense of what the neighbors are saying. Exasperated by Anneta's insistence on the superiority of her own judgment to the communal perception, Llorenç slaps her; she sees this as an unforgivable affront to her dignity and begins packing up to leave him. In desperation, he declares his repentance and determination to avoid all future offences by chopping off his hand with his butcher's knife.

Anneta and Llorenç are presented as rigid characters from different extremes of a continuum: Llorenç not yet civilized by society, and Anneta more advanced than those around her, more committed to abstract principle, to capitalist practice, and to the separation of public and private spheres.[16] The neighbors have a limited moderating effect on both, and the implication is that weaker characters would submit wholly to the collective gaze and judgment. Anneta and Llorenç succeed in resisting, but with violent consequences to themselves. Social control, by Oller's judgment, is both civilizing and levelling, frustrating the exceptional and reducing all to a mean which may or may not be golden.[17] When the neighbors' intrusive gaze penetrates the interior, the air of the street enters the house and changes its atmosphere.

Anneta's self-debate after the quarrel confirms the spatial concomitants of political dispensations. She imagines herself alone in public space while everyone she knows files past her in a "procession" or its later statist equivalent, a "parade." In this sphere of representative publicity, she is condemned. But she goes on to envision herself in two alternative, more modern spaces: the theater and the courtroom. In the former, her interiority would be made visible and her spectators would empathize with her position. In the latter space of Habermasian reasoned debate, her judgment would be vindicated. Anneta looks towards a modern public sphere that does not yet exist in Spain.

Verbs of sight and evaluation appear in every paragraph of Oller's story, along with the curtains and awnings and doors that attempt to limit access. While the state is merely an external point of reference, neighborly surveillance is constant and inescapable. Anneta's neighbors are, in effect, looking for "sleepers," a notion that presumes an engaged audience for whom normalcy must be performed, and Anneta is indeed a sleeper of a more gradual kind, insinuating disruptive new social practices under cover of her concessions to neighborhood opinion. The intensity of neighborhood vigilance marks the historical moment in which economic individualism is seen to be breaking up traditional communities; and in this story the relation between individual and social persona is Goffmanesque in its paranoia. Anneta wears a mask for a public from which she feels, to some degree, alienated, and to which her "true self" poses a risk.

The Neighbors Abdicate

Anneta embodies the contradictions of an incomplete liberal project, attempting to live by her own convictions and energies while offering anxious window-dressing to the neighborhood. Yusuf Galán's case is more extreme. Equally concerned to be independent of society, he requires the confirmation of his neighbors that he is so. Peter Suedfeld has pointed out the surprising give-away behaviors of many of the September 11 "sleepers," identifying them as an extreme instance of an ever-present tension between the power amassed through secrecy and the psychological need for self-revelation (2003). In the case of many of these men with hybrid cultural practices and no fixed audience of neighbors, one might consider these displays and the violent "awakenings" they seem to forecast as less self-revelation than self-creation. We cannot say of "Yusuf Galán" that he wore a discreet mask of normalcy concealing a threatening true identity. He represents the opposite extreme, theatrically constructing a highly performative new identity to supplant an original self too undistinguished to be worth recounting.[18]

Others arrested in the same operation, while less flagrantly self-contradictory than Galán, were ambiguous enough. Several were naturalized Spanish citizens; two had Spanish wives and one married a Finn who converted to Islam. As has been observed of the Al-Qaeda operatives in general, they did not come from a traditional background in which social control would confer an unproblematic social identity – the Muslim equivalent of the old Spanish street life. They were cosmopolitan, multilingual, often Western-educated, and the instability of their identities was dramatized in the oscillations of their everyday conduct, encompassing both drunkenness and mosque attendance.

Did those outward signs even matter? Galán's theatricality did not prevent him from acting effectively as an Al-Qaeda operative: he trained in an Indonesian camp, housed traveling Al-Qaeda members, and undertook all the other tasks shared by more discreet members of the cell. In contrast to those of our 19th century narratives, the neighbors continually interviewed in both Spanish and foreign coverage of these arrests failed to provide any conclusive interpretations. Neighbors were cited to build up a picture of the suspects through their movements, family relations, visitors, dress, grooming, demeanor, and level of participation in communal activities. The smallest details were sought to provide clues: one man was said to be "jovial," one cut himself off from observation by wearing dark glasses. Testimonies contradicted each other in tone. Ahmed Brahim, arrested in a prosperous residential suburb of Barcelona in April, was described by one as obviously intelligent, speaking six or seven languages, including French to the neighbor himself. Another called him touchy: after his car was broken into, he placed a sign in the building parking lot announcing the vengeance of Allah on racism. A third summarized the difficulty neighbors found in reading the indicators: "There was always a lot of movement in the two flats and he was a strange person with a badly groomed beard and had no interaction with anybody. But to go from that to that he was involved with Bin Laden…" (*La Vanguardia* 15 April 2002).

By contrast, the surveillance of the state was decisive. Press reports of the November 2001 arrests explained that investigating judge Baltasar Garzón and his team had had their eye on the group for years, monitoring phone calls since at least 1996, and had gradually built up a case that at last held no room for doubt. The neighbors were cited almost as if to prove their incompetence by contrast. And indeed this is a routine motif of this subgenre of the news story, the surprise arrest. In Spain as elsewhere,[19] police come in to arrest the apparently ordinary householder who turns out to be a mafioso, a drug-dealer, a serial killer, or, as in this case, a terrorist. When the neighbors are interviewed, they express their bewilderment, try to reread the information they have as indices of the now-revealed truth. As a rule – at least in middle-class neighborhoods in which the authority of police and state are recognized – the neighbors bow to the superior knowledge of the latter. Why then should the neighbors be interviewed at all?

In part they are an inheritance of genre, artifacts of an earlier identity regime. The narrative of domesticity continues to presuppose a certain norm of neighborly interaction and mutual observation. The neighbor is therefore the natural witness to identity, and himself the embodiment of community norms. The failure of the neighbor to grasp the activities of the criminal points, therefore, to a failure of social control and validates the need for state surveillance.

More than that: could the neighbors be abdicating responsibility? It might be said (oversimplifying as such narratives must) that hitherto the state has attempted to intervene in – sometimes fostering, more often obstructing – the horizontal relations of its citizens, and state surveillance has attempted to replace or coopt the neighborly gaze.[20] Today, out of exhaustion rather than desire, citizens increasingly outsource the office of social control, relying on the state to conduct the community surveillance they no longer have the means or time to undertake. On the supply side – the availability of inquisitive neighbors – the integration of the

Spanish economy into the global one has increased working hours and removed the workplace to a greater distance from the home, reducing neighborhood sociability. At the same time, it has provided consumer goods within the home, rendering private space far more attractive than it once was.[21] On the demand side – the desire to monitor others in order to reaffirm one's own individual and collective identity – the problem has grown more complex with the pluralization of norms in Spanish society, again resulting from factors such as the opening of the economy first to tourism, then to consumerism and personal mobility, then to mass extra-European immigration. The significant other need no longer be a neighbor: aspirations range far more widely for many people. In short, Galán could do as he liked. The neighbors were insufficiently interested for discretion and disguise to make any difference. Without common norms and a more determined culture of social control, the neighbors found Galán as indeterminate as the paradox of his half-Muslim, half-Spanish alias. To continue the visual metaphor, they could not resolve his image. "It seemed both impossible that he was and impossible that he wasn't what he was."[22]

Galán was once interviewed in his Madrid mosque by CNN, in search of Muslim opinion. If such representation were routinely sought on all public issues, would violence still be so widespread a strategy for achieving recognition? Liberal multiculturalism proposes a solution that should obviate the motivations for terrorism among the disempowered. The recognition of communities as distinctive, valuable, and above all, present within the state will ensure the dignity and equal opportunities of the individuals who constitute them.

In addressing the new immigration, Spanish policy makers have generally acknowledged that representation in the media is not sufficient (even supposing that it existed): real interaction in shared community space is necessary to full personhood. Urban cultural offices have generally sought to promote this by the same means used in the U.S. and elsewhere in Europe, using museums and festivals to celebrate immigrant arts as a bridge to immigrant personhood. With much success; but as is so often the case, an increase in spaces marked off as "cultural" is counterbalanced by the a larger erosion of the everyday neighborhood spaces in which immigrants and natives could meet as individuals and develop shared informal norms.[23]

Aziz Al-Azmeh observes that the reifications of Islamic fundamentalism draw upon the culturalism of the West, the "clash of civilizations" logic that assumes the incommensurability and mutual impenetrability of different cultures (1996). Even multiculturalism in its softer forms tends to reduce individuals into representatives of communities, the identity of which is based in the possession of esoteric, untranslatable knowledge – collective secrets. At the level of public recognition, there are only communities; individuals exist only at the level of surveillance. Both of these forms of visibility are the creations of the bureaucratic state, and the former can become nearly as cold and calculating as the latter. To cross through into face-to-face human recognition, with breathing bodies and individual gazes attached to it, what must the dislocated person do? Appropriate a community, first of all, making its project one's own: and this has become a strategy not now for immigrants alone, but widely pursued by the equally anonymous "majority," the Luis José Galán Gonzálezes of Western societies. The collectivity confers meaning, since collectivities have a public existence and forms of display – they have faces, or façades. But the warmth of contact is less easily recovered once the neighbors have withdrawn. In the absence of mutually negotiated ritual – structures mediating between spectacle and corporeal existence – the sleeper-terrorist replaces the trivial spectacle of "bureaucratic multiculturalism" (Scher 2003) with what Bataille saw as the ideal form of immanence, the violent encounter (1973).

The Neighbors Close Ranks

The case of Yusuf Galán suggests a dire master narrative of increasingly violent struggles for recognition against a background of ever less contested state surveillance, paradoxically legitimated by the need to protect the liberal individual. But a later series of Al-Qaeda arrests in Spain gives us a more hopeful story, of the kind increasingly being told by anti-globalization activists, which has its local roots in the resistance to the Franco regime.

On January 24, 2003 there was a second major police raid of alleged Al-Qaeda operatives. 24 men were taken and 16 held in "Operation Lake," named for the Lake of Banyoles in Catalonia, near which several of the arrests took place. Arrests were made in the early hours of the morning and the 150 officers involved caused considerable neighborhood disruption. Doors of flats were destroyed, flats searched, and materials confiscated; in one case the police broke down the door of the wrong flat. In a speech the same day, President José María Aznar cited the arrests as proving that "we are not speaking of fantasies but of realities," and that, given the threat of terrorists obtaining weapons of mass destruction, Spain must consider well "the event in Catalonia in order to avoid a tragedy in our security" (*La Vanguardia* 25 January 2003).

The press coverage of these arrests was immediately very different from that of the previous operation. Long before the supposed ricin and anthrax ingredients were revealed by laboratory analysis to be such domestic substances as couscous spices and laundry soap, long before the last of the men were released for lack of evidence four months later, strong skepticism was evident. *El Mundo*, a national newspaper generally sympathetic to the Aznar government, said little about the operation itself. But the socialist *El País* of Madrid, the centrist-Catalanist *La Vanguardia* and *Avui* of Barcelona, and the left-Catalanist *Punt Diari* of Girona told a different story. They gave an extensive account of the police operation, described as needlessly destructive and disruptive. The families of those detained were given voice and the neighbors were presented as both outraged by the conduct of the police and strong in the defense of those arrested – their neighbors. These lengthy reportages were tellingly juxtaposed with coverage of Aznar's speech, Bush's congratulatory phone call, and Colin Powell's citing of the Spanish arrests in a statement to the U.N. It did not take many days for the editorial pages to connect the dots explicitly and declare the arrests pure opportunism. In this view, the Aznar government was striving at once to sell the war to the public, to set the native population against immigrants in order to impose a more restrictive policy, and further to erode civil liberties and the presumption of innocence. *Punt Diari*, the local newspaper of the region where the arrests took place, was strongest in both its suspicion of the state and its use of the neighbor discourse, emphasizing the violation of domestic and community space as doors were broken down, children left crying in the street for their fathers, and so on.

El Punt's coverage showed, furthermore, an intensive community response to the arrests. Neighbors and coworkers declared their concern for the families of those arrested. A local businessman offered to pay for the education of the children – an education better than any Spanish policeman could afford for his children, he added. Clerics and voluntary associations protested the demonization of immigrants. The squatters' movement of Barcelona, also facing state invasion of its domestic space, declared solidarity. Festivals were held to support a legal defense fund. The local solidarity campaign quickly merged with the antiwar movement, and the detainees came home to welcoming ceremonies and places of honor in the antiwar marches. The released detainees were interviewed in the press, given individual face and voice as no "terrorist" can be (Zulaika 1995).[24] The category of terrorism was itself contextualized: some of the men were indeed involved with the Algerian Salafista movement, but public sympathy was invoked by reminders of the repressive Algerian regime – and having known a parallel situation, many Catalans do not condemn armed insurrection out of hand. Finally, both the newspaper coverage and the solidarity demonstrations embraced the carnivalesque, with extensive ridicule of the search for evidence: laundry soap was dumped in front of the civil governor's headquarters, and there was a gleeful headline when the Minister of the Interior asked the public kindly to stop making jokes about the soap.

A soberer story could have been told about the detained men; while the evidence against them was inconclusive, it was not pure fabrication. But the context had changed radically. According to the new reading of the situation, the Aznar government (easily equated by Catalanists with the Spanish state as a whole) was supporting a dangerous and illegitimate war in the teeth of public opinion in order to win U.S. recognition, much as Franco had done in the 1953 defense treaty (Elordi 2003). Another echo of the Franco regime was seen in Aznar's use of the terrorist threat to justify tighter controls on regional activists.[25]

The apparent revival of Francoist state action provoked a parallel revival of anti-Francoist community activism. A discourse of solidarity based not in common individual identities but in common resistance to an intrusive state – the *assemblea* or coalition model (cf. Noyes 2003) – came back to life in the massive antiwar movement, as more locally in on behalf of the men arrested in Operation Lake. We should note that the neighbor is not only a key metaphor of this model but in fact one of its major points of origin. The desperate living conditions of migrant labor in Madrid and Barcelona during the speculative boom of the 1960s provoked the formation of the Asociaciones de Vecinos (neighborhood associations), which gradually brought together people of different backgrounds and party affiliations in an affirmation of the de facto relationship of residential proximity. These associations, which local authorities were forced to recognize, became the earliest large-scale movement in late Francoist civil society, providing experience in democratic practice to ordinary people and fostering the more overtly political movements that brought the dictatorship to an end (Castells 1983).

Many participants remarked on the revival of devices from the transition to democracy in the antiwar protests: *La Vanguardia* summed it up as "Barcelona, de fiesta contra la guerra" (31 March 2003). As during the Transition, the ominous equation of fireworks and cannons made by Pons in 1878 was here reversed: a *Punt Diari* editorial on the Saint John's Eve celebration (after all the Operation Lake detainees had been released) noted that here was a night when everyone had explosives in the house, and each domesticity, native and immigrant, came together in a common explosion (25 June 2003).

A genre adapted from Latin America enhanced not only the festival but the neighborhood character of the protests: the *cacerolada*. Like the *tancades* or sit-ins of the Transition, the cacerolada was a façade performance in reverse: it was not outsiders demanding entry, but insiders denouncing the invasion of their private space. At 9:45 every evening from mid-March through April, citizens came out on their balconies and, for a quarter of an hour, banged pots and pans in rejection of the war: domestic chaos against a state-imposed order.[26] On a larger scale, Barcelona's reenactment with black balloons of its bombing during the Civil War was denounced by some as in dubious taste, but marked again a construction of Barcelonans and Iraqis as parallel insiders, threatened by powerful states.

State, Community, Individual

Few Spaniards I know would discount any of the stories I have detailed here as future possibilities. Although they fall in a historical sequence, this is not a progression from one dispensation to another. Rather, once created, practices and discourses remain to be recovered at need, though the material conditions that support their circulation will foster the dominance of one or another at any given moment. It may be helpful to review the broad outlines of the four stories (see table).

As a folklorist, I am led by professional interest to cheer for the fourth scenario and by professional training to doubt that any of the four will ever go away. Solidarity with distant Iraq cost Spaniards little, a skeptic might say, and the sixteen detainees of Operation Lake were thrown in as makeweights. Can the local solidarities of natives and immigrants or of squatters and bourgeois householders be sustained? Most Spaniards who lived through the Transition would doubt it, given the inevitable breakdown of that community when individual interests began to reassert themselves and use the machinery of the state to do so. There is also the question of efficacy. The antiwar protests did not succeed in changing the government position, and Aznar's Partido Popular was not significantly punished in the June municipal elections, so community press-

	Viva la llibertat!	La bufetada	Yusuf Galán	Operation Lake
Source of personal identity	The state	Community norms for the traditional; self-created for the modern	The community of choice (dissociated from residence); the covert community	The community of residence, under temporary conditions of effervescence
Status of outsiders to community	All are insiders but public unity is false	Outsiders forced into compliance or suffer consequences	Individuality asserted by becoming outsider; outsiders defined as members of covert communities; all are becoming outsiders	Outsiders incorporated: community defined as coalition uniting diverse individuals in resistance to oppressive state
Recognition	Mutual public recognition	Recognition to excess: strong social control	Absence of recognition	Post hoc recognition
Violence	Implication of future civil violence as state-based identities split community	Community maintained by violence to individuals	Individual/covert community commits violence against community as stand-in for state	Violence of state against individuals understood as assault upon community
Secrecy	Public political display valued, despite offstage conspiring to attain public position; individual interiority is denied	Secrecy valued, unattainable in practice	Extreme secrecy and extreme display: radical ambivalence	Community redefined as collective domestic realm, within which there is total visibility, outside of which they are entitled to secrecy
State surveillance	State demands public displays of individual and community allegiance: overt surveillance	State absent unless called in as guarantor of individuals	State surveillance of individuals/covert communities: legitimate	State surveillance of individuals and communities: illegitimate
Political mode and status of the public sphere	Liberalism popularized through the traditional public sphere	Incomplete liberalism: old public sphere persists, modern public sphere as yet insufficient	Liberal multiculturalism→ clash of civilizations. Bureaucratization of traditional public sphere	Liberal multiculturalism→ anti-globalization. Hybridization of traditional and modern public sphere

ure failed to control even the actions of individual voters. It remains to be seen – the antiglobalization movement provides the global test case of the moment – how far state policies or individual behaviors can be transformed by democratic, coalition-based movements, which seem to depend heavily on moments of collective effervescence. The fundamentalist movements that compete with them exercise far stricter quotidian control over individuals, and their resultant organizational strength has given them far more influence over states.

Yusuf Galán, a westerner in search of identity, participated in both types of movement and found the latter more rewarding. It seems increasingly common for liberal multiculturalism to fragment into local communitarianisms and eventually into fundamentalisms. Individuals may choose a community – based in ethnicity, religion, or other factors – but they are subsequently determined by it in the eyes of others. And having their own choice to justify, they find it in practice difficult to deal with others who have chosen differently. The given community of material coexistence becomes increasingly intolerable, the need to bring the given and the imagined communities into accordance more extreme. Fundamentalism, as many scholars have shown, is a way of stabilizing the everyday world of individuals through recourse to the rational-bureaucratic apparatus of institutions: legislating identity to provide external reinforcement against internal insecurities (e.g. Roy 1994). Political Islam attempts to resolve ambiguity by forcible erasure of incongruous elements. The Jihad warrior assumes this power at a personal level, identifying himself with the state or would-be state's capacity for violent erasure and placing both in the service of the imagined community. The sleeper becomes the most powerful instance, gaining visibility and a stable self in the act of erasing and destabilizing the world around him. With such a price to pay for an integrated identity, I cannot help feeling some nostalgia for that untidy urban neighborhood and, indeed, for that incomplete liberal project.

Notes

1. Thanks to the discussants and participants in the conference for a rich conversation; to Ernest Hakanen and Peter Suedfeld for help with sources; and to John and Regina Bendix for everything.
2. Unless otherwise indicated in the bibliography, all translations are mine.
3. See also Todorov 2001; Fabian 1999:53 gives a useful breakdown of the senses of "recognition" according to the German vocabulary; he argues that the overwhelmingly ethical emphasis of the recognition debate has forestalled the epistemological problems.
4. Goffman (1961) and Scott (1990) provide useful correctives to Foucault in demonstrating the complex dynamics in practice of "total institutions" and the modern state.
5. See for example Peristiany ed. (1966) and Bailey ed. (1971). Susan Tax Freeman's *Neighbors* (1970) inaugurated an alternative tradition emphasizing egalitarian structures of cooperation; the more usual theme has been competition, but in any case the delicate balance of competition and solidarity in neighborhood relationships is a major debate in the anthropology of Spain as it is within Spanish communities.
6. For reasons of space, many important issues such as gender and regional difference must be deferred for a later discussion.
7. To be sure, there is nothing uniquely Spanish about any of this, but such performances are a conspicuous dimension of Castilian and Catalan traditional culture.
8. See Álvarez Junco (2000) for an efficient summary of the two stereotypes.
9. "Down with those who are up!", a parody slogan current since at least 1868.
10. Reprinted in facsimile without an authorial attribution in Romea Castro, 1994:369–380.
11. The calls for amnesia here foreshadow those of the 1970s transition to democracy, when old differences seemed equally intractable.
12. For this paper I have had no access to critical work on the obscure Pons i Massaveu. The structural parallels as well as many details of urban décor and political discourse suggest that he had access to Robrenyo's play. Pons' narrator mentions the Diario de Barcelona as a source for the period, good evidence of Pons' own use of it, and this newspaper chronicled Robrenyo's activities extensively (Fàbregas 1975:131). Pons may therefore have been stimulated to consult Robrenyo's collected works, published in the later liberal moment of 1855 (133).
13. Cf. Abrahams 1981 on the differential construction of identity in a parallel context.
14. Each accuses the other of illegitimate secrecy: Bruno associates Mariano with the Masons, who were indeed the organizers of liberalism in Spain;

and Mariano notes that Bruno has just returned from a town in the Carlist hotbed of the Montseny, where conspiring was indeed going on.

15. Historians and politicians have long cited the Napoleonic resistance as the originary moment of popular Spanish nationalism (e.g. Carr 1982). Recent historiography, however, has amply documented the extent to which the famous Spanish popular resistance is a mythical construct used to legitimate the Spanish state (Esdaile 2003).

16. Anneta is repeatedly defined as "Catalan," while Llorenç's poverty of intellectual resources marks him as "a good Spaniard;" by this period there was a strong metonymic association between Catalan ethnicity and bourgeois modernization in Spain.

17. The liberal Oller's perspective is very similar to that of the Anglo-Saxon anthropologists.

18. Suedfeld suggests that relative personal insignificance may be a motivation for joining a secret organization, and much current popular culture in the U.S. treats the media-driven desire for fame as an incentive to spectacular violence: consider the film Natural Born Killers, or the debates over of school shootings.

19. I have been unable to locate mass media scholarship discussing the neighbor motif in news stories, but Wagner-Pacifici's work on the representation of neighborhood and the norms of domesticity in a similar confrontation between state, community, and "deviant" householders has been useful (1994). This genre has a rather Americanized feel to it in the Spanish context, as does the social reality it represents.

20. A history of such attempts could begin in Spain with the early modern Inquisition's endeavor to foster a culture of denunciation (Kamen 1985), and go on to such moments as the Enlightenment reforms of the late 18th century (Noyes 1998) and the proto-socialist urbanism of the mid-19th (Cerdà 1999).

21. Urban design has built upon this transformation with the multiplication of mass rather than collective public spaces and of new residential suburbs. The Al-Qaeda handbook urges its operatives to settle in new housing developments, "where people do not know one another" (Filkins 2002).

22. A measure of the perceived collapse of the neighborhood might be seen in the new prominence of the urban legend as a genre, now receiving in Spain both the popular and the scholarly attention it has long had in the U.S. (Sánchez-Carretero 2001). In contrast to gossip, which reduces the conduct of neighbors to known categories subject to evaluation, the urban legend (in which immigrants and cross-cultural encounters increasingly figure) highlights the unknowability of neighbors.

23. See, for example, the essays in Bendix and Welz eds. (1999). Several anthropologists have written on the loss of public neighborhood space in Barcelona's Barri Xino, beginning with McDonogh (1987). Much could be said, of course, about the voluntaristic community forms emerging in reaction to the privatization of urban space; but many Spaniards recognize the importance of the neighborhood as creating a given community in which modes of convivencia must perforce be collectively developed by diverse interests.

24. Their statements were prudent but not excessively so: they declared their gratitude to their neighbors and to the state for the justice eventually done; they expressed the anger with America that was also being expressed by their Spanish neighbors, and complained of economic loss and, more seriously, that their arrests had exposed their families in Algeria to reprisals.

25. Aznar's foreign policy has not been alone in reawakening public suspicion of the state. The last two years have also seen government calls for "Spanish patriotism," the Prestige disaster in which Spanish government action radically worsened the impact of an oil spill, and (in addition to the usual tensions with the historic regions) the outlawing of the Basque separatist party Herri Batasuna.

26. The protest extended into the smallest communities of Catalonia and brought out all classses and persuasions: rural towns with a dozen remaining inhabitants took pride in their universal participation, and the temporal and spatial reach of the protests was also extended by audiovisual recordings on the Web.

References

Abrahams, Roger D. 1981: Shouting Match at the Border: The Folklore of Display Events. In: R. Bauman and R. D. Abrahams (eds): 'And Other Neighborly Names': Social Process and Cultural Image in Texas Folklore. Austin: 303–321.

Al-Azmeh, Aziz 1996: "Culturalism, Grand Narrative of Capitalism Triumphant." Islam and Modernities. London: 17–40.

Álvarez Junco, José 2000: Introduction. In: José Alvarez Junco and Adrian Shubert (eds.): Spanish History Since 1808. London: 1–17.

Bailey, F.G. (ed.) 1971: Gifts and poison: the politics of reputation. New York.

Bataille, Georges.1973 : Théorie de la religion. Paris.

Bendix, Regina, and Gisela Welz (eds.) 1999: Cultural Brokerage and Public Folklore: Forms of Intellectual Practice in Society. Special Issue of Journal of Folklore Research 36(2&3):109–334.

Carr, Raymond 1982: Spain 1808–1975, 2d ed. New York.

Castells, Manuel 198: The City and the Grassroots. Berkeley and Los Angeles.

Castro, Américo 1971 (1948): The Spaniards: An

Introduction to Their History, revised ed. W. F. King and S. Margaretten, transl. Berkeley and Los Angeles.

Cerdà, Ildefons 1999: *The Five Bases of the General Theory of Urbanization*. Ed. Arturo Soria y Puig. Madrid.

Elordi, Carlos 2003: *El amigo americano. De Franco a Aznar: Una adhesión inquebrantable*. Madrid.

Esdaile, Charles 2003: Popular Mobilisation in Spain, 1808–1810: A Reassessment. In: M. Rowe (ed.): *Collaboration and Resistance in Napoleonic Europe*. Basingstoke.

Fabian, Johannes 1999: Remembering the Other: Knowledge and Recognition in the Exploration of Central Africa. In: *Critical Inquiry* 26:46–49.

Fàbregas, Xavier 1975: *Les formes de diversió en la societat catalana romàntica*. Barcelona.

Filkins, Dexter 2002: War of Secrets; Bin Laden's Guys Have Cloaks and Daggers, Too. In: *The New York Times*: September 8, Section 4, Page 3.

Foucault, Michel 1979: *Discipline and Punish: The Birth of the Prison*. Trans. A. Sheridan. New York.

Freeman, Susan Tax 1970: *Neighbors: The Social Contract in a Castilian Hamlet*. Chicago.

Goffman, Erving 1961: *Asylums: Essays on the Social Situation of Mental Patients and Other Inmates*. Chicago.

Habermas, Jürgen 1989: *The Structural Transformation of the Public Sphere*. Trans. T. Burger. Cambridge, Mass.

Herzfeld, Michael 1987: *Anthropology Through the Looking-Glass: Critical Ethnography on the Margins of Europe*. Cambridge.

Kamen, Henry 1985: *Inquisition and Society in Spain in the Sixteenth and Seventeenth Centuries*. Bloomington.

McDonogh, Gary W. 1987: The Geography of Evil: Barcelona's Barrio Chino. In: *Anthropological Quarterly* 60: 174–184.

Noyes, Dorothy 1995: Façade Performances in Catalonia: Display, Respect, Reclamation, Refusal. In: *Southern Folklore* 52:97–120.

Noyes, Dorothy 1998: "*La maja vestida*: Dress as Resistance to Enlightenment in Late 18th-Century Madrid." In: *Journal of American Folklore* 111:197–218.

Noyes, Dorothy 2003: *Fire in the Plaça: Catalan Festival Politics After Franco*. Philadelphia.

Oller, Narcís. 1979 (1888): "La bufetada." *Contes*. Barcelona: 71–94.

Peristiany, J.G. (ed.) 1966: *Honour and Shame: The Values of Mediterranean Society*. Chicago.

Pons i Massaveu, Joan 1987 (1878): "Viva la llibertat!" In: Enric Cassany (ed.): *Quadres de costums urbans del vuit–cents*. Barcelona: 73–86.

Romea Castro, Celia. 1994: *Barcelona romántica y revolucionaria : una imagen literaria de la ciudad, década de 1833 a 1843*. Barcelona.

Roy, Olivier 1994: *The Failure of Political Islam*. Trans. Carol Volk. Cambridge, Mass.

Sánchez-Carretero, Cristina 2001: "Llegendes urbanes i minories." In: *Revista d'etnologia de Catalunya* 19:86–99.

Scher, Philip W. 2003: *Carnival and the formation of a Caribbean transnation*. Gainesville.

Scott, James C. 1990. *Domination and the Arts of Resistance: Hidden Transcripts*. New Haven.

Simmel, Georg 1923 (1908): Das Geheimnis und die geheime Gesellschaft. *Soziologie. Untersuchungen über die Formen der Vergesellschaftung*. München and Leipzig: 257–304.

Suedfeld, Peter 2003: Harun al-Rashid and the Terrorists: Identity Concealed, Identity Revealed. In: *Political Psychology*: in press.

Todorov, Tzvetan 2001: *Life in Common. An Essay in General Anthropology*. Trans. Katherine and Lucy Golsan. Lincoln.

Vicens Vives, Jaime 1967 (1952): *Approaches to the History of Spain*. Trans. J. C. Ullman. Berkeley and Los Angeles.

Wagner-Pacifici, Robin 1994: *Discourse and Destruction: The City of Philadelphia Versus MOVE*. Chicago.

Zulaika, Joseba 1995: The Anthropologist as Terrorist. In: Carolyn Nordstrom, Antonius C.G.M. Robben (eds.): *Fieldwork Under Fire : Contemporary Studies of Violence and Survival*. Berkeley and Los Angeles: 206–223.

Part III

Martyrs in Visual and Linguistic Contexts

The Martyr's Way to Paradise
Shiite Mural Art in the Urban Context[1]

Ulrich Marzolph

> Marzolph, Ulrich 2003: The Martyr's Way to Paradise. Shiite Mural Art in the Urban Context. – Ethnologia Europaea 33:2: 87–98.
>
> Ever since the political changes in Iran more than twenty years ago, ideological discussions have manifested themselves in various arenas of political and societal concern. Apart from the traditional means of propaganda such as print-media and modern mass communication, Iranian political institutions employ a large range of other media to propagate their intentions and ideas. Of these, representations in writing and illustration in public spaces deserve particular attention, since they combine traditional modes of artistic expression with intentions of contemporary concern for Shiite Iran.
>
> In Tehran, walls on large buildings have been used for pictorial illustrations of moral and political standards pertaining to the presently propagated Shia ideals. Mural art serves various ends, such as glorifying the Shiite martyrs, reminding the people of the righteous leadership, and, more recently, substituting nature as a means to humanize the concrete habitat of modern cities. All of these ends aim to stabilize the present value-system by underlining its intention, outlining its basic values, or simply offering comfort in times of depression.
>
> *Prof. Dr. Ulrich Marzolph, Enzyklopädie des Märchens, Friedländer Weg 2, D-37085 Göttingen. E-mail: umarzol@gwdg.de*

Introduction

International visitors to Tehran, when traveling from the airport to the city center, cannot fail to notice a phenomenon that has spread across the megalopolis since the mid-1990s: the large, multistory, windowless exterior walls of residential and commercial buildings facing the highways and avenues are adorned with bright murals whose contours can be seen even from a distance of several miles away. These megamurals, while dominated by imagery, often also incorporate short texts. As public expression, they are utilized by different organizations to propagate their aims. Among others, municipal authorities have in recent years become aware of the medium as an inexpensive way to beautify the urban concrete habitat. In consequence, various public spaces have been adorned with ornaments or graphic designs meant to emulate nature. These designs are particularly noticeable on the concrete pillars of highway bridges.

The majority of Tehran murals have, however, been placed by political organizations that by definition in today's Iran are religiously oriented. The dominant theme in those murals is that of the martyr, or *shahid* in Persian (and Arabic). In the given context, the term martyr refers exclusively to males who have given their lives in defending the Shiite Islamic creed, or in defending the nation of Iran that in turn is firmly rooted within that creed. The murals posses artistic and aesthetic value, and would certainly deserve an art historian's interpretation (see Ahmadi 2003) positing them within the context of, say, traditional Iranian imagery versus the influence of large scale Western painting. In terms of content, they propagate a normative remembrance by depicting those individuals who have engaged in an act of martyrdom endorsed by the state. The murals thus partake in the framework of the Iranian Shiite culture of remembrance (Marzolph 1998), itself a basic value of the theocratically legitimated Islamic Republic.

In the following, I document and analyze various levels of presentation and messages implied in these murals, using data collected during several field trips to Iran between 2000 and 2002. In addition to analyzing the presentation forms they take and their ideological components, I also want to draw attention to the semiotic links between the scenes depicted in the murals and the historical events that constitute the basis of religious and political consciousness as it is defined by Iranian Shiite authorities themselves.

It may be useful, by way of introduction, to briefly recount Iranian political history since 1979 here, as well as describe some aspects of the portrayal of martyrs in Iranian art. When Shâh Rezâ Pahlavi left Iran in early 1979 for good, he was forced to do so in response to the actions taken by various opposition groups both inside and outside the country. These groups can be more or less differentiated as either nationalist, communist, or religious-Islamic (Chelkowski/Dabashi 1999: 22–29). In a relatively brief time, the religious group headed by the charismatic leader Ruhollâh Khomeini gained the upper hand and strengthened its supremacy by consciously employing a variety of media tools to promote its views. In doing so, the most effective strategy was to redefine what had been a pluralistically-oriented revolution as a decidedly "Islamic" revolution, and this interpretation has not changed since.

The internal turmoil also encouraged Iraq, Iran's neighbor to the west, to judge the country weakened and impaired. With the military and political support of the United States, Iraq, with the pretence of claiming contested territory alongside the common border, began a war with Iran. The Iran-Iraq War lasted until 1988 and ended with Iran successfully defending itself, albeit at considerable material and human loss. When Khomeini died soon after, he was succeeded as leader (*rahbar*) of the Islamic revolution by Âyatollâh Khâmene'i, who still holds the office today. Though post-revolutionary Iran was constituted as a presidential republic, the *rahbar* is the supreme political and military authority in Iran. The *rahbar* is permitted to influence, revise, or even contradict decisions taken by any other legal body in Iran, including those of the government or the head of state, both through his sheer authority and by virtue of his leadership role in various influential bodies. The rationale is that the *rahbar* oversees whether rules and actions in and by the state correspond to "Islamic" laws and rules, and the authority of his office is incontestable. While the *rahbar* is elected for life, he remains subordinate only to Khomeini and cannot question Khomeini's decisions or will.

Peter Chelkowski and Hamid Dabashi's *The Art of Persuasion in the Islamic Republic of Iran* (1999) has meticulously documented and analyzed the campaign to define the Iranian Revolution as "Islamic," and details the manner in which visual media were instrumentalized to propagate this ideological aim. The array of media employed ranged from what has been seen in the aftermath of other ideologically-based revolutions – photographs, film, wall paintings, posters, banknotes, stamps, and schoolbook illustrations – to rather less common media, including children's drawings, chewing-gum wrappers, and graffiti. While the large-sized murals of the 1990s derive from the media studied by Chelkowski and Dabashi, they were beyond the scope of their publication and have only quite recently gained scholarly attention (see Grigor 2002).

Chelkowski and Dabashi contend that political posters existed in Iran prior to the revolution of 1978/79, but argue that their conscious use for propaganda purposes only started with the revolution (see also Balaghi/ Gumpert 2002). Technically, posters are illustrations with an accompanying text printed on large-sized paper. In Iran, that illustration was often composed of artistic renderings of realistic scenes that were supplemented by symbolic components alien to the event itself. For a number of years, such posters remained the key media expression of the revolution, and though not as spontaneous as the revolutionary graffiti that covered the walls initially (particularly in southern Tehran; see *Divâr neveshtehâ-ye enqelâb* 1982; Rota 1989; Yavari d'Hellencourt 1990), posters were later institutionalized.

By the mid-1990s, the themes and topics of the posters began to appear on the murals. Yet such murals are not simply much larger versions of the earlier posters. Given their size, they are devised with a specific agenda in mind that aims to convey its message in touching images and clear messages. Moreover, the murals' very size and omnipresence render the topics they illustrate unavoidable and obtrusive. These characteristics make the mural topics themselves into inescapable constituents of daily life in Tehran, thereby firmly anchoring the propagated ideology in popular consciousness if not sub-consciousness.

The Murals: An Overview

The dominant subject of most murals are individual males who lost their lives in the so-called First Gulf War (the Iran-Iraq War of 1980–88), though there are some who are memorialized for their participation in the armed struggle for the liberation of Palestine. Some murals depict two individuals, but it is rare to see small groups of three or five or more persons shown. The largest group of martyrs portrayed shows the nine Iranian journalists assassinated by the Taliban regime in Mazar-e Sharif in Afghanistan.

The texts accompanying the murals tend to convey short and straightforward messages. These messages are of two kinds. One explains the basic facts that enable the spectator to identify the mural's subject, such as the name of the dead person(s) and the place or event at which he lost his life. The other kind prescribes how the mural should be interpreted. Such a text might be a programmatic statement from the diary or last will of the dead person, a quote from the Koran, or a quote from the *rahbar*. Thus, the image of Dr. Mostafâ Chemrân is accompanied by his exclamation: "Great God, I thank you for having opened up to me the path of martyrdom!" In the case of Mohammad-'Ali Ganjizâde, the mural includes a sentence from his last will reading: "I wish that everyone treat each other with sincerity. Do not forget to follow the right path and keep away from the evil path. This should be regarded as more important than the affection of one's family." Commander Nâser Kâzemi's depiction bears the quote: "The only way of liberating the oppressed from their oppressors is the revolutionary way of Islam" [fig. 1]. Frequently one sees the Koran quote "and by stars they will be led the right way" (16,16) or utterances by either Khomeini or Khâmene'i. Quite often, the murals include a statement of Khomeini's that has almost gained a proverbial status: *Shahâdat honar-e mardân-*

1. Tehran, Kordestân Highway.

e khodâ-st ("Martyrdom is the art of the men of God").

The portrait of the deceased person is usually of an almost photographic exactitude, while the backgrounds remain rather imprecise, with blue and white tones suggesting sky and clouds. Supplementing this, either alone or together, are two other elements. One is symbolic, a red tulip or a red rose to symbolize martyrdom, or the depiction of the blood that has been shed itself. The other is a portrait of Khomeini, or the likenesses of both Khomeini and Khâmene'i together. One never, however, sees Khâmene'i depicted without his predecessor.

As the signatures on the murals document, most have been installed at the orders of political groups and institutions. One relatively rarely sees the names of such institutions as the Tehran municipal authority, the Hezbollâh, the Foundation of the Guards (*bonyâd-e pâsdârân*), or the Foundation of the Oppressed (*bonyâd-e mostaz'afân*). Instead, the vast majority of the murals have been installed by order of the large and influential Foundation of Martyrs (*bonyâd-e shahid*). This institution was founded by Khomeini's personal decree in 1979, at the very beginning of the revolution. Since then, it has developed into a powerful national institution, its income having more than tripled from March 1994 to September 1999, comprising some $15 million for the said period (*Bonyâd-e shahid* 1999: 270). The official mandate of the foundation is to care for martyrs, invalids, and their families, as well as to keep their memory alive in society (Rahimiyân 2001). It is this latter goal that has given rise to the institutionalized public memory of martyrs by way of murals. According to the data published the foundation itself, by 1999, more than 600 of them, covering a total of 24,834 square meters, had been installed (*Bonyâd-e shahid* 1999: 90f.).

The logo of the *Bonyâd-e shahid* is a cleverly contrived combination of symbols that are essential for the contemporary interpretation of martyrdom in the Shiite context. It contains the Koran, a red tulip (which shows a striking similarity to a soldier's helmet) and a white dove in flight (symbolizing the soul) in front of an abstraction of the globe. A red border that frames the logo contains part of a Koranic utterance (33,23) whose complete form reads: "Within the believers there are men who have carried out the deeds they have promised to God. Some of them have already passed away while others still have to wait. And they have falsified nothing." With these words, martyrdom in the service of religious faith is elevated to the level of being a true believer's obligation. The key difference between a martyr and other believers is not the degree of intensity or the sincerity of belief, but rather the fact that the martyr has already fulfilled his obligation toward God by losing his life.

Martyrdom in the Context of Shiite Islamic History

This active propagation of martyrdom is alien to Western secular observers, and consequently generates a set of questions. The recent intense discussion of phenomena that are called terrorism or suicide-bombing (see Israeli 1997), or the equally recent division of the world's civilizations into the Good and the Bad on the part of various world politicians, require that one address, in its proper historical context, the pressing questions surrounding the phenomenon of martyrdom and the position it occupies in contemporary Iran (Khosrokhavar 1995; Kohlberg 1997; Butel 2002; Khosrokhavar 2003: 115–172).

At first, one might be inclined to regard the contemporary relevance of martyrdom as a result of the large number of deaths caused by the 1978/79 Revolution and the Iran-Iraq War. To memorialize these casualties means to honor those who gave their lives to help construct and safeguard today's Iran. The sheer numbers of these martyrs would seem sufficient grounds to show enduring gratitude to their heroic deeds, and acknowledge their devotion. This conclusion is as obvious as it is not exactly wrong.

Yet the historical dimension of martyrdom in Shiite Iranian thought needs also to be taken into account and placed in its appropriate context. The Shiite creed of Islam (Halm 1988) was elevated to the position of dominant creed, or to what we would call an official state religion today, by the founder of the Safavid dynasty in 1501, though most Iranians at that time would likely still have adhered to the Sunni creed. The difference between Sunni and Shiite creeds is manifested in the large number of details of both dogma and theology that have in turn generated an equally large variety of popular customs, beliefs, and practices (see Massé 1938: vol. 1, 119–169; Donaldson 1938).

Historically, the schism in the Islamic community resulted from a simple controversy over the proper succession to the prophet Mohammad (d. 632). As this controversy bears on the basis for the legitimacy of leadership in Islam, it has had wide-reaching consequences ever since. Mohammed did not leave a male descendant as heir, nor had he appointed a successor (though this last statement is not endorsed by the Shiite community). Mohammed's only surviving male descendants resulted from the marriage of his daughter Fâtima with a cousin of Mohammad, Ali.

In the Shiite view, Ali was the only legitimate successor to Mohammed. This position is expressed by their denomination, as the Arabic expression *shî'at 'Alî* literally means the "party of Ali". There were other reasons to prefer Ali, because from the very beginning, he had been a close associate and intimate friend of Mohammed's. Shiites even claim that when he returned from his last pilgrimage to Mecca, Mohammed explicitly appointed Ali as his successor. Besides, Ali was also a prominent representative of the established religious aristocracy of the original Islamic community.

But this was not the majority view, for in the discussion of Mohammed's succession, there were those who said that kinship or personal acquaintance with the prophet should be weighed against choosing a suitable or deserving person. In the end, the first and second caliphs (the Arabic term *khalîfa* literally means deputy), Abû Bakr (632–634) and Omar (634–644), were elected by decision of a board of elders. While the Shiite party already opposed these decisions, the election of the third caliph Osman (644–656) produced an open discord. After Osman was assassinated and Ali (656–661) finally became caliph, the rift between the various factions was irreparable, and Ali, too, was murdered. The developments led on the one hand to the establishment of the (Sunni) Omayyad dynasty; on the other, it resulted in the institutionalizing, within the 'Party of Ali', of the claim that Ali's direct descendants – and thus the chain of Shiite *imâms* – were the rightful and hereditary leaders of the Islamic community.

This schism did not occur without armed struggle, and it is in this early history that the tradition of Shiite martyrdom is rooted. Initially, after Ali's death in 661, Shiites claimed that his legitimate successor was Fâtima's eldest son Hasan. Hasan, however, officially declined and paid public homage to the Omayyad caliph Mu'âwiya. Hasan's death (670 or 678), as well as the succession of Mu'âwiya by his son Yazîd in 680, again raised the question of succession, and it was Hosein, Hasan's younger brother, who claimed this right.

That year, Hosein, accompanied by a small troop of warriors who supported him, crossed the desert from Mecca in the direction of Kufa, whose Arabic inhabitants he believed endorsed his claim. However, the inhabitants of Kufa, even though they sympathized with Hosein, did not support him in military terms. On the plains near Karbalâ', in Iraq, Hosein and his small troop were slaughtered and mutilated by the caliph's army, who vastly outnumbered them on Moharram 10, 61, or October 10, 680. When the battle was over, the severed heads of the males of Hosein's clan, together with the women and children, were sent to the caliph's residence in Damascus. Hosein's only surviving male descendant was his son Ali, called "Zayn al-'âbidîn" (or "Adornment of the servants of God"), who had not participated in the battle because he was ill. This Ali, and his descendants, then continued the direct succession of Shiite *imâms* that in the Iranian Shiite view lasted until the twelfth *imâm*, Mohammad al-Mahdi, who went into concealment in the year 941 and who will only return on Doomsday.

Hosein's Martyrdom and Collective Remembrance

Hosein's death during the battle of Karbalâ' in 680 constitutes the pivotal martyrdom, the central traumatic experience, of the Shiite creed. No other event has had an equal impact on both the learned and popular cultures of Shiite Iran. In particular, Hosein's death continues to exercise a tremendous effect not so much through itself and its immediate consequences, but rather by being remembered and memorized in the hearts of people. The anniversary of Hosein's death on Moharram 10 is celebrated as the highest Shiite religious holiday, and Hosein's martyrdom is remembered every year during the month of Muharram, in both public and private ceremonies and dramatic re-enactments.

Once the Shiite creed was established as Iran's "state religion" in the sixteenth century, and again during the Qajar dynasty in the nineteenth century, the collective remembrance of Hosein's martyrdom brought forth a richly documented literary genre, popularly known as *rouze-khvâni* (see Marzolph 2001: 25f.), but sometimes also called *marsiye* (lament) or *maqtal* ([narrative about a] scene of combat). This genre, which embellishes the tragic events with numerous real as well as a growing number of fantastic details, derives its name from the public performance of the popular work *Rouzat al-shohadâ'* ("Garden of the martyrs") compiled by Hosein b. Vâ'ez Kâshefi (d. 1504).

Hosein's martyrdom, together with the sense of remorse at not having been able to prevent this tragedy, is individually re-lived by men castigating and publicly flagellating themselves in mourning processions during the month of Moharram. It is also re-enacted in the dramatic genre of *ta'ziye*, often labeled the "Shiite passion play" (Chelkowski 1979), as well as being recounted in narrative performances to a broader public by professional story-tellers. These storytellers – and here we have another thematic and representational connection to posters and murals – in turn sometimes employed large oil canvasses (*parde*) to illustrate their stories (Seif 1990). Furthermore, images of Hosein's martyrdom are in evidence in numerous other forms of pictorial illustration such as the tile-work that used to adorn the Hoseiniye-ye Moshir, a nineteenth-century commemorative building in Shirâz (Homâyuni 1992), or the single-sheet lithographic prints that were sold or distributed at Shiite places of worship such as the Shrines of Karbalâ' (Vinchon 1925; Marzolph 2001: fig. 90).

Contexts and Examples

Today's Tehran murals are linked in many ways with these events, both past and present, that lie at the core of Shiite self-perception, though some links are more obvious than others. In some murals, past and present may be linked by including the image of Ali as an ideal and exemplary human being, or by portraying the righteous martyr Hosein. Other members of the Islamic "holy family" (*ahl-e beit*), such as Hosein's mother Fâtima, may also appear.

Besides the depiction of the martyr's blood, often embodied by a red tulip, the other recurrent symbol is water. This is not just a reference to water as fundamental to life, for Shiites immediately associate water with the martyrdom of Hosein and his troops. Though Hosein had been quite close to the river Euphrates, the caliph's troops would not allow him to fetch water for his thirsty men, and Hosein's standard-bearer and water-carrier Abol-Fazl was sadistically mutilated when he attempted to reach the river. Water therefore carries a semiotic charge linked to the image of the tragedy that lies at the core of belief for each member of the Shiite community.

Though the memorialization of the recent death of Iranian soldiers in the Iran-Iraq War may, through the symbols and imagery included, be explicitly linked to Shiite views of the past, the murals are also part of the present since both Khomeini and Khâmene'i, the recent leaders of the Islamic revolution, are often portrayed together with the martyrs. This bracketing not only legitimates the present, presenting it as a direct result of the past. It also presents contemporary events as normative for the future. To elaborate this point, a few murals will be examined in greater detail.

A mural on the wall of a building standing adjacent to the Foundation of Martyrs headquarters in central Tehran depicts a soldier who died in battle. Revived in the hereafter, he has put his machine-gun on the ground and humbly stands at the entrance to paradise – paradise being the reward each martyr expects immediately after death (Garthwaite 1991: 29). The incorporated text reads *Shahid avval kasi-st ke be behest vâred mishavad* ("The martyr is the

2. Tehran, Golhâ Square South.

first to enter paradise"), and the artistic style is reminiscent of classical Persian miniatures.

Paradise as the martyr's ultimate goal is also pictured in another mural that cleverly combines various layers of reality and fiction. The anonymous martyr, identified by his red ribbon, is set as a barely recognizable silhouette against a blue and cloudy sky. The viewers' gaze is drawn to two butterflies, one of which has liberated itself from the background, leaving a blank space, while the other is still struggling to do so. Besides the dove, the butterfly is a popular symbol for the martyr's soul. The butterfly's goal is an area set into a realistic landscape of mountains and seashore that is differentiated from the background by its horizontal perspective. The setting sun streaming from this area indicates its character as the promised land, one which the butterfly's shadow is about to enter [fig. 2]. The wording on the mural's left side, by Khomeini, praises active fighting (*basij*) as a "school of love" and as the natural way all those nameless martyrs who gave their lives serving its cause take.

Another mural, also placed on the wall of a government building, links Ali's exemplary character and impeccability with the element of water. Though a Western observer might be reminded of Niagara Falls, water here incorporates a dual symbol: the implicit expression of Hosein's suffering and the source of life. The quintessential expression of water in Islam, after all, is the river al-Kauthar in paradise. The water's originates from a green cloth on the left side of the image that is arranged in the form of a head-dress clothing an unidentified figure. As the green color indicates a member of the prophet Mohammed's family, there is not doubt that this figure is meant to be Ali, the exemplary and impeccable human being whose example serves as the source of life. The quotation added to the illustration underlines this interpretation. It is an admonition of Khomeini's reading: *Shomâ varzeshkârân bâyad be-'Ali eqtedâ' konid*, "Sportsmen, take Ali as your example!" [fig. 3]

Another mural neatly combines several of the aforementioned elements by showing the portraits of three martyrs who are set as stars in front of a field of tulips. They are framed by the two leaders of the revolution, with the name of Ali placed in the upper middle and emanating light like the sun. The motto is again Khomeini's: "Martyrdom is the art of the men of God!" It is

3. Tehran, Vesâl-e Shirâzi Street, Corner of Beheshti Ave.

4. Tehran, Golhâ Square West.

5. Tehran, Modarres Highway.

worth noting that this mural is on a wall in front of large faucets from which the tanker trucks hired by the municipal authorities fill up the water sprayed on the numerous lawns and green areas in the city [fig. 4].

Probably the most emotionally moving poster in Tehran has been installed next to one of the more heavily frequented city highways that heads north [fig. 5]. It shows a little girl holding a red rose in her hand, mourning her dead father, who lies in front of her, with the words: *Bâbâ-ye shahidam – hich goli khoshbutar az yâd-e to nist* ("My martyr father – no rose smells sweeter than your memory!"). This mural includes a number of stars that contain invocations addressed to the full set of characters most revered by Shiite Islam: Mohammed, his daughter Fâtima (implied in her cognomen Zahrâ'), Ali, his sons Hasan and Hosein, and the twelfth *imâm* al-Mahdi, who watches the world's fate from his place of concealment. The upper right-hand corner shows what appears to be a crack in the sky, permitting a glimpse of paradise, the future residence of all martyrs and the ultimate goal their way will lead them to. The writing on the left side comforts the martyrs by assuring them that the community will never forget their victory. A separate plate, placed next to the mural at a later date, adds both Khomeini's image and his interpretation. The founder of the Islamic Republic is placed before a wall adorned with an ornament representing the stylized name of Ali, pointing out that Ali serves as a constant model to all true Shiite believers, "in piety, faith, and support for the suppressed" (*shi'e bâyad moshâye'at konad 'Ali-râ [...] be zohd, be taqvâ, be residegi be mazlum ...*). It is worth noting that this mural, for as yet unknown reasons, was whitewashed in early 2003.

Finally, another powerful mural is affixed to the wall of a building immediately adjacent to the "Square of the Revolution" (Meidân-e enqelâb), the most frequented public space in Tehran where hundreds of thousands pass by and see the mural every day [fig. 6]. The city campus of the University of Tehran lies in the vicinity, a location that even before the revolution had often been the scene of civilian intellectual protests, and that since then has been used as the arena for the programmatic Friday prayers. This mural's center is occupied by a young soldier who is flanked by masses of soldiers ready for war. The young man's red ribbon signals his readiness to die as a martyr. On the

6. Tehran, Enqelâb Square East.

right side, to the rear of the martyr, stands Khomeini, depicted in about the same size and looking in the same direction, while stretching out his right arm in a gesture of blessing and protection for which he was famous during his lifetime. At the mural's left side, in front of the martyr, the artist has placed the smiling (if somewhat inward-looking) head of Khâmene'i, who faces the future with an air suggesting confidence. The mural's lower edge is shown dripping with blood, while the upper edge is dominated by green, the prophet Mohammed's color. That green gradually melts into the black turban that indicates Khâmene'i (and Khomeini) are *seyyid*, thus among Mohammed's descendants. The space in between these two colored edges is dominated by white that gradually turns into the revered grey of Khâmene'i's beard. Taken together, the three colors represent the Iranian national flag. The writing, centered in the image's upper half, reads: *Parvaresh-e javânân-e khodâ-juy basiji-ye fath ol-fotuh-e emâm ast* ("Educating the God-seeking youth means mobilization for the final battle of the *imâm*"). The rectangular mural has ingeniously been placed on a wall whose left side is lower than the right, thus visually suggesting an emphasis to the left that signifies the future.

Conclusion

The Tehran murals, whether regarded individually or as a collective phenomenon, are strong evidence for the popularization of martyrdom as a constitutive element of the Shiite creed in today's Iranian interpretation. In combining current events with references to Hosein or Ali, they rely on the past as a foundation for contemporary identity while also aiming to perpetuate this interpretation into the future. Martyrs, though depicted as named individuals, are turned into de-personalized stereotypical models by their enormous size and omnipresence, and the symbols included make clear that their individual fate is subordinate not just to the public interest but to the pivotal importance of martyrdom as a constitutive element of Shiite Islam. A mural underlining this interpretation shows various martyrs who are explicitly labeled as adhering to creeds and religious communities other than Islam, including an Armenian, a Syrian Christian, a Jew, and a Zoroastrian. In this way, the mural claims universal validity for the concept of martyrdom as serving a just cause.

Further research is needed to illuminate the ideological motivations of the institutions and organizations that use murals. While the murals are installed at a time when Iranian politics is showing signs of becoming more liberal, the murals themselves are indicative of a conservative trend aimed at propagating and firmly rooting specific religious values and interpretations in the population both now and in the future. In this respect, the Tehran murals illustrate a phenomenon Werner Schiffauer (2001), in his recent essay on Kurdish martyr imagery, has called the "esthetic evidence."

By using a particular set of symbols and imagery in a visually attractive form, the Tehran murals aim to both create and solidify identity. The identity they propagate is not an individual and isolated one; it is highly complex and draws on religious and national elements, while using the past to project its values into the future. Furthermore, by combining a set of commonly acknowledged and unquestioned Shiite values together with more recent manifestations, such as the rise and position of the leaders of the Islamic revolution, along with the suggestion of death in the service of patriotic defense, the murals aim to create an aura of legitimacy for revolutionary politics and for self-defense as much as for martyrdom and sacrifice in the name of the faith.

It remains to be seen whether the murals should be taken to indicate a strong self-consciousness on the part of the conservative elements in Iranian politics. The active promotion of the heroics of past martyrs could also mean a sign of weakness towards a young population that appears increasingly indifferent towards religious values, as they conflict with their notions of modern life. The conditions of production, along with the reception of the murals by the surrounding society, require further examination. While the Foundation of Martyrs actively admits to pursuing propagandistic aims, empirical research among the Tehran population would have to be undertaken to establish what effect the murals have among either sympathizers or opponents of the ideological system portrayed.

Iranian society continues to be in transition, and those who judge phenomena they encounter in Iran from a Western or non-Muslim background may feel disoriented if not alienated. At the same time, in light of recent political and societal events, it is vitally important not to jump to rash conclusions. In this respect, studying the particular art-form of the Tehran murals affords us a chance to engage in a more refined or more adequate evaluation of the Iranian, and, in the broader context, of the Islamic Other.

Notes

1. This paper is the first published version of a presentation that has been given orally at various occasions.

   German versions were presented at the September 2001 meeting of the Deutsche Arbeitsgemeinschaft Vorderer Orient (DAVO) in Göttingen ("Schiitische Wandmalerei als politische Propaganda") and in the context of the Ringvorlesung of the "Sonderforschungsbereich Erinnerungskulturen" in Gießen in January 2002 ("Der Märtyrer und das Paradies: Schiitische Megaposter als Ausdruck des normativen Gedenkens").

   English versions were presented at various occasions in Rochester, N. Y., Osaka, Tokyo and Cambridge. I would like to thank the respective audiences for their comments and criticism. Also, I am grateful to Shahnaz Nadjmabadi and Yuriko Yamanaka for supplying information and references that would otherwise have remained inaccessible to me.

   The reproduced photographs have been taken by the author in September 2001.

References

Ahmadi, Mahnâz 2003: *Bar-resi-ye divâr-negârhâ-ye shahre-e. Tehrân.* Thesis. Dâneshgâh-e âzâd-e eslâmi. Tehran 1382.

Balaghi, Shiva, & Lynn Gumpert 2002: *Picturing Iran: Art, Society and Revolution.* London, New York.

Bonyâd-e shahid 1999 = *Bonyâd-e shahid: hasane-ye jâriye-ye Emâm (s).* Tehran 1378.

Butel, Éric 2002: Martyre et sainteté dans la littérature de guerre Iran-Irak. In: C. Mayeur-Jaouen (ed.): *Saints et héros du moyen-orient contemporain.* Paris.

Chelkowski, Peter J. (ed.) 1979: *Ta'ziyeh: Ritual and Drama in Iran.* New York.

Chelkowski, Peter, & Hamid Dabashi 1999: *Staging a Revolution: The Art of Persuasion in the Islamic Republic of Iran.* New York.

Divar neveshtehâ-ye enqelâb 1982 = *Tasâvir-e divâr-neveshtehâ-ye enqelâb. be-monâsebat-e chahâromin sâlgerd-e piruzi-ye enqelâb-e eslâmi-e Irân.* Tehran 1361.

Donaldson, Bess Allen 1938: *The Wild Rue: A Study of Muhammadan Magic and Folklore in Iran.* London.

Garthwaite, Gene R. 1991: Popular Islamic Perceptions of Paradise Gained. In: Sheila S. Blair, Jonathan M. Bloom (eds.): *Images of Paradise in Islamic Art.* Hanover, NH: 25–31.

Grigor, Talinn 2002: (Re)Claiming Space: The Use/Misuse of Propaganda Murals in Republican Tehran. In: *IIAS Newsletter* 28 (August 2002) 37.

Halm, Heinz 1988: *Die Schia.* Darmstadt.

Homâyuni, Sâdeq 1992: *Hoseiniye-ye Moshir.* Shirâz 1371.

Israeli, Raphael 1997: Islamikaze and their Significance. In: *Terrorism and Political Violence* 9,3: 96–121.

Khosrokhavar, Farhad 1995: *L'islamisme et la mort: Le martyre révolutionnaire en Iran.* Paris.

Khosrokhavar, Farhad 2003: *Les nouveaux martyrs d'Allah.* Paris.

Kohlberg, Etan 1997: Medieval Muslim Views of Martyrdom. In: *Koninklijke Nederlandse Akademie van Wetenschapen, Mededelingen van de Afdeling Letterkunde, Nieuwe Reeks* 60,7: 281–307.

Marzolph, Ulrich 1998: Islamische Kultur als Gedächtniskultur: Fachspezifische Überlegungen anhand des Fallbeispiels Iran. In: *Der Islam* 75: 296–317.

Marzolph, Ulrich 2001: *Narrative Illustration in Persian Lithographed Books.* Leiden/Boston/Köln.

Massé, Henri 1938: *Croyances et coutumes persanes, suivies de contes et chansons populaires.* Vols 1–2. Paris.

Rahimiyân, Mohammad Hasan 2001: *Dar harim-e lâlehâ: moruri bar resâlat-e Bonyâd-e shahid dar nezâm-e eslâmi.* Tehran 1380.

Rota, Giorgio 1989: L'importanza delle scritte murali nell'Iran rivoluzionario. In: *Majmu'e-ye Bahariye.* Rome: 155–195.

Schiffauer, Werner 2001: Das Märtyrergrab in der Landschaft: Zur Rolle von ästhetischer Evidenz bei der Konstruktion einer nationalen Identität. In: Behrend, H. (ed.): *Geist, Bild und Narr. Zu einer Ethnologie kultureller Konversionen.* Berlin: 192–203.

Seif, Hâdi 1990: *Naqqâshi-ye qahve-khâne'i.* Tehran 1369.

Vinchon, Jean 1925: L'imagerie populaire persane. In: *Revue des arts asiatiques* 2,4: 3–9.

Yavari d'Hellencourt, Nouchine 1990: "Etranger" et "identité collective" dans les slogans révolutionnaires en Iran. In: *CEMOTI* 9, pp. 63–78.

Martyr vs. Martyr
The Sacred Language of Violence

Galit Hasan-Rokem

> Hasan-Rokem, Galit 2003: Martyr vs. Martyr. The Sacred Language of Violence. – Ethnologia Europaea 33:2: 99–104.
>
> This paper attempts to capture the violence and immediacy of current events by applying semiotic analysis. The mutual cruelties acted out by Israelis and Palestinians is analyzed in terms of the growing usage of words from religious contexts to legitimize violence and to attach powerful collective emotions to it. The focus is on the use of the term "martyr" to refer on the one hand to Palestinian victims or suicide bombers, on the other hand to Israeli victims. A concise historical analysis of the word "martyr" in Jewish sources points at its contingent changes in various situations. In the twentieth century the vocabulary of death has radically changed in European discourse, but probably specifically in Jewish discourse. The analysis points to mechanisms of appropriation of individual lives and deaths as a result of the application of the term "martyr". The analysis of such language use hopes to contribute to some better understanding and greater tolerance.
>
> *Prof. Dr. Galit Hasan-Rokem, Head of Institute for Jewish Studies, The Hebrew University, Jerusalem 91905, Israel. E-mail: hasan@h2.hum.huji.ac.il*

The events of 9/11/01 in New York City heightened the awareness of human frailty and the limits of control of even great empires. They sharpened the general consciousness of the power of images and words to shape not only the concepts of individuals but also to instantly reshape the behavior of millions of individuals and a great number of governments, public agencies, and commercial corporations worldwide. In the following paper I wish to touch upon an aspect that is present in the specific media complex regarding those events in New York City, but that is even more visible and audible in the public discourse in the Middle East where the named events have deep roots. I shall trace the semiotics of one specific term, "martyr", that has played a fatal role in the molding of images between Israelis and Palestinians in their longtime strife over the territories of the Holy Land. The way the concept of martyr functions in the communication between these two identities infuses the word dialogue with a different tone than the positive value that most of us are used to attach to the term in the wake of European humanist and existentialist traditions represented by thinkers as different from each other as Martin Buber, Mikhail Bakhtin and Hans Georg Gadamer.

The paper will not encompass the entire historical width and depth of the phenomenon of martyrdom. It has been part and parcel of religious phenomenology as long as we can trace it back, but was consolidated and institutionalized by Christianity and Judaism in the early centuries of the first millennium. It should, however, be mentioned that in the historical perspective it becomes very clear that the term martyr, derived from the Greek "witness", has always served in the generation of mutual relationships of entities contesting their legitimacy over a specific legacy, be it sacred texts or sacred territories. This fact as well as its phenomenal relationship to communication, and especially mass communication, may be illuminated by the following observation made by Daniel Boyarin on the "cooperative" emergence of martyrdom, under very different circumstances and power relations, in late antiquity:

"Martyrdom, even more than tragedy, is *Thanatoi en tōi phanarōi*, 'deaths that are seen,' murders in public spaces. Insofar as martyrdom is, then by definition, a practice that takes place within the public, and therefore, shared space, *martyria* seem to be a particularly fertile site for the exploration of the permeability of the borders between so-called Judaism and so-called Christianity in late antiquity" (Boyarin 1999).[1]

I shall in the following resort to the tools of the ethnographer who uses herself as the source of information, thus appropriating the witnessing function from those who have used it in death to one who hopes to do it in the service of life.

At five in the afternoon on the Sunday when I obtained the consent of the Dean of the Humanities to take off a week to go to Göttingen for the conference on "Sleepers, Moles and Martyrs", I participated in the funeral of Daphna Shpruch. She had died on Saturday, ten days after a bomb exploded at the Hebrew University Mount Scopus Cafeteria, at the Frank Sinatra Student Center, situated at the Nancy Reagan Plaz, on July 31, 2002. Daphna died of a severe head injury caused by the explosion that destroyed the front part of her head.

Some secularized Jews in Israel today, to whom the form of the ceremonies of death are a matter of principle and of deep feelings, create an individually styled ceremony with music, poetry reading, etc. At Daphna's funeral it became clear that her stricken family had not made an extra effort to salvage the ceremony from the hands of the orthodox religious authorities. As a result, the raw pain of the family was laid bare by the harsh contradiction between the formality of the orthodox officials and the introvert lack of communication of the family members and close friends with the undertakers. The official cantor who recited the traditional texts of the Jewish funeral ceremony introduced Daphna Shpruch as a martyr, *qedosha*. Although the usage somewhat disturbingly alerted my attention, it was familiar enough from the prevalent public discourse so that no explanation was needed. The cantor obviously considered Daphna a martyr because her death had occurred within the context of the national conflict between Palestinians and Israelis. Her death was caused by a bomb in the current wave of terror.

In the original usage of martyrdom in early Christianity and rabbinic Judaism (*qiddush ha-shem*), the agency of the martyr who chooses death to witness her or his belief was reportedly of central significance. Political manipulation of individual agency seems to characterize the contemporary discourse of martyrdom. Perhaps we should not rule out the possibility that such manipulation lies also behind some of the martyrological discourse of earlier eras. However I cannot deal systematically with this last question in the context of the present paper, and will rather return to my short ethnographic account.

Upon hearing the word *qedosha*, I made an instant comment turning to one of Daphna's closest friends standing next to me. Incidentally the friend's father is one of the chief ideologues of the Canaanite movement that was especially active in Israel in the late forties and the early fifties of the twentieth century (Diamond 1986; Shavit 1987; Kuzar 2001). The major platform of this minuscule cultural movement, however of some consequence, was to diminish the influence of Jewishness and to ground Israeli identity in the territorial aspect of Canaan and the common heritage of the peoples of the land west of Jordan valley prior to the Moslems, Christians, and the Jews. The Canaanite ideology failed to incite the masses. However, its secularist, almost pagan, message infiltrated such enterprises as the reshaping of Jewish holiday traditions in the context of the agricultural life of kibbutzim. It is therefore noteworthy that the secularizing tendency of some parts of public language has with regard to the language of public mourning, especially concerning violence occurring in the context of national conflict, suffered a blatant failure. The way martyrs figure in public uses of language is a major example of this.

Let us return to Daphna. By the current language usage, applied for instance by the Rector of the Hebrew University (at least outwardly a perfectly secularized person) in his words of lament at the funeral, her name may or perhaps "should" be appended by the cliché *hashem yiqqom dammah* "may God revenge her blood" – routinely added to the names of victims of terror in speech as well as writing (obituaries, ads of mourning etc.). One could assume that the forwarding of the act of revenge to the Almighty in those words expresses a belief in the governance that will restore some kind of moral balance into the grim reality experienced by mourners. Conceivably it could then serve to cancel any ideas about human revenge meted out by official agents of the state or others. There is, notwithstanding, a danger for another alternative to emerge, that will find some footing from biblical traditions onwards, that the collective "we" of the speaker envisages itself as the legitimate tool for the fulfillment of divine justice, dictated by internal group interests.

Since the religious language of the present quotes heavily from classical and medieval sources, I will now sketch some of the historical connotations emerging from the linguistic usages of *qedosha* (masc. *qadosh*) and *hashem yiqqom dammah* (masc. *dammo*).

The main usage of *qadosh* according to the dictionary of the Hebrew Bible concordance is "holy" as an attribute of God (translates into the *sanctus* of the Latin mass, according to Isaiah 6:3 *Qadosh, qadosh, qadosh adonai tsevaot*). Imparting the idea of emulation of the divine, anybody of great righteousness and adherence to God, and in special cases also Israel as a people (Exodus 19:6) may be described by the term. It also denotes places, objects, and persons who are not in any way defiled, and serves generally as the antonym for impure and secular.

In Rabbinical literature of late antiquity the connection between *qadosh* and martyrdom is created in complete dialogue with the emergence of martyrdom in Christianity, as shown in the above mentioned work of Boyarin. The main semantic extension of the concept consists of an act of sacrificing one's life to testify (the Greek etymon of "martyr") to the existence of God, an act that sanctifies His name and elevates it. The expression in rabbinic literature is indeed the verbal compound "to sanctify His name", rather than an attribute of the martyrs themselves. The holiness of the martyrs is thus derived from their own act and from the holiness of its addressee, God, rather than from the atrocity meted out to them by others. This may be understood as intimately associated with the change in mentality occurring in late antique culture, first in the eastern part of the Mediterranean and later in most of the Roman Empire. This change may be best formulated as a new stage in the development of subjectivity and individual responsibility, expressed especially in the texts of Early Christianity and Rabbinic Judaism in parallel.

In medieval Jewish texts there is a slow but clear semantic shift that turns over the agency to create martyrs, *qedoshim*, to the executors. One could speculate on the transformation and varieties of Jewish identity, subjectivity, and agency in the transport from the land of origin, to first the Moslem, then the Christian Diaspora. Spanish-Jewish Maimonides (11th century Moslem Spain) in his essay on conversion calls those who prefer to die rather than embrace another religion "saints" (*qedoshim*) thus still retaining the exertion of a free will (Kellner 1991: 49–59). The chronicles describing the pogroms against the Jews of the Rhine valley (notably Speier, Worms and Metz), as a result of the zealotry of the crusaders on their way to the Holy Land, also apply the term for those who refused to Christianize, often in the context of cruel torture and desperate acts such as suicide and slaughtering their own children (Yuval 2000: 108–218; Einbinder 2000). From the fifteenth century onwards in Jewish texts from Germany (the emic term being Ashkenaz) *qedoshim* and *qadosh* have become standard usage for Jews being killed by non-Jews in a variety of contexts. Thus in the seventeenth century autobiography of the remarkable woman Glikl Hamel, two Jewish thieves who were caught and repudiated the clemency of conversion are called by her "saints". In a number of epic poems of historical topics, for instance the victims of a great fire in Frankfurt are called *qedoshim* although there is no indication in the text that the fire was anything else but a calamity (Lowenthal 1977; Davis 1995).[2]

The earliest occurrence of the dictum *hashem yiqqom dammo* that I have been able to identify is the 13th century Spanish poet-hermeneutic Moshe Ibn-Ezra's elaboration on Deuteronomy 32:43: "Rejoice, o you nations, with his people, for he will avenge the blood of his servants, and will render vengeance to his adversaries, and will be merciful to his land and to his people". This first half of the final verse of Moses' lengthy prophetic and didactic valediction (in which he outlines all the calamities that will befall Israel due to their disobedience before God will finally absolve them) is commented by Ibn-Ezra with the above mentioned exhortation, in plural: *hashem yiqqom dammam.*

In the twentieth century a completely new vocabulary for death, especially Jewish death, was created through the lethal industry of World War II and the Shoah. Ethical and political texts referring to the victims of Shoah often call them *qedoshim*. A forest of six million trees planted in the mountains close to Jerusalem, to commemorate the victims of Shoah, is consequently called "The Martyrs' Forest" – *ya'ar ha-qedoshim*. The very term "Holocaust" denotes a religious connection. This is a deplorable association to sacrifice, atonement, purgation. It constitutes a reply to the metaphor of defilement attached to the victims by the Nazis and thereby resumes it. This discursive act has aptly been critiqued by Giorgio Agamben:

"The wish to lend a sacrificial aura to the extermination of the Jews by means of the term 'Holocaust' was, from this perspective, an irresponsible historiographical blindness. The Jew living under Nazism is the privileged negative referent of the new biopolitical sovereignty and is, as such, a flagrant case of *homo sacer* in the sense of a life that may be killed but not sacrificed. The truth – which is difficult for the victims to face, but which we must have the courage not to cover with sacrificial veils – is that the Jews were exterminated not in a mad and giant holocaust but exactly as Hitler had announced, 'as lice', which is to say, as bare life. … If today there is no longer any one clear figure of the sacred man, it is perhaps because we are all virtually *homines sacri*" (Agamben 1998: 114–115).[3]

The final sentence of this quote may be interpreted as a sinister description of the reality of terror of state, religious, political as well as individual nature.

I offer this all too concise historical excursus because it seems absolutely necessary to keep these facts in mind if we wish to even try to understand the complex resonance of the usage of *qedosha* for a woman like Daphna Shpruch. What the performer of the funeral service (not a rabbi, by the way, but a member of the hevra *qadisha,* 'the holy association" – an ancient institution responsible for the handling of the corpse and the funeral) did not know was that Daphna Shpruch was a fervent peace activist, one of the Women in Black of Jerusalem's Paris Square, women who in their body and presence have for fifteen years, since the beginning of the first Intifada, stood at the heart of Israel's capital, voicing (if mostly in silence) their resistance and disagreement with the occupation and oppression of the Palestinians. Her death thus signals a double appropriation: that of her murderer who appropriated her as an enemy, as part of the occupation, a fact that no Israeli can avoid whatever the degree of her resistance to the majority politics is. The other appropriation is by the rhetoric of occupation, especially by applying on her the tag *qedosha,* communicating a rhetoric and state of mind fed and fueled by every act of terrorism.

The enormous impact of the peoples of the Middle East and especially the Holy Land for the religious history of Europe and the entire world resonates again through the dialogic double construction of the qedoshim and the *shuhada* (sing. *shahid*), the Arabic term for martyr.[4] The complexity of the lethal dialogue between those two concepts of martyrdom would need a much more thorough ethnography and especially a study of mass media than can be provided here. However, a theoretical insight that seems fruitful in this context is Homi Bhabha's concept of "mimicry", in his cultural analysis of colonialism inspired by Lacanian psychology:

"In mimicry, the representation of identity and meaning is rearticulated along the axis of metonymy. As Lacan reminds us, mimicry is like camouflage, not a harmonization of repression of difference, but a form of resemblance, that differs from or defends presence by displaying it in part, metonymically. Its threat, I would add, comes from the prodigious and strategic production of conflictual, fantastic, discriminatory 'identity effects' in the play of a power that is elusive because it hides no essence, no 'itself'" (Bhabha 1994:90).

The threat mentioned by Bhabha reminds us of the powerful effect of religious language when geared into the business of stereotyping the other in creating the fantasy of averting the threat. The discursive transformation is perceptively described by Paul Ricoeur:

"Defilement itself is scarcely a representation, and what representation there is is immersed in a specific sort of fear that blocks reflection. With defilement we enter into the reign of Terror. Thereupon the philosopher recalls Spinoza's *nec spe nec metu*: hope for nothing in order to fear nothing; and he learns from the psychoanalyst that this fear is akin to an obsessional neurosis" (Ricoeur 1969: 25).

The moral, religious interpretation of terror results then, according to Ricoeur, in a problematic apology: "If it is true that man suffers because he is impure, then God is innocent" (31–32). Ricoeur's dilemma, that has been reiterated by him numerous times, whether in dealing with Shoah or the biblical book of Job, sharpens the problematic arising between the canonized forms of religion and their potential for either interpreting the violence of the other religiously, or the worse case, in turning violence into a religious act.

This essay cannot be brought to its inconclusive end without mentioning a private nightmare of mine that was sharpened by the reactions on the Israeli raid in the Jenin refugee camp in 2001. Is it possible that by legitimizing the foundation of Israel on the martyrdom of the Shoah, Western consciousness may have set a challenge for the Palestinians to produce a martyrdom of the same magnitude in order to establish Palestine? If so, are the Jews again cast in the taboo-laden role of the Sacred Executioner traditionally allotted to them by European culture? (Maccoby 1982). The inflamed effect of the usage of *martyr-shahid-qadosh* on all sides of the Middle Eastern conflict, the Western, European and Third World "audiences" included, becomes thus a dangerous weapon. How will the Jews in Israel harness the moral traditions of Judaism in order to subvert and counteract this karma?

The following poem by Israeli poetess Agi Mishol does not conclude this essay but rather adds another uneasy voice into the complex and multi-vocal discourse on the terror of martyrdom:

"The afternoon darkens,
and you are only twenty."
Nathan Alterman, *Afternoon in the Market*

"You are only twenty
and your first pregnancy is an exploding bomb.
Under your broad skirt you are pregnant with dynamite
and metal shavings. This is how you walk in the market,
ticking among the people, you, Andaleeb Takatkah.

Someone changed the workings in your head
and launched you toward the city;
even though you come from Bethlehem,
the Home of Bread, you chose a bakery.
And there you pulled the trigger inside yourself,
and flung yourself into the sky
together with the Sabbath loaves,
sesame and poppy seed.

Together with Rebecca Fink you flew up
with Yelena Konreeb from the Caucasus
and Nissim Cohen from Afghanistan
and Suhila Houshy from Iran
and two Chinese you took with you
to your death.

Since then, other matters
have obscured your story,
about which I speak all the time
without having anything to say."
(Translated from the Hebrew by Lisa Katz)

Notes

1. Also see the following groundbreaking works: Frend, 1967, and Bowersock, 1995. Whereas Bowersock's historical approach situates the origin of the phenomenon strictly within early Christianity, Boyarin's cultural method opts for a dialogic, mutual emergence of the phenomenon in a way that breaks down the dichotomy between the two entities in their early phases of formation.
2. The information regarding Glikl as well as early modern German Jewish historical poetry has been generously shared by my friend Hava Turniansky, the greatest expert on these things and many others.
3. The centrality of sacrificial violence is the focus of discussion in Girard, 1977, especially relevant for our discussion is chapter 6, "From Mimetic Desire to the Monstrous Double".
4. Due to ignorance I cannot venture a similar reconstruction of the historical roots and associations of the Arabic term *shahid* as I have tried to provide for the Hebrew *qadosh*.

References

Agamben, Giorgio 1998: *Homo Sacer: Sovereign Power and Bare Life*. Translated by Daniel Heller-Roazen. Stanford, Calif.

Bhabha, Homi 1994: *The Location of Culture*. London.

Bowersock, Glen 1995: *Martyrdom and Rome. The Wiles Lectures given at the Queen's University of Belfast*. Cambridge.

Boyarin, Daniel 1999: *Dying for God: Martyrdom and the Making of Christianity and Judaism*. Stanford, Calif.

Davis, Natalie Zemon 1995: *Women on the margins: three seventeenth-century lives*. Cambridge, Mass.

Diamond, Janes S. 1986: *Homeland or Holy Land? The "Canaanite" critique of Israel*. Bloomington.

Einbinder, Susan 2002: *Beautiful Death: Jewish Poetry and Martyrdom in Medieval France*. Princeton.

Frend, W.H.C. 1967: *Martyrdom and Persecution in the Early Church: A Study of a Conflict from the Maccabees to Donatus*. Garden City, N.Y.

Girard, René 1977: *Violence and the Sacred*. Translated by Patrick Gregory. Baltimore.

Kellner, Menachem 1991: *Maimonides on Judaism and the Jewish People*. Albany.

Kuzar, Ron 2001: *Hebrew and Zionism: A Discourse Analytic Cultural Study*. Berlin.

Lowenthal, Marvin (ed. and translator) 1977: *The memoirs of Glueckel of Hameln*. New introduction by Robert S. Rosen. New York: Schocken Books.

Maccoby, Hyam 1982: *Human Sacrifice and the Legacy of Guilt*. London.

Ricoeur, Paul 1969: *The Symbolism of Evil*. Translated by Emerson Buchanan. Boston.

Shavit, Yaacove 1987: *The Hebrew Nation: A Study in Israeli Heresy and Fantasy*. London.

Yuval, Israel Jacob 2000: *'Two Nations in Your Womb' – Perceptions of Jews and Christians*. Tel-Aviv. (Hebrew. The English version is in press at the University of California Press 4.)

Part IV

Murmurs and Silences

Making Sense of Memory

Monuments and Landscape in Croatian Istria[1]

Jonas Frykman

> Frykman, Jonas 2003: Making Sense of Memory. Monuments and Landscape in Croatian Istria. – Ethnologia Europaea 33:2: 107–120.
>
> When the actual terror is over, how do you reconcile without trying to pay back? With the falling apart of Yugoslavia, past, suppressed injustices remerged and were frequently used to connect the present with bitter memories. In the ethnically diverse region of Istria, however, it has been difficult for any group to claim its interpretation of history to be superior to others. Seeking to explain the Istrian case and within it the role of the *esuli*, the article juxtaposes the material discourse represented by monuments with the workings of memory and the dynamics which jostle sleeping, hidden, or private memory into public discourse. It is argued that in Istria, the absence of an ethnic "master narrative," and the coexistence of many different groups sharing the territory has been useful for keeping nightmarish memory of ethnic violence at bay. Instead, place has come to matter more than history. Within landscapes and monuments, experiences of terror and narratives of martyrdom find a resting place, however uneasy.
>
> *Prof. Dr. Jonas Frykman, Dept. of Ethnology, University of Lund, Finngatan 8, SE-223 62 Lund. E-mail: Jonas.Frykman@etn.lu.se*

"Say a hawk came out of the blue and seized one of your chickens. What can you do? You can't get it back. The hawk has flown away. You have no means of hunting it down, or killing it. All you can do is accept and go on with your life. But you don't really forgive, you don't really forget. You simply accept that there's nothing you can do to change what has happened" (Jackson 2003:100).

Keeping Memory Alive

This story takes place in the region of Istria in Croatia. It is mainly devoted to the politics of memory and how particular kinds of sleepers – the victims from the Second World War – were used in an ongoing argument over the ethnic or political belonging to places and territories. Memory can be perceived as symbolic power, which can be used to support different discourses and claims striving for dominance and legitimacy (Müller 2002:25).[2] In this process the dead support memories: they are looked upon as part of the landscape, the soil that has received them. What was culture has now become nature.[3]

Memory is not really what people recollect, but how they manage to make sense of the past. Memory is "not a vessel of truth or a mirror of interests, but a process of constructing meaning" (Müller 2002:30). There must be a context that promotes a particular interpretation of past experiences that make them fit into the present. In this article I look at the recycling of memories" (Bet-El 2002) or the "constant return of the same" (Ćolović 2002) in relation to the war during the 1990s in Croatia. Memories from the Second World War were not allowed to be history; instead they were used to explain present events. In Istria, however, the past slowly passed into history, leaving the present open to a multitude of interpretations and the hope for a future between warring factions. The monuments and lack of linkage between Istrian identity, sense of national belonging and the memory of past atrocities both shed light on Istria's circumstances during the conflict in the 90s.

In the summer of 2001, I met a man from the city of Motovun in the center of Istria. He was born in 1947, the son of a mother who spoke a

Venetian-Italian dialect and a father who spoke Čakavian-Croatian. At home they switched between the two languages. His statements open up the complexity of Istrian existence:

"Trying to understand people in Istria will be very hard for you," he said defiantly while looking at me, the stranger, "because you will only end up in confusion, and being a scientist, you want clear-cut answers." "Very few people here in Motovun," he said pointing to the huge flagstones covering the open square in front of the church, "could look at this square and say that my great grandfather laid those stones. The identity that you people look at is not a matter of who you are but where you are and how you manage on this poor land." And he continued on with a parable, which in its condensed symbolic content had real, personal meaning. "When I was born, my mother went to the social services in Buzet to ask for aid for her poor household. The person at the desk did not give her any money, but found an old flag. I do not know if it was Italian or Yugoslav, but it was handed over to her. Mother washed it till all the colors went out and it became soft enough. Then she used it for my diapers and I did everything a child could do in it."

Foundation of the State

Memory had a very peculiar importance for the shaping of the Yugoslav state, writes sociologist John Allcock (2000). The political legitimacy of Yugoslavia was founded on the experience of the "National Liberation Struggle," which produced an identity in sharp contrast to the interethnic atrocities of the Second World War. The slogan "Brotherhood and Unity" united the peoples of the many ethnic groups comprising the pre-war Kingdom of Yugoslavia together with those who belonged to the short-lived Nazi puppet states in Serbia and Croatia. The victory over fascism won by fighting partisan was established as the founding memory, and was crucial in lending the state legitimacy – but appeasement meant throwing hatred into history's deep-freeze (Bet-El 2002:208). This engendered lasting dilemmas that contributed to the break-up of Yugoslavia. One concerned time: memories could hardly be passed on to a generation that did not share the experiences. "The 'partisan generation' could have no successors. In this respect, Yugoslavia epitomized Max Weber's observations about the necessary crisis which attends succession to charismatic authority" (Allcock 2000:421).

Alternate memories had had to be actively suppressed and made illegal – although they were bound to surface sooner or later. People became aware of their memories as politically important, but also as not to be communicated openly, only in private "while fields were tilled or over a family meal" (Bet-El 2002: 208). They became part and parcel of people's habitus, shaping their attitude toward life and everyday practice. Suppressed in public, memories forged connections to objects and places. The strong tradition of attending family graves was part of this process of keeping unspeakable memories alive.

Only after Tito's death and the slow dissolving of the state, did the suppressed resurface. Personal memories bore the mark of true experience, and now people could come out and say, "I remember", "I was there!" (Bet-El 2002: 209ff). The rarely uttered personal memory became public, and eventually – in distorted form – nationalized, as the true memory of the various oppressed ethnicities in the republic. Istria's ethnic composition, however, is too complex for such a waking-up to nationalism.

Contested Territory

Istria is the peninsula that thrusts into the northern part of the Adriatic Sea. For hundreds of years it was part of the "imperial borderland" between the Danube Monarchy and the Ottoman Empire (Lampe 1989, Allcock 2000). Stable state-formation or ethnic homogeneity is structurally difficult in a borderland. The maritime power of Venice had dominated Istrian towns and marketplaces along the coast, exercising cultural influence since medieval times; Habsburg had ruled the inland areas. After World War Two, the Iron Curtain fell close to Trieste, there where Istria ends and Italy begins. Istria was under fascist Italy between the wars, and was now a borderland to the West.[4]

The beauty of the landscape is surely the

first thing that strikes the visitor today. In marketing it as the most successful tourist region in Croatia, the tourist board of Istria relies on concepts such as ecology, magic, exoticism, and the "exploration of your true self". With its undulating hills, Istria resembles a less exploited and more mysterious Tuscany, its long beaches forming an imagined Mediterranean landscape.[5]

The tourist image mirrors and supports the creation of a regional identity in the context of contemporary European regionalism. Istrians have been quick to ignore the twentieth century and dwell on almost forgotten Habsburg, Venetian, Roman, or Illyrian roots instead, for archaeology here serves as a better guide to the past than history. The recent past is so problematic, so traumatic, so filled with uncertainties and problems that a mythical history with a strong connection to the landscape is more appealing. Medieval towns, old folk customs, and ancient folk music and instruments still prevail (Frykman 2002). The new narration of Istrian identity is told in poetic terms that allude to this mythical past, and it is articulated in objects or souvenirs, and by "colonizing" the extant territory of Istria with a history open to the multitudes and to the many (Frykman 2003).[6]

The borderland experience has meant Istrian popular culture remains extremely local, for the population cowered through the ages while the great rulers were fighting. The abundance of dialects, music, food habits, and variations in material culture is still striking today. The place where you lived provided continuity, while capital cities changed and emperors played with language and names.[7] Even now there are no dominant urban centers, just a larger commercial town on the west coast (Pula), and an inland administrative center (Pazin).[8] People continue to live in small towns or in the countryside.

After the Second World War, the majority of Italian-speaking Istrians were forced to leave, and some of the houses left empty were nationalized or taken over by people moving in from Medjimurje in northern Croatia, or from Macedonia or Serbia or other far-away places. The actual number of *esuli* – Italians – forced to leave has been hotly debated, since their number is politically important in claims over the contested territory. Anthropologist Pamela Ballinger suggests it may have been from 200,000 to 350,000 people, though this includes Dalmatian refugees (2003:1). Other investigations have suggested there were only half or a third that number.[9]

But this was not the only exodus, for after Mussolini's takeover, some 70,000 Croats were forced out of their Istrian homes. In the Croatian cities of Karlovac and Zagreb, entire blocks carried names of Istrian towns. To fill the gap, some 50,000 Italians, mostly from southern Italy, moved in; many *esulis* were thus actually newcomers. The man from Motovun cited above held the opinion that 70,000 of today's Istrian population were "parachutists" with no roots in the place. On these grounds, any story of who the territory "belongs" to and whose roots are the deepest is easily challenged. As a result, all groups compete over who had been most victimized. Only on political grounds – the victory over fascism – was it possible to write a message into the landscape.

A Partisan Monument

Istria was the scene of intense fighting at the end of the Second World War. Numerous memorials, monuments, and graves are devoted to human sacrifice and the victory over fascism. Detailed notes from my field-diary show how such monuments are given a predominant position not only in the cemeteries where they are found but also in the entire landscape.

"Easter is the time of death, burial and resurrection. 2002 was the coldest in living memory in Istria. Istrians, as well as many holiday-makers from Germany, Austria and Italy preferred to stay indoors. The *bura* – a northern wind that sweeps icy weather down from the Alps and makes the trees sway and the tiles clatter – even brought snow some days ago. My wife and I were staying at one of the two well-equipped hotels in Opatija for its convenient location for this project. On Maundy Thursday, we drove along the curvy road to the nearby village of Veprinac, trying to get a view without the wind chilling us to the marrow.

The customary churchyard, sheltered by the church and surrounded by a wall, was defended by a row of cypresses. We were the only visitors. Most of the graves bore post-1970s dates, with names hinting that those interred here were of Croatian origin. Only a few faded, moss-covered stones with Italian names remained from earlier generations. In the center of this small churchyard stood a huge square block of pure white marble. As with many of the partisan monuments, the stone had been brought in from the island of Brač, its marble renowned since Roman times for its luster and durability. Crowned with a red, five-pointed star, the porous, almost living marble had such a majestic presence it involuntarily caught the eye. As we drew closer, we saw that the huge block was surrounded by smaller blocks, all with the same cubic form, but made of granite and polished to near-perfection.

The marble block carried the inscription '1945' and to highlight it, a red star crowned the year. Each small stone bore a name, but no date or place of birth. Perhaps they were so well-known by every villager that nothing more was needed? Or perhaps not? Several of them carried the inscription *Nepoznat* – unknown. The blocks commemorating the unknown contributed to the impression of a completely symmetrical archipelago, a solar system where all the planets rotated around the sun at right angles, or perhaps a Roman army clustered around its centurion.

The monument depicted an insistent, idealized picture of a State and its citizens where everything is a carbon copy of the State, where every individual – to use Althusser's expression – is interpolated by power. Men had died for a good cause and even the death of the unknown had contributed to the cause. Their sacrifice had not been in vain, their otherwise fragmented, risky life had direction and purpose: The Cause and not Foolishness had won. As things appeared here, in the churchyard at Veprinac, so they should be perceived in the country as a whole, the small scale reflecting the larger scale. Rudoljub Čolaković, in his diary of the partisan battles during the National Liberation Struggle, writes about the symbolic importance of granite:

"To have spent oneself and fallen in a senseless struggle leading nowhere would have been terrible. Yet nothing could have been more glorious than thus to give one's whole self to a cause ... From the blood my lost comrades had shed had sprung the triumph of the revolution. By their death they had placed their noble lives into the foundations – firmer than granite – of a new and brighter world, which it was now for us to construct" (1962:415).

Most graves were decorated with daffodils, as an Easter symbol and token of respect for the dead. Even the partisan monument was decked with a wreath bearing the red, white and blue ribbons of the Croatian flag, but without greeting from either the party or the city council but instead from "The Association of Opatija Fighters" honoring their former comrades. They were now commemorating something private that justified their lives, rather than something that concerned society as a whole.

In the Land of Monuments

Those who fell, as victims on the losing side, however, were not commemorated. As in all of former Yugoslavia, monuments and politics went hand in hand, creating a cultural web so dense that any deviation would be unthinkable. In market places, at road crossings, parks, and on individual buildings, the same messages were spelled out. In Istria today they are more numerous than churches and chapels. Working the fields, transporting the harvest of grapes, meeting at the café and in church entailed passing a memorial of some kind. They became not only a part of the landscape and its architecture but were also intertwined with body movements and everyday tasks and practices, part of peoples' life-worlds. Perhaps they are not something to think *about* or reflect over, but something people think *with* (cf. Frykman & Gilje 2003:37; Gillis 1994:5).

Monuments are a strange kind of material culture – with lives of their own. To see a monument in Istria is like striking a key on the piano and listening to the full resonance, or like a choir with high, low, and loud voices all singing the same tune. They were meant to create the memory that the State rested upon, yet victory over fascism was only the beginning of a larger collective story. Just as a single church could extend its message through all of Christianity, so every local partisan monument could call to those in Pazin and Zagreb, in Belgrade, in Sarajevo, in Skopje, Titograd and Ljubljana, as well as to those in socialist Eastern Europe. Ideologically connected, these monuments emphasized that power and real life had been created somewhere else – while at the same time shrinking Marshal Tito to local proportions.[10]

Monuments are not the equivalent of memories. Usually they remain a part of everyday life, something you pass when going to work. But under what circumstances do they come alive? The war in the 1990s documented and clarified the answer, for many of the half-forgotten partisan monuments throughout Croatia took on a different life. What had been integrated into village life for decades suddenly became visible and laden with meaning, reminding all of long-suppressed injustices.

The ancient town of Solin is situated a few kilometers from the Dalmatian coastal town Split, and is a former Roman settlement filled with archaeological remains and monuments. Solin also held memories of partisan fights that had slowly seeped into local cultural heritage, and a partisan monument, in the form of a bridge parapet, stood over a small river in Solin's central park. Names of townsmen killed in the fighting were cast in copper and mounted together on a perforated wall background, and the fast-flowing water of the river glittered through the names. As a monument it was simple, tastefully designed, and unpretentious. Passing the bridge meant being made aware of the suffering. In the war that started in 1991, the Yugoslav Navy blocked the harbor of Split while the Army occupied the hinterland. Anti-Yugoslav sentiment ran high. And during the conflict, someone blasted a big hole in the middle of Solin's partisan monument.

Symbolically, this vandalism could be interpreted as a sign that people had become aware of the missing past, of the memories the monument was supposed to repress. To gain access to a local identity, a historic continuity, another memory, the monument had to be pierced. Solin was not the only place where such iconoclasm took place. According to a survey recently published by *Savez Boraca* (the "Association of Anti-Fascist Fighters"), 731 partisan monuments in Croatia were destroyed during the 1990s – most in places where active fighting took place and sentiments of national belonging were thereby provoked – and 2,233 other war memorials demolished (*Rušenje antifašističkih spomenika u Hrvatskoj 1990–2000*, 2001).

Invisible Monuments

Perhaps violence is needed to make certain monuments visible, for there is such a self-destructive capacity built into them. Monuments are built to create clarity and unity where doubt prevails – irrespective of the ideology of the regime – and they are expected not just to have the power to commemorate but also to forge and sustain a single version of the past (Gillis 1994).

Yet memorials are often over-explicit, repeating the same message in different forms. Solin's bridge parapet was an illustration: Cast in bronze and stretched over the flowing water, the names were meant to create stability in the midst of movement, with stone laid on stone and names cast in copper. Monuments seldom commemorate variation, multiplicity, or the transitive, but rather are aimed to create continuity and confidence. Yet confidence has a strange capacity to remain unseen, unless of course it is no longer there. As phenomenology points out, the life-world that we encompass has to be invisible in order to be open and manageable (Frykman & Gilje 2003).

Therefore the life of a monument is much more precarious than any other kind of public art, as it depends on its ability to be itself through its expression while at the same time representing something else. Martin Heidegger points out that art has a particular capacity to "transport us out of the realm of the ordinary," as "artwork opens up a world and at the same time allows us to see that something is concealed" (Polt 1999:138) in its transgression of immediately available interpretations.[11] Monuments generally do not create a multitude of interpretations through their own expression and are a mere representation or a cliché; they also seldom serve as an expression of the place where they stand, nor do they interact with the surrounding landscape.

The general idea is *not* to let the landscape and its people emerge, but to challenge them instead to tackle the past in such a way as to make it appear as quantifiable or offering a clear message. Showing the exact number of the fallen gave the state, or the cause, added credibility and confidence by creating memory. The intention was to give to the everyday, to people, animals and nature – everything we call *hic et nunc* – a framework that would transform it into a personal recollection of private and collective suffering.

Yet when political intention meets an over-explicit artistic expression though socialist realism, monuments become paraphrases rather than original works of art. Once you have seen Comrade Tito on hundreds of stones, with fist outstretched in front of fluttering standards, and red stars, and tensed arm muscles lifting rifles, or swords, or hammers, or axes, you start to wonder why the message has to be so all-embracing. An over-explicitness actually diminishes the melancholy nature of the many partisan monuments of Istria, as if they intended to deprive the past of its secrets rather than reveal them.

In the late 1940s, large red letters were daubed on the walls of most towns, proclaiming: "Long live Free Yugoslavia. Long live Tito. Long live Stalin. Our dead haven't given their lives in vain. We want to belong to Yugoslavia." Such slogans were meant to justify and convince everyone that the region should come under socialist rule.

For many years after the war, it was unclear if Istria really should belong to Italy or Yugoslavia. As time went on, these stirring messages became self-evident, and in practice invisible. Today, only pale pink fragments of the letters remain, blending in with numerous alternate and later layers of lime wash and plaster. No destruction of partisan monuments took place in Istria, for in a number of ways these memorials were so much part of the everyday that they had become invisible. No acts of violence could make them come alive again.

Opposing the Slavs

The majority of the Italian-speaking population of Istria was forced into exile. A coherent narrative took shape among them, highlighting their pain and losses but also identifying the perpetrators as ethnic Slavs operating under the banner of Communism. The official Yugoslav version says: the Italian minority "chose" to emigrate, since as fascists they had to save their necks.

Pamela Ballinger has movingly described how the stories were not only kept alive in ghettos, refugee camps and among the many *esuli* in exile, but also how they were supported by right-wing political parties that had reason to despise the communist regime in Yugoslavia. In exile, the vision of an Istrian landscape, never to be seen again as it had been, somehow became truer. It was not possible to visit and thus remember the places where they had once lived and where their relatives were buried. In Italy, as well as among those who remained – the *rimasti* – centers for collecting life histories were organized, and documentation of a life once "Italian" was conducted. Being *esuli* was often understood as being a victim, and as such, certain about your belonging and cultural identity: it promoted an essentialist understanding of who Italians were and who their opponents were. Communists who had taken over Istria were viewed as barbaric Socialist Slavs – *schiavi* – from the Balkans, and the antithesis of Europe, of Culture and Civilization, which were what the Italians possessed (Ballinger 2002:245). Yet such stories could easily be countered by tales about what Italian fascists had done to the Croats and Slovenes living in Istria. After all, the landscape had been impregnated with memorials to the victory over fascism.

With the beginning of the war in the 1990s, the stories told by the *esuli* in Italy started to resemble the ones told by Croats of the Communist Serbs, to say nothing about what the Serbs were saying about the fascist Croats. Out of this confusion – of stories about the *chetniks*, the *ustashi*, the partisans, and the fascists – the *esuli* could tell was this was all about: It was the Slavs doing it again! It was the ever-repeating pattern of the Balkans! When the Bosnian atrocities in Srebrenica and Omarska hit the front pages, exiled Italians could say: "What the Slavs are doing to one another they did to us fifty years ago" (Ballinger 2003:146). Gruesome stories about how Communists engaged in ethnocide were revived: how they rounded up Italians, tied their hands together with metal wire and threw them down, still alive, into deep caves (*foibe*) to die a slow, cruel death. Such mass executions were the preferred method in the process of ethnic cleansing, and symbolically, *esuli* were siding with Jewish victims of the Holocaust (Ballinger 2003). No other argument can gain such instant moral support in today's political rhetoric, and thus old accusations gained new credibility in the 1990s, and voices were raised to put the perpetrators guilty of old crimes finally on trial, and to finally force official admission that past atrocities had been inflicted on the Italians.

The Eternal Return of the Same and Truths More True

Yet while the *esuli* worked to form a coherent interpretation of their past as one of ethnic victimization, there is always the possibility of simply being a victim in a destiny of greater magnitude than man can affect. The Serbian anthropologist Ivan Čolovič has described it as a step beyond historical time into mythical time. People in Serbia realized that what were once private memories now fit a pattern that was the fate of "our people" – an ethnic group beyond history. Events during the break-up of the Yugoslav federation gave meaning to events fifty years before, and from that it was easy to slip deeper into a mythical time. People were faced *not* with factual events, but with the eternal presence and eternal return of the same: It started for the Serbs with Kosovo Polje in 1389, but each ethnic group had its own story of victimization (Čolović 2002:13).

When Slavonia (bordering Serbia) was invaded in the spring of 1991, one of my interview partners received a telephone call from his elderly aunt, who like him lived in the capital city of Zagreb, and who sobbed into the receiver:

"Now it has started! Look at what they are doing to us again," *Us* was the Croatian family, where since the days of Maria Theresia, Hungarians, Croats, Serbs, Germans, Slovaks, and French had produced a remarkably multiethnic mix that was the hallmark of the Danube basin. *They* were yet another instance of the returning Serbs who marched in waves through her home village.

My interview partner was a retired Senior Administrative Officer who had moved to the capital from his Slavonian home village a long time ago. As a young boy he had watched his village being invaded by armed men. The educated bourgeoisie and civil servants, the pharmacists, doctors, veterinarians, school-teachers, lawyers, shopkeepers, and businessmen, about three hundred of them, were rounded up that first evening at one end of the small marketplace. "They weren't further away than this," my partner said, spreading his arms out wide. As state and local government employees, these men were connected in different ways to Ante Pavelić's fascist vassal state, and some were also *Volksdeutsche*. To the partisans, these were by definition enemies: class enemies, political enemies, collectively guilty, ethnically suspect. They were taken to the rubbish dump of the village and proceedings were kept short. As a token of contempt, their bodies were dumped into the village sewers. Some time later, a monument was erected in the village to commemorate the victory of the partisans and the destruction of fascism.[12]

In this family, the memory of those prominent villagers was kept alive through half-whispered stories, was alluded to among relatives, formed the basis of their understanding of the world: The remembrance was obvious yet seldom expressed. It is said that every generation has to live through its own war, yet the aunt lived long enough to live through three of them. Like so many others, she carried a memory that was hard to manage simply because it was so seldom articulated. It would have been politically dangerous, and a threat to her own safety to articulate that memory during the Yugoslav era, so that the "they are doing it to us again" complex could only be communicated to someone close, or to someone who had experienced the many transformations that same place had gone through, and who carried similar recollections. And now it was made obvious through the war: this story was told to me in visible, intense anger. The past was not dead; it had only been biding its time.

When people grow accustomed to the loose-endedness and superficiality of what is recorded in books, they live in increased fear of the past returning. When a new conflict breaks out, what has long been pushed aside will float to the surface as a commentary upon the present. In the former Yugoslavia, the past was therefore ready to wend its way back in, through a door standing ajar, with a nagging dread that the door might be flung wide open. In the many whispered narrations, everything was boiled together into a witches' brew of publicly acknowledged acts (some commemorated in monuments) and privately acknowledged cruelties and horrors. Secret information was handed down through families or heard from friends, and the fear thus conveyed made it reliable, physically tangible, yet with all the gory details. It was recognition rather than critical assessment that shaped the reception of the stories, for if you believed in the person, then you believed in the story: the accuracy did not need to be questioned.

The Dutch anthropologist Mattijs van de Port (1998) says that in the Balkans the past has a strangely formless character, present everywhere and yet nowhere. In his study of Novi Sad in 1990–92, he witnessed hatred and kinship suddenly blossoming alike. For generations, ill-treatment had been meted out by *them*, and an almost forgotten solidaristic *we* was suddenly triggered among ordinary businessmen, academics, bourgeoisie, and workers alike. People saw themselves as being at *their* mercy and living through a familiar, tragic fate.

Van de Port says something similar to Čolović, that the past is not so much something to be *understood* intellectually, as it is be *remembered* – and unfortunately, also to be *repeated* – but he turns the argument around. To Čolović, mythical time is a time of no war, while real time appears less often but bears the terrible hallmark of authenticity. But people in Novi Sad in the early 1990s lived instead with a dual chronology, a virtual one of Peace, Civilization and Culture and a real one of war, one where nightmares appear in the daytime and have a face. For in real time, you reconnect to a deeper truth, an inevitable insight into the fragility of human existence and to the realization that civilization is only a thin varnish on a harsh reality – and it is self-deception to deny it. Van de Port thus turns Norbert Elias' ideas about the process of civilization upside down. Elias's argument is only an ideology of the well-to-do in the Western world, a middle class belief that human nature is an ongoing project of progress and education. War makes the urgent undercurrent of barbarianism all too visible.

Thomas Hobbes would have agreed; peace is only a pause in Leviathan's heavy breathing. The culture Van de Port describes shows the eternal return of the same, an imagination heavily impregnated with the idea that war will repeatedly be unleashed, like the dark rain cloud hanging in the sky throughout Milcho Manchevski's film *Before the Rain*. When the rain cloud bursts, it is both expected and as impossible to stop as war itself; it washes everything clean as naturally and inevitably as the sun dries it up. Unreason temporarily takes over the power to control life, and while there is a bitterness in realizing "that which exists in me but also in you", there is also a strange sweetness.[13] War then serves the purpose of creating clarity in what, paradoxically, has been obscured in daily, peaceful life. Friend can now be differentiated from foe, good from evil, the brave fighter from the cowardly terrorist: "it is only in war that the true can be separated from the false" (van de Port 1998:222).

If so, then the draught from the door standing ajar is always wafting round your legs in an otherwise warm house. That understanding opens up no possibility of reconciliation, and no possibility of letting past terrors be instances of a unique combination of circumstances that we later will call history. Trying to make past horrors fit a pattern is like trying to control the past, and that is a road well travelled in narratives and tradition. It is a more dangerous conviction to hold to this notion of "the truer truth".

Off the Beaten Track

It is also not altogether true that the past was turned into history in an uncomplicated way or that past ills were forgotten. The pain was still there. Field notes from my visit to a grave – this time the first "illegal" commemoration of the fallen Italians – could serve as a basis for understanding the possibilities for reconciliation.[14]

"On Good Friday, we pointed our car in the direction of the town of Motovun, one of a number of small towns that crown the hills in this undulating landscape. In recent years it has become a popular tourist attraction. But it was the road to Motovun that was our goal, not the town itself. The day before, the archivist at the Istrian Center for the Registration of Cultural Memorials in Pazin had told us such an improbable story that we wanted to investigate it for ourselves. We drove by the village of Čiže, to find the memorial for the Italians who had fallen in the Second World War. We had never seen anything like it during our fieldwork excursions through the countryside mapping partisan monuments.

During the autumn of 2001, the road had been rebuilt to carry the increased traffic between Motovun and the regional center of Pazin. As the works' manager had driven along the road to inspect the upcoming tasks, he came across a newly built, enclosed space in a place that later became known as a 'Park of Remembrance' or memorial grove. Stones were exposed on which Italian names – and thus allegedly Fascists – were engraved.

In the summer, the authorities in Pazin had received a petition from a group of Italians – *esuli* from Istria, allegedly belonging to the Famiglia Montonese, in other words of Motovun origin – who had asked for permission to build a memorial. It was likely their relatives or neighbors had been killed here on May 10th 1945, but as yet these esuli had no place to go where they could mourn them. An agreement recently had been reached between Croatia and Italy concerning the protection of war graves, which in practice meant that esuli were given the right to commemorate their countrymen who had been executed during the war.

The Mayor of Pazin didn't know what to do. No one had ever considered that anything other than monuments for partisans could be built in the commune. One hardly needed permission for that – although it was a long time since one had been erected. In the old days, a monument was by no means a private thing but a concern for decision-making bodies like Savez Boraca. In the previous era, a monument had wider purposes: a token of appreciation or faithfulness to the Party, or to the whole idea of 'Brotherhood and Unity' – which could come in handy when asking for favors or privileges. If a costly road needed to be built, or water pipes laid and sewers constructed, an appeal was easier to accept if it came from people who had previously proven their reliability and citizenship. Besides, financial support could be obtained for building a partisan monument locally. It was a political statement aimed at the future.

The new request was made at a time when the authorities were not so much afraid about which monuments should be built, as they were considering which ones should be demolished. This was a region trying to repair its image among tourists after the recent war. Many a potential tourist was still afraid of coming to Croatia because warfare continued in Kosovo, Macedonia, and other distant parts of former Yugoslavia. For obvious reasons, many of the tourists who did come were from Italy – Trieste is only about an hour's drive away.

In towns like Motovun, newly painted road signs are in both Croatian and Italian. The names of the great partisan heroes now adorn not the center but the periphery, used to name 'donkey-paths,' as a local member of the Savez Boraca said with contempt. Joakim Rakovac is now the name of a back street, while the main road by the city wall has regained the old, Italian sounding toponym of Barbacan. This bilingualism does not really give in to the claims of the many esuli or right-wing parties, but to the fact that the Italian language and European belonging happen to coincide. Tolerance and multiculturalism are the politics of the EU. This implies that gratifying memories from fascist Italian times coincide with cultural heritage and the defense of ethnic minorities. How can one, if one is decently compassionate, prevent anybody from mourning their nearest and dearest at a place special to them?

Though the request caused some surprise, there was much that spoke against denying it outright. The result, therefore, was a very pragmatic decision: Erecting the Italian memorial site did not disturb the plans for further roadwork, so it was allowed to proceed. The applicants took this to mean they were given a free hand – provided that they didn't make a big fuss about it. So on May 10th 2001, the 'Park of Remembrance' – which the road manager had discovered – was inaugurated. A priest arrived from Italy to give a sermon, together with a local priest, a streamer was unfurled to blow in the wind, local dignitaries from Pazin and Motovun were present – and a few days after the ceremony, the local paper carried a short news item about it.

After a thorough search we found the memorial. The road runs through an agricultural landscape here, where cultivated fields alternate with shrubs and pine groves. If it had been partisan fights to be commemorated, this would not have been the place for a monument. While it was easy to find stretches of road with views extending for miles on either side, right here the countryside was undulating – hardly anything more – and there was nothing extraordinary about it. In the shadow of towering pines and next to a smaller road, was a green, waist-high, ordinary mesh wire fence with a gate, surrounding an area about half the size of a tennis court. As we opened the gate, we noticed a sign with an inscription in both Croatian and Italian that declared that though this was private property, those who wished to enter to pray were welcome to do so.

On the recently cleared, red Istrian soil, lay twenty white and roughly-hewn small stones, with one side inscribed with the names of the men to be remembered here – Tullio Stefanutti, Mario Reser, Giuseppe Belletti, etc. With one exception, they were all men who had died on the same day, May 10th 1945, the day after the official last day of the war. Their dates of birth and home districts were noted, all of them indicating surrounding villages and small towns – Trevisio, Montana (Trviž, Motovun) – and the men were all young. No other information was given.

The occasional visitor might stop to ask: Why here, in this comparatively out-of-the-way place? Was it a platoon of soldiers, a fascist *lega*? Were there as many as you could make room for on a lorry? Had there been a battle? Or was it an execution? It was difficult to find a context in which to fit the circumstances. There was no placard visible, as is usually the case for partisan monuments, and no standard holder for the three flags of Yugoslavia, the Republic, and the Party. Nor was there any sign of a Cause for which they had died, no company or country that they had fought for, no ideal.

Lying in front of each stone, on the grave, was a red, burnt-out candle and a bouquet of those strange churchyard flowers specially made so they never wither – obviously placed there by the same visiting party. In the center of the memorial grove, an altar had been built with the Latin inscription *Fiat voluntas tua*, "Thy will be done". The resurrection cross had been placed to the right of the altar, and someone must have given it a severe blow as it had fallen over on its side. To the left of the cross stood a simple marble tablet with a poem in Italian inscribed on it. While the altar expressed one expectation of a hidden Godly will, as it was unclear what significance the deaths held, the poem itself expressed only the grief and distress of the surviving relatives.

You did not hear the cries
of spouse or mother
when darkness fell upon you
and the horror.
A pain, bereft of word and end
became the lot of us
who stayed behind,
by force dispersed
around the world.

It was private, and not an official mourning, that pervaded the landscape, the grief of families once part of the region, and from their scattered diaspora in Australia or South America or the USA, the *esuli* had claimed their right to be remembered where they had once lived, and to bury their dead accordingly. Now, though the dead are commemorated in their rightful place, the memories have to be protected by fences, and constantly run the risk that they are more important to their old opponents than their relatives. Quietly provocative, the 'Park of Remembrance' challenged the ideological hegemony established by the partisan monuments. A message had surely been written into the landscape that had much wider implications than mere personal grief. Čiže was one of a number of mapped *foibe* where crimes against Italians had supposedly been carried out. For a long time, this and other places should have been made into real sites of mourning, the *esuli* claimed.

Thus, this was a successful statement that was bound to be followed by others, and the politicization of Istrian territory by monuments was about to begin once again. But this presupposed that the provocations were being registered as such. Silvio Delbello, President of the *Unione degli Istriani* (Association of Istrians) in Trieste gave a speech at the inauguration, defiantly stating that people in the abyss should have been treated as prisoners of war. The head of the Famiglia Montonese said instead that for them, creating this park ended the war, because they could now come without any fear to these graves and leave flowers.

Later that year, the chairman of the Istrian Committee for Old Partisan Combatants protested that by allowing this park of remembrance, an attempt was being made to rewrite history and honor unduly being rendered to wartime criminals. Those cast into the (alleged) *fiobe* were supposedly all well-known fascists. So the eternal return of the same could have been going on, if it were not for the fact that this was no longer part of a discussion where anyone could make sense of connecting past memories to contemporary situations. Who would listen? The strongest nationalist voice came from a group in the diaspora who had no real opponents left: the Yugoslav state was being put as much into question by the Croats as by the *esuli*. Only the old partisan fighters might feel insulted, but they in turn were more in the nature of local Istrian nationalists – and being Istrian implied today that you were connected to a more tolerant tradition of multiculturalism . . ."

A Multicultural Region

During the war in the 1990s, Istrians were searching for cultural and political distinctiveness they could use or lean on – and many found it in the history of diversity, and it became an almost classic example of a "difference that could make a difference". In registering their national identity during 1991, people in the area were sensitive to the hidden suggestions of homogeneity the act implied. "Like many others, I did not want to register as a Croatian national", a high-ranking local tourist official told me, "so I wrote 'Istrian' instead. Others just wrote Human. No one has to tell me that I'm not as good a Croat as any, but I also didn't want to have it be forced down my throat. Like many others, I knew a war was coming and I did not like it. To write 'Istrian' meant taking a stance against forcing destiny on people. Coming out as a nationalist opposes our entire tradition. Striving for freedom from any oppression is characteristic for the region. People have been exposed to the presence of many lords – Venetian, Austrian, Italian, German… They might change, but we won't."

From the point of view of the ruling HDZ-party in Zagreb, Istrians were sometimes seen as "selling out to the Italians". When Franjo Tudjman visited Pazin in 1991, he accused Istrians of not being "Great Croats" – a wartime term used to characterize those who were strongly, or particularly, nationalistic. "I guess he was met with whistles!" an 80-year old former partisan from Pazin remarked. "My family has been here for hundreds of years. We were fighting the fascists when the *Ustasha* state was selling out to Mussolini. 17 000 Istrians fell on this soil and none of them had any connection to the Ante Pavelič regime.[15] We would also have fought the English, if need be, to keep Istria free. My mother went to an Austrian school trying to keep her Croatian, I went to an Italian school trying to keep my Croatian, and my children went to a Yugoslav school, and my grandchildren to a Croatian. We certainly know who we are."

The *rimasti* – the Italians who stayed – made similar statements about the dexterity of living with a reality that seemed to be ethnically diffuse or unclear only on the surface. The

Mayor of Brtonigla belonged to a family that had lived in the same village for more than 400 years. This is an Italian-speaking town, and he therefore had to use Italian at work although he mostly spoke Croatian at home. He had sent his son to study economics in Trieste, while his daughter had gone to an Italian school in nearby Buje; now she attended a Croatian business high school in Višnjan.

People in Istria looked for a workable compromise – convivenza or *suživot* – in the post-1945 era. Diversity has defined people in terms of *where* they were rather than *who* they were, without raising exclusive claims to territory on ancestral grounds. The experience of managing different dialects or languages was a necessity and not a sign of excluding belonging. People knew perfectly well about their family, its legacy and the group they came from, but this did not give them a right to dominate or any idea of a "hybrid identity" or "creolization". The identity of being Istrian opened a variety of possibilities rather than clear-cut identities. In resisting Zagreb homogenizing efforts, Istrian politicians chose to pronounce the entire region as "multicultural and tolerant," and it was a message which worked both locally and for elections to the Croatian Parliament. By stating that Istria should recognize the rights of all its major linguistic groups, it was in practice giving the large Italian-speaking population the right to use its language in education and administration. When Istria applied to become a Euroregion, it was bound to comply with the entire rhetoric of contemporary EU politics of Unity in Diversity.

More importantly, no acts of war were carried out in Istria during the 1990s. In making sense of the past, in creating a real memory that spoke of and to the present, the Istrian experience radically differed from that in the rest of Croatia. What came out of the process was not a "constant return of the same" but an instance of the different. The past was turned into history, and a slow process of recognizing the suffering without wanting to justify the many wrongdoings seems to be underway.

Notes

1. This essay is part of the project Borders of Europe, financed through the Centre for European Studies at the University of Lund. The fieldwork was made possible by the comparative project Annerledslandet (The Different Country) at the University of Bergen, Norway. The collection and compilation of material has, for the most part, been the result of teamwork with Maja Povrzanović Frykman.
2. For a discussion of the politics of dead bodies in Romania, see Verdery 1999; for the use of similar arguments among the Istrian *esuli* in Italy, see Ballinger 2003.
3. Letting landscapes speak about the dead is not merely a matter of blood-soaked European fields where ancestors have made their sacrifices for the living. The September 11 attack on New York City has shown how even urban landscapes can come to resound with memories of loss and terror connected to national identity. "Memories of this landscape have been reflected in narratives of New Yorkers since the event and will be referred to in historical accounts for years to come" (Stewart & Strathern 2002:10).
4. In a rather confusing 20th century, Istria belonged to Habsburg until the Treaty of Rapallo in 1920, when it was handed over to Italy. The fascist period under Benito Mussolini lasted from 1922 to 1943, after which it fell under German military command. From 1945 to 1947, Istria was divided into Zones A (Allied) and B (Yugoslav) control, and it was not until 1954 that the entire region became part of Yugoslavia. With Croatian (1991) and Slovenian (1990) independence, the major part of Istria became Croatian.
5. The Croatian Tourist Board, in marketing the Adriatic coast, uses the slogan: "The Mediterranean as it once was".
6. As Ballinger (2003) has pointed out, a latent risk exists of creating a new "multicultural Istrian identity" that takes the shape of still another form of regional essentialism.
7. Slovenian ethnologist Borut Brumen (2001) has argued that the experience of living under so many rulers made people extremely aware of place itself, with its nature and particular memories. Historical time has been overtaken by virtual and social time, merging people and place into one.
8. There is a pre-history of how Istrian identity became rooted in landscape and material culture rather than ethnic and national difference. Towards the end of the 19th century, when Austrian ethnologists started to investigate this province of the empire, they became convinced they had captured the last remains of an archaic, pre-national phase of European popular culture (Nikočević & Škrbić 2001). In the widely read newspaper *Glas Istre* (The Voice of Istria) and in

the dominant local political party, *Istarski Demokratski Sabor* (Istrian Democratic Assembly), the idea of Istria as multicultural and multilingual is taken for granted – even as it is factually constantly challenged.
9. Davor Mandič, Director of the War Museum in Pula and historian of Croatia, gives 89,000 as the number of applications accepted from those who "opted for Italy" in all of Dalmatia and Istria, although he also estimates the total number to be 101,000.
10. Unlike the parish church that made something beyond visible and present, a monument openly proclaimed the Promised Land was realized and the results could be seen all around.
11. Polt is particularly good on Heidegger's *Sein und Zeit,* and I draw here as well on Rüdiger Safranski's masterful intellectual biography (1998).
12. There are countless similar stories throughout Eastern Europe today: "What occurred in my village happened to the Don Cossacks and the Sudetendeutsche to the same or greater extent", my interview partner said, as if to generalize his own experiences (see also the discussion in Verdery 1999).
13. Rebecca West, in her classic book of travels *Black Lamb and Grey Falcon* (1941), makes similar observations where she brings out both the magnificent and tragic in the Yugoslavian culture of the time. The book "is an attack on the Christian doctrine of the Crucifixion and the atonement, in which our sins are forgiven by God in return for the sacrifice of Jesus on the cross", she writes, for "All our Western thought is founded upon this repulsive pretence that pain is the proper price of any good thing". But is there really any meaning to pain and to sacrifice? See Kaplan 1994:4.
14. The interviews revealing the events that had taken place in 1945 and 2002 were carried out by the Director of the Ethnographic Museum of Istria in Pazin, Lidija Nikočević.
15. A reference to the many references the HDZ made to the "Independent State of Croatia" led by Ante Pavelić.

References

Allcock, John, B. 2000: *Explaining Yugoslavia*. London: Hurst & Company.

Ballinger, Pamela 2003: *History in Exile. Memory and Identity at the Borders of the Balkans*. Princeton and Oxford: Princeton University Press.

Bet-El, Ilana, R. 2002: Unimagined communities: the power of memory and the conflict in former Yugoslavia. In: Müller, Jan-Werner (ed.): *Memory & Power in Post-War Europe: Studies in the Presence of the Past*. Cambridge: Cambridge University Press.

Brumen, Borut 2001. Imagined Tradition at the New State Borders. *Proceedings of the SIEF Conference in Budapest.*

Čolaković, Rudoljub 1962: *Winning Freedom*. London: Lincolns-Prage Publishers Ltd.

Čolović, Ivan 2002: *The Politics of Symbol in Serbia*. London: Hurst & Company.

Feldman, Allan 1992: *Formations of Violence*. Chicago: Chicago University Press.

Frykman, Jonas 2002: Place for Something Else: Analysing a Cultural Imaginary. *Ethnologia Europaea* 32:2.

Frykman, Jonas 2003: Between History and Material Culture: On European Regionalism and the Potentials of Poetic Analysis. In: Frykman, Jonas & Nils Gilje (eds.): *Being There. New Trends in Phenomenology and the Analysis of Culture*. Lund: Nordic Academic Press.

Frykman, Jonas & Nils Gilje (eds.) 2003: *Being There. New Trends in Phenomenology and the Analysis of Culture*. Lund: Nordic Academic Press.

Gillis, John (ed.) 1994: *Commemorations. The Politics of National Identity*. New Jersey: Princeton.

Jackson, Michael 2003: The Politics of Reconciliation. Reflections on Postwar Sierra Leone. In: Frykman, Jonas & Nils Gilje (eds.): *Being There. New Trends in Phenomenology and the Analysis of Culture*. Lund: Nordic Academic Press.

Kaplan, Robert, D. 1994: *Balkan Ghosts: A Journey through History*. New York: Vintage Departures.

Lampe, John R. 1989: Imperial borderlands or capitalist periphery? Redefining Balkan Backwardness, 1520–1914. In: Chirot, Daniel (ed.): *The Origin of Backwardness in Eastern Europe*. Berkeley: University of California Press.

Müller, Jan Werner 2002: Introduction: The power of memory, the memory of power and the power over memory. In: Müller, Jan Werner (ed.): *Memory & Power in Post-War Europe: Studies in the Presence of the Past*. Cambridge: Cambridge University Press.

Nikočević, Lidija & Nevena Škrbić 2001: Österreich-Mythen in Istrien. In: Istrien: Sichtweisen. *Kittseer Schriften zur Volkskunde 13.*

Polt, Richard 1999: *Heidegger: An Introduction*. London: UCL Press.

Port, Mattijs van de 1998: *Gypsies, Wars and Other Instances of the Wild. Civilization and Its Discontents in a Serbian Town*. Amsterdam: Amsterdam University Press.

Safranski, Rüdiger 1998: *Martin Heidegger: Between Good and Evil*. Cambridge: Harvard.

Stewart, Pamela, J. & Andrew Strathern (eds.) 2003: *Landscape, Memory and History. Anthropological Perspectives*. London: Pluto Press.

Verdery, Katherine 1999: *The Political Lives of Dead Bodies*. New York: Columbia University Press.

Silences, Cultural Historical Museums, and Jewish Life in Sweden

Barbro Klein

> Klein, Barbro 2003: Silences, Cultural Historical Museums, and Jewish Life in Sweden. – Ethnologia Europaea 33:2: 121–132.
>
> The silences surrounding Jews and Jewish culture within the Swedish folklife sphere and within the historiography of Swedish folklife studies are examined in this paper. Emphasis is placed on one national institution, the Nordic Museum in Stockholm. The sleep at issue, then, is the undergrowth of embarrassed, taken-for-granted or hostile silences concerning ethnic/religious difference that could be found more or less throughout the 20th century, not only among the majority of the population but also among experts in the study of culture. It is argued that the silences and the lack of clear stances at a national cultural institution contributed to legitimizing xenophobia in the past and might well continue to do so among people who are lost, violently inclined, looking for scape-goats, and waiting to strike when the time is right.
>
> *Prof. Dr. Barbro Klein, Director, SCASSS, Götavägen 4, SE-752 36 Uppsala.*
> *E-mail: Barbro.Klein@scasss.uu.se*

The extensive immigration into Sweden during the last few decades has affected all societal and cultural sectors, not least the aging cultural historical museums and other institutions devoted to the study, preservation and presentation of vernacular traditions. Not only were these institutions planned as the bastions of national consciousness, they also came to serve a country that, for a long time, regarded itself as extraordinarily homogeneous, religiously, linguistically, and culturally. The pressure on the museums increased during the middle of the 1990s, when the government enjoined all public institutions to take into consideration, in all their activities, that Sweden is "multicultural". The emphasis on cultural diversity contributed to a renewed interest (both within the cultural historical sector and elsewhere) in the minorities who have a long history in Sweden – in spite of the country's perceived homogeneity. The changing demography has now brought about a re-discovery, or even re-invention, of Saami, Roma, Finns, Travelers and Jews as ethnic groups both by members of the groups themselves and by outsiders.

This paper concerns one of the historical minorities, Jews, and their role within the cultural historical museums and other components of the Swedish "folklife sphere".[1] In focus is the largest of the cultural historical museums, the Nordic Museum, and its open-air extension Skansen in Stockholm, founded in 1873 and 1891 respectively. Using the case of rabbi Gottlieb Klein and his son, folklorist and museum teacher Ernst Klein, I wish to examine different aspects of the silences surrounding Jews and Jewish culture at this national museum and within the folklife sphere in general[2]. The silences represent, I argue, many problems and contradictions. On the one hand, it is hardly surprising that the social discourses within a nation-state such as Sweden was in the first half of the 20th century would emphasize a public sphere of an ethnically pure – but culturally varied – Swedishness. On the other hand, it is troubling that folklife scholars, ethnologists, and other experts in cultural study would have been as unreflective of the constitution of that Swedishness as they were and, to some extent, have continued to be.

To some Swedes my task would seem absurd; to them it is self-evident that Jewish culture could (or should) have no place in a museum concerned with Swedish folk culture. To others the topic is puzzling: they take it for granted that Jews are "just like everybody else". To others still, in particular to young ethnologists, the task is uncomfortable: they detect essentialism in it. A few have also asked if it would make any difference at all to Jewish-Swedish history or to the understanding of the Swedish folklife sphere, if we were to identify a Jewish presence in the cultural historical museums. But regardless of the reasons they cite, the result is silence about Jews and Jewish culture in the Swedish folklife sphere, i.e. the very sphere that has continuously professed that its object of interest is cultural variation in Sweden.

The "sleep" at issue in this paper is then differently constituted from what the title of the symposium at first would seem to point to. As the discussion in the conference on "Sleepers, Moles, and Martyrs" confirmed, the term sleeper is exceedingly elastic and laden with a variety of metaphoric and mythic overtones. On one end of a scale, there are various "weak" meanings and uses of the term, such as its use in the antiquarian book trade where it refers to items that have not been of interest to anyone for decades and then suddenly are in demand and, therefore, move quickly. On the other end of the scale, is the "strong" sense of the term as used after September 11, i.e. to connote secret agents from another world who, although seemingly integrated in the culture in which they live, in a silent rage commit acts of unimaginable horror when the time is set for them to reveal their true nature. This paper might seem to have little to do with either of these extremes. It is not the potential agency of a seemingly assimilated minority that concerns me, but rather the discursive undergrowth or murkiness within the majority culture, a murkiness that is hidden but close to the surface. The everyday suspicions and prejudices, the seemingly taken-for-granted silences concerning people who may or may not be regarded as different Others or as possible inner enemies constitute this murkiness. I am assuming, however, that there are potential connections between such simmering everyday suspicions and the violent acts of sleepers in the strong sense. These suspicions and silences do not emerge out of thin air, but are deeply rooted in history. And in the case at issue here, the Holocaust and its long pre-history inevitably echo (Karlsson & Zander 2003), as they echo in the acts committed by Mohammed Atta and the others on September 11, 2001.

Public Recognition and Diffuse Silences

Since the late 18th century, Jews have been granted permission to live in Sweden without demands to convert to the Lutheran State Church. In the 19th century, a small and eventually well integrated group of Jewish families became important in such fields as publishing, banking, and the sciences. Indeed, a number of Sweden's foremost scholars and intellectuals were and are Jewish. But also Jews of other backgrounds arrived in different immigration waves, not least during the late nineteenth century when poor East European Jews fled from pogroms.[3] Even so, the number of Jews remained small. In the 1930s there were perhaps 7 000 Jews in Sweden and today around 20 000 people in the country call themselves Jews. Many scholars have remarked that the virulence of Swedish anti-Semitic attacks against well-known and well-integrated Jews during the first decades of the twentieth century stand in no reasonable proportion to the modest number of Jews actually living in the country (see, for example, Andersson 2000, Hedling 1999).

Also during the last few years, contradictions and ambiguities have continued to dominate. On the one hand, Jews and Jewish culture have been more visible and received more official recognition than perhaps ever before. A Jewish museum and a Jewish theater were recently founded in Stockholm, and books on Jewish humor and other aspects of (American-)Jewish culture have circulated widely among young Swedes, in part as a result of the popularity of American films and television sit-coms. Furthermore, the Swedish government has recently established a civil service department devoted to information in schools about the Holocaust and related issues and it has allocated substantial funding to the scholarly study of genocides. In 2000, it also sponsored a high level conference on the subject.⁴ Also, the Nordic Museum contributed to the measures designed to inform people about World War II by initiating a project in which the reminiscences of Jewish war victims residing in Sweden were collected and published (Johansson 2000).

However, parallel to this recent flurry of activities linked to the echoes of the Holocaust, silence reigns at the Nordic Museum and elsewhere within the folklife sphere concerning Jews and Jewish culture. Indeed, one could easily get the impression that there have never been any Jews nor any Jewish culture in Sweden. With a few small exceptions, ethnologists, folklorists and anthropologists have written next to nothing about Jewish life and everyday Jewish culture in Sweden. No questionnaires have ever been sent out from the Nordic Museum archives or other folklife archives concerning Jewish culture in Sweden, although questionnaires have been distributed concerning other historical minorities, in particular the Saami, Sweden's celebrated exotic others. No Jewish festivals or rituals have ever been described in any of the many books that folklife scholars have regularly published concerning the annual cycle and life cycle customs of peasants and contemporary Swedes (just as little as the festival calendars of other minorities and immigrant groups have been described in these books). Actually, historians, linguists and sociologists have conducted more research on the everyday culture of Jews than have the presumed specialists on the topic, i.e. the ethnologists, folklorists, museum scholars and anthropologists. One might say that within the Swedish folklife sphere Jews are more interesting "as dead victims" than as people with a living culture and religiosity.⁵

Museum Builder Hazelius and Rabbi Klein

The Nordic Museum, founded by Artur Hazelius 1873, is the foremost among the cultural historical museums established in Sweden at the end of the nineteenth century to represent both regional peasant cultures and urban upper class cultures. One would assume that Jews and Jewish culture would have been entirely absent from this effort to create a symbolic rallying point for the Swedish nation and all historiography about the museum would seem to confirm that assumption. However, careful investigation renders other insights. One is that eminent Jews were active in the work to gather together and preserve the Swedish cultural heritage. Carl Robert Lamm, for instance, was a member of the executive board of the Swedish Homecraft Association, but like other Jews in similar positions, he participated as a learned professional, not as a Jew.

But there are also other aspects to the question of Jewish participation in the early efforts to establish cultural historical museums. It turns out that not only Artur Hazelius in Stockholm but also Georg Karlin who founded the Museum of Cultural History in Lund, worked actively to acquire Jewish objects for their budding museums. Particularly interesting is the relationship between museum builder Artur Hazelius and rabbi Gottlieb Klein. Born into a poor family in Hungary, Klein became a brilliant scholar and teacher and was appointed rabbi in Stockholm in 1883 at the age of thirty-one. He was highly appreciated in Sweden and was awarded the title of professor by King Oscar II. "*Gott liebt Klein*" – God loves Klein – was one expression that circulated about him (Josephson 1998). He was Sweden's foremost representative of reform Judaism, an anti-Zionist and a friend of liberal intellectuals such as archbishop Nathan Söderblom and publicist Torgny Segerstedt, senior (E. Klein 1933a: 239).

In the 1880s, Gottlieb Klein donated to the Nordic Museum a ritual object which he had brought with him from his hometown, Humenné in Hungary (accession number 47081) and, possibly, also other objects. For a few years, Hazelius exhibited this object in the "Upper Class" department (*högreståndsavdelningen*) of the Nordic Museum, thereby signaling that he regarded Jewish culture, as it was represented by the learned rabbi, as urban and cosmopolitan. (The classification is doubtful in light of the fact that the synagogue in Klein's hometown was poor and hardly cosmopolitan). It might even have been Klein who inspired Hazelius to continue acquiring Jewish artifacts. Hazelius eventually gathered together a collection of Judaica consisting of some 150 items, primarily in the form of ritual artifacts from the Alsace. Why Hazelius did this – and exactly why museum founder Georg Karlin in Lund collected Judaica – I do not yet know.[6] But whatever Hazelius' motivations, it is clear that his Judaica collection eventually became enveloped in silence; the objects to do not seem to have been exhibited during the twentieth century.

Jews contributed to the creation of cultural historical museums in Sweden in other ways as well. For example, Selman Neuman, an itinerant salesman from Eastern Europe, worked as a buyer for Karlin in Lund and acquired some significant objects for his museum. At the same time as Jews – intellectuals as well as itinerant salesmen – participated in the efforts of museum founders to save Swedish folk culture and at the same time as these founders gathered Jewish objects, Jews were frequently described in negative terms. Such descriptions are revealed in an exchange of letters between Artur Hazelius and journalist and folklore collector Eva Wigström. In 1879, when on a tour in the province of Skåne to buy artefacts for his museum, Hazelius complained: "In Skåne Jews have come looking for silver, and there is not a single cottage which has not been visited by twenty Jews looking for silver". And in 1885, while travelling in the district of Östra Göinge in Skåne, Wigström wrote to Hazelius: "In these districts you could still see whole rooms covered from floor to ceiling with tapestries painted in various colors, with motifs taken from the early history of the Israelites. But Jews buying up articles for foreign museums negotiated with the owners so that these hangings, probably along with many other objects of cultural historical value, have already been sent abroad" (cited after Bringéus 1992:127–128).

It is striking how, on the hand, Hazelius collected Jewish ritual objects while, on the other, he would carelessly subscribe to a common prejudice, thus singling out Jews as unscrupulous sales agents prepared to buy cheaply the finest of Swedish folk art treasures and sell them dearly in foreign lands.[7] But regardless of whether their role is seen as praiseworthy collecting or as misappropriation, it is evident that Jews played a considerable role in the building up of the holdings of Swedish cultural historical museums. Yet, this role is acknowledged neither in the standard histories of ethnology as a discipline nor in the histories of cultural historical museums and other areas of the folklife sphere. One might well ask if it is important to be cognizant of the role of Jews in the early phase of the folklife sphere. Is this the kind of insight that makes a difference?

One of his Race – at Skansen?

It is hardly surprising that very little was written about Jewish-Swedish culture within the folklife sphere during the 1920s and 30s and that few, if any, museum employees identified themselves as Jews (although there were some). The only exception was Ernst Klein, Gottlieb Klein's son. He must have made a great impression on his colleagues. I remember my teachers speaking about him fondly when I started studying what was called "Nordic and Comparative Folklife Research" in the late 1950s; at that time he had been dead for more than two decades. But I cannot remember anyone ever mentioning his Jewish background, and it would never have occurred to me to ask.

Ernst Klein was born in 1887 and became a man of many talents and interests. Between 1910 and 1920, he worked as a journalist, in part as a foreign correspondent in the Soviet Union and Finland. For a while he taught at *Brunnsviks folkhögskola* (Brunnsvik's "folk high school") with Karl-Erik Forsslund, one of Sweden's foremost students of local history (*hembygdsforskare*).[8] In 1921, Klein was hired at the Nordic Museum and its open-air extension, Skansen (the two constituted one administrative unit at this time) where he remained until his death in 1937. Throughout this period he continued to be active as a journalist. A primus motor at the spring festivals and other public programs at Skansen, he was eventually appointed museum lecturer, a role in which he broke new pedagogical ground. He also created folklife films, not least about dance and music; he was a birthday poet and the life of a party. He published continuously and quickly (way too quickly according to his critics) on boats, fishing gear, Saami culture, and many other topics. In 1925 he was awarded the equivalent of a master's degree *(fil.lic.)* in "Folk Memory Research" *(Folkminnesforskning)* on the basis of a book on the traditions of Swedish speakers in Estonia (1924). This book which was based on extensive field research in Estonia became highly acclaimed. It is sought after and read to this day as are some of Klein's other works, among them his innovative studies of Swedish folk dance and an often praised history of Sweden "from below" (1931–32, see also Svensson 1982).

In addition, Klein published works on Jewish culture and traditions, among them a collection of Jewish folktales with a long and learned introduction (1929). However, none of these works have become known within the Swedish folklife sphere and none of them have been reviewed in folklore or ethnology journals, although they were discussed in Jewish periodicals and occasionally also in Swedish dailies. Particularly interesting, not least as an ethnography of Eastern and Central European Jewish life, is the book *Genom sju riken* ("Through seven countries", 1933b). Here Ernst Klein describes a trip he undertook in the spring of 1933 together with his wife, Olga Boedecker and a Dr. B.; the party traveled through Poland, Czechoslovakia, Hungary, Yugoslavia, Austria, Germany, and Sweden. The book is unsentimental, amusing and full of astute observations. But it also contains a partially shocking portrayal of life in Central Europe a few years before World War II. The main purpose of the trip was to visit Gottlieb Klein's hometown on the slopes of the Carpathians. Ernst Klein had never been there and the long awaited trip had become urgent, due to the increasingly difficult situation in countries in which Jews had come to be "regarded as less desirable immigrants and strangers" (p. 192). "Through seven countries" is full of fearful premonitions but also contains lively descriptions of life in Jewish country villages and small towns, forms of life that were soon to be extinguished. At the same time, in this book perhaps more clearly than in any other of his works, Klein communicates his simultaneous devotion to Jewish religion, culture and history and to Swedish culture and history.

"Through seven countries" was well received in Swedish newspapers and in the Jewish-Swedish press. But not a word was said about it in print within the folklife sphere. This silence is perhaps to be expected; probably the book was regarded more as journalism than as serious academic research. Yet it seems to me that, in 1933, things must have been said or whispered in the everyday conversations and interactions at Klein's workplace, the Nordic Museum. What political discussions were held there? What did Klein say to his colleagues about his Jewish identity and to what extent did they speak about it? It could hardly have been a secret: he and his father were well known personalities. How did Ernst Klein react to the onslaught of anti-Semitic representations in films, literature, comic magazines, and oral tradition during the 1920s and 1930s (Andersson 2000, Gerner 2000, Wright 1998)? Were his wit and irony ways to handle suspicions and prejudice? Or did he speak out to his colleagues at the museum? As a journalist he wrote unequivocal protests and as such he was one of many writers – Jewish or not – who did so. The Swedish newspapers of the 1930s are full of stories and debates concerning the so-called "Jewish question" *(judefrågan)*.

In any case, it is hard to imagine that silence was total within the folklife sphere. Indeed, there is evidence that Ernst Klein acted inside the walls of the Nordic Museum to further and protect Jewish culture. For example, he led an appeal to the museum's executive board requesting a transfer of its collection of Judaica, (i.e. the collection to which his father had contributed) to the Synagogue of Stockholm *(Mosaiska Församlingen)*.[9] The request was granted on December 2, 1931 and the minutes are signed by museum director Andreas Lindblom, and incoming director, Gösta Berg. In other words, the museum leadership was clearly aware of Klein's background and interest in this matter.

But there are also more problematic signs that silence was not total at the museum with regards to "the Jewish question". Now living, retired employees who were present at the time (or a few years later) admit that some colleagues were quite "brown" and that many ideas were not only whispered but also spelled out aloud. Ernst Klein's friend Karl-Erik Forsslund, director of *Brunnsviks folkhögskola*, notes that "there were those who were shocked that a Jew was hired at the Nordic Museum" (Forsslund 1937:56). Furthermore, there is indication that Ernst Klein encountered discrimination. On July 7, 1924, the head of the department of cultural history at Skansen, Nils Keyland, died. On July 24, i.e. a few days later, Gustaf Upmark, director of the Nordic Museum and Skansen 1913–1928, commented on the matter of Keyland's successor in handwriting in the margin of a typed letter to a colleague: "Keyland's death was a heavy blow and the choice of successor will be difficult. – Klein is a candidate, of course, but do you want a person of his race as head of the department of cultural history at Skansen?" Klein did not get the job. Instead, a young bachelor of arts, Sigurd Erixon (the future giant of Swedish folklife studies) was immediately appointed as temporary head of the department; a few months later the job was permanently his (*Fataburen* 1925:4). Ernst Klein was given the task of arranging "folk music, story telling .. and cultural historical events" etc. at Skansen (*Fataburen* 1926:5). I do not wish to suggest that Klein was better suited than Erixon for the more prestigious position. However, the sources justify questions regarding possible racial discrimination on the part of the museum leadership. Did Upmark, like many contemporaries of his class, regard Ernst Klein a foreign mole, an infiltrator with roots in Eastern Europe, a Bolshevik spy who ought not to be involved in the work to gather, refine and exhibit the finest products made by the Swedish folk? After all, Ernst Klein's political leanings were leftist and toward Social Democracy, whereas many people at the museum were of aristocratic or bourgeois background and "were obsessed with a fear of *les classes dangereux*".[10] Was Klein aware of Upmark's views and, if so, did he choose to ignore them?

Ernst Klein died in 1937, on April 30 (*valborgsmässoafton* or "Walpurgis Eve"), only fifty years old. Some questions about him and his position at the museum are illuminated in the handful of obituaries written by colleagues at the museum soon after his death. All the texts are appreciative and a couple of them are long and detailed. However, with one exception, all of them are silent or use paraphrases or code words, when it comes to describing Klein's Jewish identity and his commitment to Jewish culture and religion. For example, Sigurd Erixon, the central figure in Swedish folklife studies, expresses himself with utmost care and refers to Ernst Klein's father not as head rabbi, but as "a teacher of religion and a scholar". Klein's trip to the seven countries is described as "a physically and psychologically most demanding study tour" and, at the end of the article, Erixon writes that "an idealistic seriousness always lay behind even the seemingly most high-spirited of his jokes and amusing rhymes … Perhaps this was connected to his unshaken solidarity with that religious community to which he belonged because of birth and inclination" (Erixon 1937: 125). Erixon never uses the words "Jew" or "Jewish" and neither does another important folklife scholar, Sigfrid Svensson, who had been a close friend of Klein. In his moving obituary Svensson alludes to Klein's background on only one occasion: "The last few years of illness did not break down his courage and confidence. But even so, there was no lack of pessimism and bitterness in Ernst Klein's life … But the reasons for that emanated from the outside. His sensitive nature intensified the persecutions of his race out in the world transforming them into a tragic experience of a personal kind" (Svensson 1938: 204).

To my knowledge, folklorist Gunnar Granberg is the only colleague at the museum to write about the importance of Judaism and Jewish culture for Ernst Klein, in both a scholarly and personal sense. Granberg, who writes at length about Klein's 1933 visit in his father's hometown, also emphasizes that it "is truly remarkable that, in the midst of all the gory nationalism and racial fanaticism, Ernst Klein was able to enter into our inherited Swedish culture to such an extent that, in the deepest sense, he became one of our own, making our culture come to life in a way which no one had managed to do before him. … To this deep understanding of and devotion to Swedish cultural tradition Ernst Klein added his inherited loyalty to Jewish culture and religion. He … worked as teacher of religion at the synagogue ... and in his written works he often took up Jewish issues" (Granberg 1937:172). Perhaps Granberg could write so openly about Klein's commitments to both Jewish and Swedish culture, because he published this obituary in the radical review, *Studiekamraten* ("The Study Comrade") to which both he and Klein had long been contributors. Perhaps Granberg would have held back, if he had written for a museum periodical or a folklore journal? Perhaps he, too, would have felt it inappropriate to foreground, in that kind of context, the Jewish-ness of an employee at a bastion of Swedish national culture. I can only compare these texts with the obituaries in the daily press and non-academic publications the authors of which (regardless of political color) were far more open than writers within the folklife sphere about Klein's Jewish background and about using the word "Jew".

Silences

The silences surrounding Jews and Jewish culture were to continue to dominate in the folklife sphere for many more decades. Indeed, there is indication that the silences grew deeper and wider in time. In the few texts that ethnologists and other scholars wrote about Ernst Klein long after his death nothing is mentioned about his studies of Jewish culture or about his Jewish background. Among these texts is museum director Gösta Berg's long and detailed entry published 1977 in a standard biographical encyclopedia. Here Berg refers to "Through Seven Countries" as a "captivating" description of an "extended study tour" through Europe (Berg 1977: 266) but does not mention the main contents of the book. And the pattern prevails. In 1998, in a lavishly illustrated book celebrating the 125th anniversary of the Nordic museum, Klein is called "socially engaged", "radical", "verbally gifted", and "the happiest among friends" (Stavenow-Hidemark 1998). But not a word is said about his studies of Jewish culture.

Why was it, in the 1970s, 1980s, and 1990s, neither interesting nor possible to reveal that an important and popular colleague had studied Jewish culture and history (in Sweden and elsewhere) as well as Swedish peasant culture and history and that his Jewish identity was significant for him? Had all the years of silence had the effect that the Jewish aspects of Klein's life and scholarship had become forgotten? Or were these aspects regarded irrelevant? Or dangerous or shameful? Are we speaking about silences and secrets that all parties found best withheld for the benefit of all?

Here we return to the contradictions and ambiguities of the last few years mentioned at the outset. In one respect, Jews have become more visible and received more official recognition than perhaps ever before, both in scholarship and in public life. A great deal of this interest is connected to a governmental engagement in the moral lessons to be learned from the Holocaust. Like many other countries, Sweden – including cultural historical museums (Jönsson 1998) – is shaping its very own Holocaust profile (Young 1993). It would seem that Sweden has belatedly begun participating in that which has sometimes been called the Holocaust industry (Finkelstein 2000, Hoffman 2000).

Yet little of the interest today concerns everyday, religious, or learned culture among Jews in Sweden, in the past or at the present. In many contexts, not least within the cultural historical museums, Jews remain better known as dead victims than as people with a living culture and religiosity.[11] There is on the part of the Swedish majority, especially on the part of young people, little awareness that there could be anything distinctive at all about contemporary Jews in Sweden. Aren't they the same as everybody else? I know of an instructor in ethnology at a Swedish university whose students once asked: "How do Jews celebrate Christmas?" – "I suppose they do it like everybody else", was the answer. And I know of young Swedes who have seen Ingmar Bergman's film *Fanny and Alexander* without understanding that a central character is Jewish; this is a character whose role is pivotal and highly ambiguous. And older people who do understand keep silent. Indeed, silence predominates all around.

We are dealing here with the kind of taken-for-granted silences that confirm stereotypes or ignorance and, therefore, serve to make the objects of silence invisible. Silences are not innocent, they conceal. They can conceal conflicts, ambiguities, and indifference. They can conceal prejudices such as Gustaf Upmark's. They can conceal shame or fear to utilize the word "Jew" as a positive marker as was the case in the obituaries and other writings of the folklife scholars cited above. Silences can establish excluding boundaries which become so self-evident that people cannot imagine transgressing them. One can only speculate as to what would have happened if the Nordic Museum had pursued another policy than that of silence. What would have happened if Sigurd Erixon, Sigfrid Svensson and other friends and colleagues of Ernst Klein had been willing to review "Jewish folktales" or "Through seven countries" in a professional journal? What would have happened, if his friends and colleagues had thought that it would be possible to study Jewish-Swedish culture and to exhibit it? Perhaps not *that* much might have happened. But the silences of indifference, fear, shame, prejudice, and suspicion, might have had less of a chance to become constitutive markers of Sweden's hidden (folklife) sphere.

The old silences have not disappeared. Recently, when I have given talks about Gottlieb Klein and Ernst Klein, the reactions indicate that not only are the silences still present but also that the words "Jew" and "Jewish" are tainted with negative connotations, with an aura of something unmentionable that might even be reinforced by some of the recent mass media interest in the Holocaust. At the Nordic Museum, one commentator noted that he was bothered by my presentation, since he "knew the family". What he indicated was that he was disturbed by my blunt use of the word "Jew" about Ernst Klein. To him the word has as negative a ring as it did for Erixon and Svensson. Indeed, an elderly scholar, who knew personally several of the people mentioned in this paper, emphasized that he always avoids the word "Jew" out of "politeness" and "consideration". He is also certain that his Jewish friends would want him to do exactly that. And perhaps many would. Another person who listened to my talk wrote to me saying, "I don't care whether Klein was Jewish or not! It is not important, the main thing is that he was a good scholar and teacher!" This commentator seemed to say that we in our enlightened and "multicultural" Sweden ought to be above essentializing people by giving them ethnic labels. Indeed, several people said that ethnic identity is something private that has nothing to do with people's professional work.

All these and other, similar comments are problematic. For one thing, we cannot assume that we know what people's possible ethnic identities might mean to them in different contexts and what they might mean to those with whom they interact. It is part of our task as students of culture to be able to distinguish between all those contexts in which ethnic and other differences are immaterial and all those in which difference makes all the difference – as it did to Ernst Klein when he could no longer wait to visit with the people in his father's hometown. And to be able to make such distinctions we need knowledge, research, and open debate. This does not mean that individuals and societies do not need their secrets (see Regina Bendix, in this volume). But the opposite cannot be desirable either, i.e. that people because of their ethnic or religious background should be surrounded by frightened, shameful, xenophobic, racist, or (even) polite or considerate silences that go on for decades and conceal a murky undergrowth of ambiguous ideas, animosities and suspicions.

I am certain that this murky undergrowth under a blanket of silences which occasionally sends out messages in marginal notes or whispers in the corridors, is linked to the violent acts of sleepers. The lack of open speech and clear stances at a national institution might well help to legitimize dangerous ideas in minds so inclined. To what extent will the innuendoes and the silences justify acts of violence among people – be they neo-racists or "ordinary schoolboys" - longing for the "warmth of *Gemeinschaft*" and blaming such historical scape-goats as Jews whose everyday lives continue to be surrounded with a hush-hush attitude. It is not far-fetched to suggest, as Marianne Gullestad (2003) does, that some of the sleepers in Europe today are to be found among the young and the lost. Indeed, the leaders guiding these young people are no longer as easy to spot as skinheads. They take care not to stand out but to appear to be integrated, well-dressed, and well-behaved young people at the same time as they move in a thicket of darkness, perhaps waiting to strike when the time is right.

Concluding Remarks

I do not think that it is immaterial to know that Jewish itinerant salesmen and Jewish intellectuals played a role in the establishment of the Swedish folklife sphere and I do not think that it is immaterial to know that ethnologist/folklorist Ernst Klein published studies of Jewish folktales. Such insights must be seen as an enrichment in a country which must now abandon seemingly self-evident silences and learn new ways to "know and respect the others version of the past" (Gillis 1994:20).[12] Not all the people in Sweden today with an "immigrant background" will be interested in exhibiting their traditions and expressions in a Swedish national museum. Perhaps very few will want to do so. But for those who wish to do it, the doors must not be closed a priori or be surrounded by embarrassed silences as the case has been for Jews. This will have to be important in a democracy that says that it is eager to protect openness and integration *and* the rights of citizens to live in accordance with their own religious beliefs and traditions.

Notes

1. Elsewhere, I have used the Habermas-inspired term "folklife sphere" to describe several intellectually and historically closely related enterprises, such as the folklife museums and the folklife archives, the academic disciplines of folkloristics, folklife research and ethnology, and the movements dedicated to "home crafts" (*hemslöjd*), local history, folk dance, and folk music. All of these have had as their object, in different ways and proportions, to study, preserve, celebrate, present, promote, redesign or sell aspects of vernacular, expressive life forms. Like many other peoples, Swedes selected some of their most cherished national symbols from the folklife sphere: the peasant costumes, the fiddle tunes, the midsummer festivities (Klein 2000).
2. This article builds on two previous studies (Klein 2002, Klein 2003). Like them, it has been written within the framework of the projekt "Folklore, Heritage Politics, and Ethnic Diversity" financed by NOS-H. I thank several friends, relatives and colleagues for their contributions to my ongoing studies of Jewish culture and the Swedish folklife sphere: Lotten Gustafsson, Cecilia Hammmarlund-Larsson, Jakob Klein, Ingrid Lomfors, Hans Medelius and Christian Richette. Special thanks to Thomas Hauschild for sending me a number of texts on German-Jewish ethnology and anthropology. My deepest thanks go to Eva Eliasson, Ernst Klein's daughter. Without her powers of memory and her artistry as a narrator, my understandings of the events I describe, would have been poor indeed. I am also grateful to her for lending me her manuscript on Gottlieb Klein (Eliasson n.d.) and other materials (Levy n.d.). I am, however, not related to the Klein family discussed in this paper.
3. The foremost historian of Jewish life in Sweden is Hugo Valentin whose main works were published in the 1920s. A compact study by Valentin was issued in 1964.
4. The immediate impetus for this and other activities was a (now partially disputed) research report according to which an astonishingly high percentage of youngsters in schools cited total ignorance of the Holocaust and the events that led up to it. A much acclaimed informational booklet (Bruchfeld and Levine 1998) has since been distributed in Swedish schools; it has also been translated into a number of languages.
5. I owe this last formulation to Barbara Kirshenblatt-Gimblett (conversations, spring 1999). A handful of references to smaller texts published within the folklife sphere could be cited as the exceptions that confirm the rule (for example, Jacobowski 1967). However, Jewish culture and Jews are not at the center of attention in one single of the Swedish ethnological texts in which they play some role. Rather the authors have come to touch upon the subject more or less inadvertently (see, for example, Ek 1971). Thomas Hauschild (1997) has noted a comparable paucity of research in German *Volkskunde* and *Ethnologie* and emphasizes that Jewish culture was neglected, because it fell between disciplinary boundaries. Jews were not regarded German enough to be studied within *Volkskunde* and not exotic enough to belong to Ethnologie (Hauschild 1997). Nevertheless, it would still seem that Jews and Jewish culture have played a more important role in German *Volkskunde* and *Ethnologie* than in the Swedish counterparts, at least recently and during the founding stages of the disciplines. Not only was the *Gesellschaft für jüdische Volkskunde* founded in Hamburg in 1896, Jewish topics were actually taken up in *Volkskunde* journals in Germany. Bernd Jürgen Warneken has noted that about 5% of the articles

printed in *Zeitschrift für Volkskunde* during the years 1891–1932 concerned Jewish culture and religion (Warneken 1999). Nothing comparable happened in Sweden.

6. Perhaps the collecting and exhibiting of Judaica indicate that the folklife museums (and perhaps also folklife research) in Sweden, as well as in Germany, "in seiner Institutionalisierungsphase kein völkisch-germanophiles Project darstellte" (Warneken 1999: 165).
7. The selling of folk art abroad was (and remains) a significant problem. But Jews were (and are) not the only people involved in these activities.
8. In the 1830s, Svend Grundtvig in Denmark began envisioning folk high schools as centers for civic education of adults. The idea took root also in Sweden where some of the folk high schools, such as Brunnsvik, came to play a significant role in the education of industrial workers.
9. The collection is now housed at the Jewish Museum in Stockholm.
10. Jonas Frykman used this expression in his comments to my paper at the Reinhausen conference. I wish to thank him, Marianne Gullestad, and Thomas Hauschild for their helpful and insightful comments.
11. This does not mean that there are no exceptions whatsoever to these observations. There are a few. For example, in 1996 there was a fine exhibition on Jewish Culture in Sweden at the Museum of Cultural History (Kulturen) in Lund (Landberg 1997).
12. Cf. Frykman's contribution to this volume.

References

Andersson, Lars 2000: *En jude är en jude är en jude. Representationer av "juden" i svensk skämtpress omkring 1900–1930*. Lund: Nordic Academic Press.
Berg, Gösta 1977: Klein, Ernst Immanuel. In: *Svenskt Biografiskt Lexikon*, red. Erik Grill. Band 21. pp. 264–268. Stockholm: Norstedts.
Bringéus, Nils-Arvid 1992: Folk Art in Peasant Society. In: *Ethnologia Scandinavica* 22: 119–133.
Bruchfeld, Stéphane, and Paul A. Levine 1998: *... om detta må ni berätta ... En bok om Förintelsen i Europa 1933–1945*. Regeringskansliet: Levande Historia.
Ek, Sven B. 1971: *Nöden i Lund. En etnologisk stadsstudie*. Lund: Gleerups.
Eliasson, Eva. N.d. Gottlieb Klein (1852–1914). Unpublished manuscript.
Erixon, Sigurd 1937: Ernst Klein *1887 + 1937. *Rig* 20:121–125.
Finkelstein, Norman G. 2000: *The Holocaust Industry. Reflections on the Exploitation of Jewish Suffering*. London: Verso.
Forsslund, Karl-Erik 1937: Ernst Klein in memoriam. *Brunnsvikarnas midsommarskrift*: 54–58.
Gerner, Kristian 2000: Antisemitism var central för definitionen av svenskhet. *Svenska Dagbladet*, 20 april.
Gillis, John (ed.) 1994: *Commemorations. The Politics of National Identity*. Princeton, N.J.: Princeton University Press.
Granberg, Gunnar 1937: Ernst Klein. *Studiekamraten* 19:171–172.
Gullestad, Marianne 2003: Mohammed Atta and I: Identification, discrimination and the formation of sleepers. In: *European Journal of Cultural Studies*, No. 4.
Hauschild, Thomas 1997: Christians, Jews, and the Other in German Anthropology. *American Anthropologist* 99(4): 746–753.
Hedling, Erik 1999: Antisemitism i populära svenska filmer. *Svenska Dagbladet*, 26 februari.
Hoffman, Eva 2000: The Uses of Hell. *The New York Review of Books* (March 2000): 19–23.
Jacobowski, C. Vilh. 1967: Svenskt-judiskt herrgårdsliv. *Rig* 50: 33–44.
Johansson, Britta (ed.) 2000: *Judiska minnen. Berättelser från Förintelsen*. Stockholm: Nordiska museet.
Josephson, Ragnar 1998 (1967): Den vise på Wahrendorffsgatan. I: *Det judiska Stockholm*, ed. David Glück, et al. Stockholm: Statens kulturråd.
Jönsson, Lars-Eric 1998: Förintelsen och Sverige. Om ett museum. In: *Rig* (4): 193–199.
Karlsson, Klas-Göran and Ulf Zander (eds.) 2003: *Echoes of the Holocaust. Historical Cultures in Contemporary Europe*. Lund: Nordic Academic Press.
Klein, Barbro 2000: Foreigners, Foreignness, and the Swedish Folklife Sphere. In: *Ethnologia Scandinavica* 30: 5–23.
Klein, Barbro 2001: More Swedish Than in Sweden, More Iranian Than in Iran? Folk Culture and World Migrations. In: *Upholders of Culture*, ed. Bosse Sundin. Pp. 67–80. Stockholm: Kungliga Ingenjörsvetenskapsakademien (IVA).
Klein, Barbro 2002: När skillnad gör skillnad. Reflektioner kring museipolitik, tystnader och judisk kultur i Sverige. In: *Saga och Sed. Kungl. Gustav Adolfs Akademiens Årsbok*, 2002: 47–61.
Klein, Barbro 2003: 'One of his Race' – at Skansen? Reflections on Heritage Making, Museum Politics, and Cultural Difference. In: *Dynamics of Tradition. Essays in Honor of Anna-Leena Siikala*, ed. Lotte Tarkka. Pp. 75–92. Helsinki: Finnish Literature Society.
Klein, Ernst 1924: *Runö. Folklivet i en gammal svensk by*. Uppsala: J.A. Lindblad.
Klein, Ernst (ed. and tr.) 1929: *Judiska sagor*. Stockholm: Hugo Geber (= Judiska Litteratursamfundets Skriftserie IX).
Klein, Ernst. 1931–1932. *Bilder ur Sveriges historia. Svensk kultur från urtid till nutid*. 2 volumes. Stockholm: Nordisk Rotogravyr.
Klein, Ernst 1933a: Gottlieb Klein. Ett femtioårsminne. *Judisk Tidskrift* (6 september): 234–239.

Klein, Ernst 1933b: *Genom sju riken*. Stockholm: Nordisk Rotogravyr.

Klein, Ernst 1978: *Om Folkdans*. Essays edited by Mats Rehnberg. Stockholm: LT:s förlag.

Landberg, Anna 1997: Röster om judisk kultur. In: *Samtid & Museer* 21(3): 4–5.

Levy, Sophie. N.d. Berättelser ur mitt liv. Unpublished manuscript.

Stavenow-Hidemark, Elisabet 1998: Ernst Klein. In: *Nordiska museet under 125 år*, ed. Hans Medelius, Bengt Nyström and Elisabet Stavenow-Hidemark. P. 175. Stockholm: Nordiska museets förlag.

Svensson, Sigfrid 1938: Ernst Klein. In: *Fataburen*: 203–208.

Svensson, Sigfrid 1982: Ernst Klein och hans historieverk. Ett halvsekelminne. In: *Folkets historia* 10(1): 27–31.

Valentin, Hugo 1964: *Judarna i Sverige*. Stockholm: Bonniers.

Warneken, Bernd Jürgen 1999: 'Völkisch nicht beschränkte Volkskunde'. Eine Erinnerung an die Gründungsphase des Fachs von 100 Jahren. In: *Zeitschrift für Volkskunde* 95(2): 169–196.

Wright, Rochelle 1998: *The Visible Wall. Jews and Other Ethnic Outsiders in Swedish Film*. Uppsala: Studia Multiethnica Upsaliensia 11.

Young, James E. 1993*: The Texture of Memory: Holocaust Memorials and Meaning*. New Haven: Yale University Press.

Other Sources

Dagens Nyheter, fall 1933, spring 1937.
Svenska Dagbladet, fall 1933, spring 1937.
Fataburen, 1925, 1926, 1934, 1938. Redogörelse för Nordiska museet.
Nordiska museet. Archives, selected letter exchanges.
Nordiska museet. Accessions catalogue.